THE
CRUSADES

BOOKS BY HILAIRE BELLOC

Available From The Publisher
In This Series

Europe and the Faith

William The Conqueror

The Crusades

How the Reformation Happened

Characters of the Reformation

Essays of a Catholic

The Great Heresies

Survivals and New Arrivals

The Crisis of Civilization

THE
CRUSADES

THE WORLD'S DEBATE

By

Hilaire Belloc

TAN BOOKS AND PUBLISHERS, INC.
Rockford, Illinois 61105

Copyright © 1937 by Hilaire Belloc.

Published c. 1937 by Bruce Publishing Company, Milwaukee.

Retypeset and republished in 1992 by TAN Books and Publishers, Inc.

Library of Congress Catalog Card No.: 92-60960

ISBN: 0-89555-467-4

Cover picture: Godfrey de Bouillon and his knights on their way to the Holy Land, from William of Tyre's *History,* c. 1280.

Printed and bound in the United States of America.

TAN BOOKS AND PUBLISHERS, INC.
P.O. Box 424
Rockford, Illinois 61105

1992

Manzikert,* the shock that launched the Crusade, would have destroyed us—but for the Crusade. Constantinople would have fallen; all Europe would have been involved—but under that stimulus the West moved. Gaul and the Rhine, Normandy, Flanders, Aquitaine, Lorraine armed, faced east, and went forward.

The issue was the life or death of Christendom.

—From Page 17

---

*Great battle in 1071 at which the Christian forces in the East suffered a crushing defeat at the hands of the Turks, leading to years of pillage, killing and wholesale destruction of civilized life.—*Editor,* 1992.

TABLE OF CONTENTS

vii

AUTHOR'S PREFACE

There are a score of ways in which a man may treat of the Crusades. They were, in their entirety, a continuous struggle between our civilization and the hostile world of Islam, which all but overwhelmed Europe. The contrast, in its vividness, has struck all minds in any degree awake to the past. The color and the drama of medieval warfare fill the story. Or, again one may speak of the Crusades in their deepest aspect as the conflict between Christendom and that undying Anti-Christ which desires to kill Christendom. One may regard the Crusades (and that is the commonest fashion) as subject for romance; it is in this aspect that they have been introduced to the world that reads English and mainly so introduced by the genius of Sir Walter Scott in his excellent novel (and grotesquely unhistorical work) *The Talisman*. Or, again, one may make the Crusades a text for exemplifying the strength and weakness of the Gallic temperament; or, again, a text for exemplifying the permanence, the exaltation, and the vices of Islam.

In this study the author has concerned himself with another limited but essential side of the story. He has attempted to know why and how, as a military effort, through military errors, the original great experiment failed: why and how from the military excellence of its first leaders it came so near to success and might perhaps have attained it. He deals with the story as essentially one continuous campaign, or even one battle, a battle of ninety years, a battle with a political objective, the Holy Places, a battle which in attaining its objective might have secured a political result that would have changed the world, a battle that began with a victorious offensive and ended in full defeat.

This being his theme, he has confined the affair to the effort to retain what the first Crusaders set out to grasp, and with their loss of the Holy Sepulchre he closes the record.

H. BELLOC

King's Land

THE
CRUSADES

1

THE WORLD'S DEBATE

Human affairs are decided through conflict of ideas, which often resolve themselves by conflict under arms. To understand those decisions under arms which determine in succession the fate of the world, three things should occupy the mind: first, the nature of the issue and its launching, that is, the occasion of its coming to battle; second, the military character of the opposing forces; third, the strategy and tactics of the campaigns.

It is proposed in this book to deal with that major conflict under arms between Christendom and Islam which took the form of the First or Great Crusade: its triumph, the exhaustion of the result it had achieved, and the final catastrophe of an episode of victory and defeat covering the very long lifetime of a man—eighty-eight years. Gibbon, in a phrase as concise as any of his packed sentences and far more exact than most of them (for he was ignorant of the religious temper he attempted to judge), called this major episode in our history, "The World's Debate."

An effort was made after centuries of peril and invasion, during which civilization had lost half its area, to react and impose upon the Mohammedan world the domination of the Christian; its initial success, which we call the First Crusade, occupied the last years of the eleventh century (from 1095 to 1099). That initial success was gained by great hosts ill-organized but ardent; and in spite of divergent personal ambitions, consequent delays, continual and at last rapid melting away of forces, the goal was attained. The Holy Sepulchre, to rescue which near a million men, first and last, had risen, was carried and held by the last few thousands who had survived and endured till Jerusalem.

The swarm settled; the Western warriors, two thousand miles from home, cut off by such long sea passages and by such months of marching over such burnt, alien land, struck root and might feel that they had permanently grasped the vital belt of the Orient. All seaboard Syria was theirs and *nearly* all that bridge of fertile land which unites the rivers of the north, the fields of Cilicia, the pastures of the Armenian valleys with the green wealth of Egypt, the Delta and the Nile. That "bridge," a narrow band pressed in between the desert and the sea, was the all-important central link joining the Moslem East to the Moslem West; giving Mesopotamia, Persia, and the Mohammedan mountaineers beyond, their access to the wealth of Cairo, of Tunis, of all Barbary, and to the wealth also of half-conquered Spain.

Should the link be broken for good by Christian mastery of Syria, all Islam was cut in two and would bleed to death of the wound.

But though the Crusaders had *nearly* occupied all the narrow band, it was "nearly" and not "quite." There ran down the edges of the desert a string of cities and their connecting road—Aleppo, Homs, Damascus—which remained wholly in Moslem hands and still threatened the seacoast belt and its Christian garrisons.

Their inability, through lack of numbers, to hold *all* the corridor between the sand and the waves left all the effect of the Crusades incomplete, and to this must be added the effects of blood.

The Christian, Western host which had seized the "link," the "Bridge," in the First or Great Crusade was mainly French. Its fighting corps of armed knights and their followers was mainly Gallic; Norman, Provençal, Angevin, Lorrainers and Picards, with Flemings and some few Rhinelanders as well. National divisions had hardly yet arisen among Christian men, who were all of one strict religion and therefore of one habit of mind. But the blood told, and the *Franci* (whom the court of Constantinople called the "Gauls") had the weakness as well as the strength of their race as it has been known throughout history. They had its intense energy, its aptitude for arms, its sudden enthusiasms and, in such moods, exalted unity of aim; they had further its aptitude for interpenetrating the society of the conquered. But they had also its violent personal conflicts, its vice of faction and recurrent civil war: the private ambitions and greed of individual leaders: the sudden distractions and the following of some new thing.

All this would weaken them: but more still the lack of reinforcement in so very distant and isolated an advance guard. Merchants and pilgrims came in numbers, the Italian galleys enlarging Eastern trade. Armed adventurers singly and by bands reached the "Francs of Over-sea"—the men of *Outre-mer*. But not enough. The harvest garnered by the Great Crusade remained insufficient and precarious; its results were already shaken when within fifty years there came a loss of critical territory, the northern bulwark of the realm the Crusaders had founded—Edessa. The spasmodic attempt to recover from the check was what we call the Second Crusade—a brief and insufficient effort at reinforcement which filled the middle of the twelfth century, 1147-48.

There followed another somewhat briefer period of less than half a century, in which all runs down to ruin, the attempt to hold what had been won grew more and more difficult, and the immediate military objective of the Crusaders was lost through the fall of Jerusalem in 1187 after the overwhelming, in 1187, of the last Christian rally at Hattin.

Hattin was the end.

That disaster did, indeed, rouse the men of our race and religion to a final effort which fills the latter years of the twelfth century, as the First Main Crusade had filled the latter years of the eleventh century; but it was of no avail. The defeat of Hattin had been final.

This belated effort, in which all the strength of Western Christendom rallied to the saving of a lost cause, is known as the Third Crusade.

Its expeditions, led by the three great sovereigns of the West, the French King, the Plantagenet, the German Emperor, set out from a civilization which had grown greatly in stature since the Oriental war began, and so grew through the new life aroused by the Crusades. Europe in the century of the Crusade had become far more learned and more brilliant—also more wealthy.

Therefore this "Third Crusade" is most fully related and stands out most vividly in our history and fiction. It is Saladin and *Coeur-de-Lion.*

But the picture is out of perspective. The battle was lost before these last crusaders landed. Their belated and unsuccessful effort is but an epilogue, of no great interest to the prime question "Why did the Crusading effort fail?" It had already failed. When the main forces of the newcomers had withdrawn, by the autumn of 1192 all was over.

Points upon the seaboard of the Levant were maintained with difficulty for a hundred years more; sundry efforts against this and that point of Mohammedan territory were continued fitfully, generation after generation, right on till the end of the Middle Ages and the beginning of modern times.

They still bore the name of Crusades, but they were true Crusades no longer. The initial clear attempt to break and master the Mohammedan pressure upon our civilization was in ruins.

Therefore it is the First or Great Crusade which is essential to an understanding of the struggle; it alone was victorious; its success advanced for less than fifty years. Whatever followed on it was but the rear-guard action of a defeat.

*   *   *

In considering the nature of an armed issue, the military character of the opposing forces, the strategy and tactics of the campaigns, each division of such a statement requires expansion.

The nature of any military issue, even the sharpest and briefest conflict, includes three separate considerations; we have to consider the immediate and conscious motive which led men to engage in the shock; we have also to consider the large underlying instinctive forces at work, of which the conscious and immediate motive is, as it were, but the spearhead; lastly, we have to consider the deflection of both motives and their results—for invariably, in the story of a human struggle, however definite the original aims, however clearly seen the target, something other than the mere reaching of it, or the mere missing of it, results. Two things always breed a third; and the two opposed forces, though as clearly divided as black and white, will never present the mere victory of the one or the mere defeat of the other. Something which neither the attacker nor the defender intended issues from the turmoil.

Then again, the military character of the opposing forces in these great duels of history means much more than the nature of their armament and of the personnel which waged the war on either side. To understand the military character of any large event in war, one must consider race, climate, economic circumstance, and all that properly enters the mind of a competent military leader engaged in battle, short or prolonged, against another. One must consider the ground, the possibility of defense and its nature, and all the circumstances that make for triumph or disaster.

The last title, the strategy and tactics of the particular campaigns, is more definite and narrower than either of the first two; yet that also needs some expansion. The strategy on either side is never fully planned, the part played by accident must be remembered, and the constant sudden surprising alliance between genius and good fortune, as also, for that matter, between good fortune and incompetence.

All this we shall observe during that living story through the course of which our fathers all but re-established the spiritual mastery of Europe over the East: all but recovered the full patrimony of Rome.

That story must not be neglected by any modern, who may think, in error, that the East has finally fallen before the West, that Islam is now enslaved—to our political and economic power at any rate if not to our philosophy. It is not so. Islam essentially survives, and Islam would not have survived had the Crusade made good its hold upon the essential point of Damascus.

Islam survives. Its religion is intact; therefore its material strength may return. *Our* religion is in peril, and who can be confident in the continued skill, let alone the continued obedience, of those who make and work our machines?

2

THE ISSUE AND THE OCCASION

THE ISSUE

The Roman Empire, from which we all derive, stretching from the Scottish mountains to the Euphrates, from the Rhine and Danube to the Sahara, was gradually converted to the Catholic Faith in a period of three centuries: from about A.D. 30 to A.D. 330. By this last date in the fourth century, the New, and first Universal Religion, had become predominant in administration and social life. The emperors, the monarchs of the world, accepted the Creed: their subjects followed them.

Unfortunately that vast creative change came too late to save altogether a society perishing of pagan despair in its old age. The Church saved all that could be saved. Through the Empire's conversion we have been able to survive. What had been Rome, what became Christendom, though divided in government and sinking lower and lower in crafts and culture, cohered. The western half of our Europe suffered from the chaos of permanent civil wars between various bodies of Roman Federated troops under their chieftains. The Roman army, in which the whole structure of society depended, had been more and more recruited (for their cheapness) from the half-civilized tribes: Slavs and Germans, who lay upon the borders, who were permeated with Graeco-Roman ideas even in religion, but these insufficiently absorbed.

With such a soldiery in power, with central authority broken down, we entered the Dark Ages. We had grown weak. The outer, savage world raided and harried what was left of Europe. But we fought hard to maintain our nearly ruined heritage, and through those phases of constant raids from the outer pagan savagery we still carried on.

After the year 1000 the tide turned. The siege was raised— Western Europe awoke. Building, the arts, learning expanded. Soon we were to arise in the splendor of the Middle Ages after the material decline of the Dark. The Faith had carried us through.

But it had been a close thing. In the Western half of the Empire where the great common act of religion, the Mass, was Latin in form, and where various generals of the barbarized Roman army had taken over local government and the levying of local taxation, society broke into local fragments, from the gradual coalescence of which were to arise, much later, the western European nations. In the Eastern half, where the Liturgy was mainly Greek, but where also the Mass was said in Armenian, in Syriac, in Coptic, etc., the unity of society was maintained by the strength of Monarchy. There was an all-powerful and all-revered Emperor at Constantinople, who was still regarded in a vague way as being the Emperor of the whole of Christendom. But he was only actively powerful, he was only obeyed, within a fluctuating border which included, at its widest, parts of Italy, Greece and the Balkans, Asia Minor, Syria, North Africa, Egypt and Spain.

Half a lifetime after the year 600 this Eastern part of the Empire, the most highly civilized, the wealthiest, and the only united part, was challenged in an unexpected fashion.

Hitherto, its only dangerous enemy had been the Persian power to the east, which had sometimes pushed raids as far as the Mediterranean coast of Syria, taking Antioch and even Jerusalem, but not permanently holding them. The Roman Empire—its most highly organized, Greek-speaking part—held Syria normally and Egypt and Asia Minor, as well as its European mainland, until there came this new, quite unexpected force out of the desert.

One Mohammed had preached in desert Arabia (outside the

effective boundaries of the Empire) a powerful new heresy, to which he and his eager followers converted by force and zeal the pagan Arabs and which was to prove violently attractive to great masses of the Eastern population.

This new movement was, on its religious side, an intense simplification of the Catholic body of doctrine, eliminating nearly all that had seemed difficult to the untrained masses: the Trinity, the Incarnation, above all the mysterious Sacrament, and therefore the priesthood. On the political side it got rid of the burden of debt, the shame and suffering of slavery, the toils of an elaborate legal system and the lawyers who battened on it. It also ministered to the jealousy felt by outlying parts for the despotic central power at Constantinople. The message of Mohammed promised easy thinking on the religious side, freedom on the political; freedom not only to the individual but to local groups—the Egyptians, for instance. The individual was relieved from his debts and from legal constraint; the social groups from their domination by a distant imperial government with its arbitrary rule and its heavy weight of taxation.

The new creed came to be called Islam, that is, "The Acceptation," and has retained that name. Those who followed it were the "True Believers." We call them also, from the name of the great heresiarch who launched their effort, "Mohammedans." We also talk of the culture they founded as the "Moslem" world.

Not long after Mohammed's death, in A.D. 634, his Arab followers broke forth, a swarm of eager desert cavalry sweeping northward and making converts wherever it passed. Those who joined it, if they were slaves or debtors, recovered their freedom and could henceforward boast their independence of the imperial government. They were the more enthusiastic for their new creed because it seemed to them so simple of comprehension after the Christian affair of sacrifice and renunciation and difficult strain: its hierarchy of priests and its mysteries. The new enthusiasm, sweeping the Oriental world much as Communism proposes to sweep the Western world today, enthusiastically preached one God. It revered Jesus Christ as the greatest of the prophets, but rejected the complication of the Trinity. It revered Our Lady highly—far the highest among women, but not the Mother of God. It offered comprehensive worship to the Deity, but it swept away the Mass with its Communion and all the rest. It had hardly a ritual; only prayers that all could follow, and a social system which men could easily adopt and find just.

Within a century of the first change, the soldiery of this new thing, Islam, had mastered and garrisoned and were governing Syria, North Africa, and much the most of Spain. They had even for a moment thrust into the heart of France, whence they were thrown back to the Pyrenees. They had thus dismembered the Roman Empire of the East and had overrun North Africa and Spain in the West.

There remained, of course, in the countries they thus garrisoned and held, a great number (for generations a large majority) of subject orthodox Christians; but these pretended to no political power. They paid tribute to their Arabian masters and those of their own fellows who in great numbers had joined themselves to these new Arabian masters. Through these Christians and renegades the old culture went on, for they could build and they could write and calculate and do all that had been done by civilized men. But political power was in the hands of the Moslem soldiery and their chiefs.

Islam mastered not only Syria and Egypt and North Africa and most of Spain but rapidly extended itself eastward, seizing the very fertile plain and wealth of Mesopotamia, flooding with its religion and arms Persia and the tangle of mountains on the borders of India and up into the steppes of Asia; and here it was, on this Asiatic border (which Western soldiers had visited after the campaigns of Alexander but had never colonized nor transformed in their own image), that Islam, this new power and expansion, did a fatal thing: it introduced the Mongol: it opened the gates to a racial force of murder and destruction.

The Mongol of the Asiatic steppes, nomadic hordes of mounted men, horrible in the eyes of all Westerners, detestable to the European, were favored by Islam in the following fashion:

The original Arabian conquest looked to be short-lived. As a political power it had no sense of unity save such as was given by a simple, widespread religion. Native commanders here and there took over the government of towns and districts, fought each other and combined in alliances that dissolved almost as soon as made: hardly a lifetime's lease. There was a moment when it seemed as though the power of Islam would break up into an anarchy, making possible the recovery of Africa and the Near East by the Christian power of the Empire seated in the Imperial City on the Bosphorus. Suddenly out of the steppes of Asia came one band, then another, of these hideous, swift, fighting, mounted Mongol hordes, brought up wholly to combat, archers and swordsmen, pouring out in clouds.

Centuries earlier these same Asiatics had forced their way into the heart of Europe. They had been beaten back; they had come again and again and still been beaten back. Many of them remained in permanent fashion in the neighborhood of the Black Sea and on the Middle Danube, where today the word "Hungary" perpetuates their name of Huns. But here they never governed; in the East, they did. They mastered, by their fighting quality, their physical endurance, and their ruthlessness, the central power of the Moslem world. They became the bodyguard and afterwards the supplanters of the caliphs of Baghdad. They were the real power, acting in the name of the Commander of the Faithful. *That* is the prime business which led at last to the Crusades: the Mongol, the Turk.

The Issue to be joined was the issue between the main bulwark of Christendom on the east, Byzantium, and the pressure of these savage horsemen upon its frontiers.

Byzantium had held out bravely. Asia Minor had been stoutly maintained and great Christian armies were recruited from it. But the pressure on its eastern border was constant and severe. That border might crack and let in the Turkish torrent of death.

It is remarkable that the Mongol hordes, from their first wave onward, had fitted in at once with the social structure and creed of Islam. Why and how this was so has never been explained. It has not even been described. Their own bloody or absurd superstitions, barbaric as they were, without substance or philosophy or reason, yielded at once to the religious spirit of the

society into which they came. They became not only Mohammedan, but fanatically Mohammedan, and through their military
power what had already begun to be the decline of Mohammedanism recovered.

The best general name for them is the name "Turk." They
had no conscious unity; they came in bands fighting for immediate gain. They were possessed, as the original Arabian horsemen
out of the desert had *not* been possessed, of a fierce lust for
cruelty and mere destruction, and the letting in of that spirit
and all its armed agents was the great and almost mortal wound
delivered indirectly by Islam to the civilization of Europe. They
burnt and unroofed and massacred everywhere in their campaigns. Successive arrivals of them were to continue in that
mood which was inherited from them by their mixed descendants
in whom the Mongol language (Turkish) remained, though the
Mongol features and habit of body had been transformed by perpetual intermarriage. Their function was the function of the
Destroyer, and from the first of the great names among them,
Attila, to the very last modern massacre of the remaining Christians in Asia Minor, they have brought with them nothing
constructive—only death.

But their fighting power, though it was merely murderous, was
of such energy that for centuries it continued dominant, and even
so late as little more than two hundred years ago it had
penetrated to the heart of Europe, besieged Vienna, and threatened to reach the Rhine. Of these successive Turkish waves, of
this Mongol abomination to which the original Arabian Islam
had opened the door, the one which here concerns us was the
Seljuk, for this it was, coming forward out of Asia in the eleventh century, which almost overwhelmed what was left of the
Christian East and which provoked the Crusade.

The Seljuk clan took their name from a chieftain three generations back from the moment of which I am here writing, the
last part of the eleventh century. He had extended his power as
the leader of all those bands one after the other until starting
from the steppes around the Aral Inland Sea, he had built up
a sort of loose empire based on nothing more than the terror

of small but fierce garrisons, the commanders of which soon quarrelled among themselves but, in coalition, could bring forward formidable armies.

Being the latest of the Mongol hordes, the Seljuk Turks had least benefited by intermixture with more civilized people. They were still dwarfish, slant-eyed Tartars, crouched on the saddle of their small, swift horses, riding with the absurd short stirrup of the nomads, kneeling over the horse's neck, as, do (or did) certain jockeys of our own day.

Their tactics were simple. Thousands of them came on, not in a close line but in a sort of thin extended flock, galloping closely at top speed, shooting with their short bows from the saddle then wheeling back again, while a second relay did just the same thing and then a third. Only when the enemy thus attacked was thoroughly shaken would they all come forward and charge with the curved, thin-bladed, very sharp sword, which, with their light bows, was their chief weapon. Mounted, mobile, and not dependent upon exact dressing, they would in this final charge work to envelop either wing of the strict, dense Byzantine line.

During the tenth century, at the end of what was for the West of Europe the Dark Ages (the generations when the Swabian German kings were wrangling for control of the Papacy, and when the Scandinavian pirates came so near to destroying our civilization in northern Gaul and in Britain), Imperial Byzantium, the last heir of the Roman Empire, the last island of the ancient culture, passed through a period of military and political resurrection. It owed this to the vigorous character of its Macedonian emperors. These had not only stood up to the pressure of Islam on the eastern borders, they had found it possible to carry the counter-offensive into what had so long been Mohammedan territory. Christendom under their leadership pushed back Islam in spite of the successive waves of Turkish invasion. The Turks would raid into Byzantine territory in Asia Minor, but never came near to establishing a permanent foothold—until one fatal day, the day of Manzikert.

A Byzantine counter-attack upon Mohammedanism even

reached halfway down the Syrian coast. There was a moment when it threatened Mesopotamia.

But the strength of this revival in the Christendom of the East, in the Christians of the Greek rite, was sapped by political intrigue at the center. That political intrigue was mixed up with an "intellectual" disease comparable to the movement called today in Europe by the barbaric names of "Pacifism," and "Anti-Militarism." The coming into power of such politicians as batten upon movements of that kind undermined the whole new strength which the Macedonian Emperors had built up. The last fighting emperor could no longer be certain of proper support in the field against the Turk.

They still had admirable recruiting material in what was still the numerous peasantry, and ample finance from what were still the wealthy towns of Asia Minor. Their generals and leaders in the field were drawn mainly from the great landowners of that same Anatolian land which was still the bulwark of Christendom against Islam. But the politician had done his work; the armed power was sapped: a collapse must come and did. The whole situation disastrously changed in one decisive action. At Manzikert[1] on August 19, 1071, the great-grandson of Seljuk, the Turk, Alp Arslan, struck the fatal blow.

* * *

After so many invasions of the base Mongol stock, apt at nothing but destruction, thus fell—for the misfortune of the world— one far worse and to be of far greater consequence than any that had come before. The Seljuk Turks, coming in very great numbers, a mounted horde to be counted by the hundred thousand, now poured down southward to the loot in the last third of the eleventh century. Until that moment Asia Minor had stood well rooted, the bastion of the Christian world. We have seen how it furnished the economic basis of Constantinople and its

---

1. Of the several ways in which the name is spelled I adopt what has long been commonest. The latest and, I am told, most scholarly form is "Manazgerd"—but "Manzikert" is the more familiar and shall be retained.

military basis as well; revenue and the recruitment of armies. Its high central plateau, its fertile well-populated seacoasts, its many cities holding a continuous tradition from Greek and Gaulish ancestors, filled with the remaining great buildings of antiquity, the region which had been the early seedbed of the Christian religion, formed, as it were, the pedestal upon which the strength of Byzantium reposed. Occasional raids from Islam had pierced Asia Minor, but they had not affected in the main that wealth in men and goods and agriculture, seaports and commerce, nor divided them from the central discipline of the great capital on the Bosphorus when this new Turkish horde, far larger and more savage than any that had gone before it, increased the menace on the northeastern frontiers.

The Roman Emperor, Romanus Diogenes, went out to meet it with good hope of succeeding, as our civilization had always hitherto succeeded against the black menace of more barbaric Asia. We had failed to save Syria and Mesopotamia for Christ, but they had not been ruined, the high tradition of culture remained with them: this last menace was another matter. It needed to be dealt with at once, for if Asia Minor were overrun, Constantinople would come next and Europe be open to the destroyer.

The Emperor raised against these horsemen a force of the highly disciplined Byzantine sort—heavy cavalry in numbers greater than any that had hitherto marched out against the barbarian. He had sixty thousand highly trained men, drawn from all the provinces of the Empire, and aided by some small proportion of mercenaries recruited from the west, French and German and other. When the clash came, near the frontier fortress of Manzikert, our world was reaching the end of that long generation in which all Europe had been stirred with a new life. The stirring had begun with the Norman organization of Sicily and South Italy, continued through the vital reform of the Church under the man who was later to be pope, as St. Gregory VII, bringing remote Britain back into the high new life of Europe through the Norman conquest.

The Emperor who thus marched out against the Mongol

hordes was a great soldier, in temperament certainly, and perhaps in science as well—but his political position was precarious.

Byzantine succession passed sometimes through marriage, sometimes through usurpation; this last Romanus Diogenes had become emperor but a few years before, succeeding by marriage with the widow of his predecessor. He was the object of fierce enmities and jealousies at the Byzantine Court, and of continual intrigue, through which all the while ran that rising hiss of academic hostility to the military spirit. The force which marched out to its doom by Manzikert was coherent and well-disciplined; numerically inferior to the enemy in the proportion of perhaps three to five but superior in defensive armament and in training for tactical movement upon the field. The light-armed, light-horsed Mongol marauders, skillful with the bow, had not yet proved the equals of the civilized Greeks in formal war.

The Emperor committed the initial error, against which the textbooks of military science in the Eastern Empire had warned generals for centuries. Strongly armed, well-disciplined coherent forces will miss their prey if that prey be loosely organized, highly mobile horse which can retire (after doing its utmost of damage) more rapidly than the heavier opponent can pursue. It should be essential, in meeting the lighter and more mobile force, to guard against envelopment and to drive the enemy towards some obstacle against which he can be pinned. Fighting in open country without such an obstacle to check his retirement, the light and mobile enemy may retire indefinitely.

The Emperor did indeed advance successfully in front of Manzikert; he also secured himself against envelopment from the more numerous and lighter horse opposed to him by placing at the proper distance in the rear a strong reserve prepared to move right or left at a moment's order and check any effort at turning either wing. But he had apparently made no plan for backing the Turkish myriads against something that could check their retirement. He shepherded them towards no defile of mountain pass or river crossing or morass; he engaged in country where they were free to retire indefinitely. And retire they did, still continually fighting; he pressed on past their camp, and still they eluded him though still harassed.

At last, with his men exhausted by an overpressed forward movement and in great heat, he had no choice but to retire upon his own camp far behind. That retirement was made at first (apparently) in reasonable order, but as it proceeded the intervals grew confused and the line irregular; the detachments at the extremities (notably the foreign mercenaries from western Europe) got cut off from the main center. The whole force was in danger of dislocation, and the retreat might turn into a rout.

The day was ending; but the reserve might yet have restored the action, permitting the Emperor to save his army and to fall back securely behind the entrenchments of his camp. He was destroyed through the jealousy of his rivals. The commander of that reserve abandoned the field, saying that the Emperor had lost his battle and must suffer the consequence. As for the main command under Romanus, one portion of it fled and the center was overwhelmed. With the approach of darkness and during the night there was a general massacre. The Emperor himself was wounded and taken prisoner. The bulk of the Byzantine army was no longer in being; Asia Minor lay open to a swirling tide of Mongol barbarians.

Such was the battle of Manzikert. . . .

It is not possible to say of any one action in history, "On this the fate of the world depended," though certainly of each great critical action one can say that the future for generations to come was molded by its results. What one can certainly say of Manzikert is that the remaining Greek and Christian civilization received a mortal wound. The Mongols overran, devastated, and destroyed all that land of hither Asia which had been the solid foundation of the Byzantine power; the reservoir of Byzantine landed wealth, the nursery of our religion. The victorious Turks pillaged and killed wholesale. They overthrew permanent buildings wherever they went. They so cut at the roots of all civilization that it withered before them. Within much less than a lifetime the whole vast district of interior Asia Minor was ruined. In such strongholds as remained, Turkish garrisons and governors established themselves. The menace came to the gates of Constantinople.

Manzikert, the shock that launched the Crusade, would have destroyed us—but for the Crusade. Constantinople would have fallen; all Europe would have been involved—but under that stimulus the West moved. Gaul and the Rhine, Normandy, Flanders, Aquitaine, Lorraine armed, faced east, and went forward.

The issue was the life or death of Christendom.

THE OCCASION

The occasion which launched the Crusade was the action of one man.

It is not often that one can say this so positively in history as one can say it of 1095. Great movements of their nature rise from the profound and infinitely complex organic mass of human things. You see a tendency arising, confused forces at work, some general convergence, a movement of upheaval, the whole thing is like one of those larger waves which heave their shoulders up out of the deep, monsters and blind. So it was with the religious revolution of the sixteenth century, so it was with the Western collapse of central government from Rome in the fifth. So was it *not* with the great Crusade.

All the tendencies were there, all the confused convergences of force; but the striking out of action, the setting forth was the work of one will and one voice acting upon the material thus prepared. Had not that individual determination been taken and that one speech delivered, the march into the Orient would not have begun.

The man who so willed and acted was he who had been made pope to continue the work of the great Gregory. He had taken the title of Urban II, and now, on November 8, 1095, the center of the Gauls at Clermont in Auvergne, he gave the word.

For near a hundred years Europe had been prepared against such a moment. The pagan assault on Christendom had been beaten off and tamed; the Danish pirates of the North Sea, few in numbers but viciously desperate in destruction, had failed to destroy Britain and northern France. They had easily been bridled and settled down in the Second Lyonnese, which took from them a new name—Normandy—ever since; but there was little admixture of Scandinavian blood. The pagan Slavs on the Eastern Marches had ceased to be the enemies of the civilized and Christian thing. The Hunnish Ugrians, pagan also, had been stopped on the Lech. Their king had accepted Baptism, and the government of the Dacian Plain, thenceforward to be called Hungary, was after 1000 an outlier of our culture and its faith.

In this new relief from the siege that had been threatening our destruction all around at the hands of wild men who could neither build, write, nor frame laws, the menace from Islam became isolated and more prominent. The whole of the eleventh century was filled with that contention.

The field in which the struggle continually raged was the field south of the Pyrenees. There Christendom, by bands in turn isolated and associated, in repeated blows, in alternate advance and retreat, gradually hammered back the Moslem. There the new knighthood of Europe, the new conception of an armed and mounted nobility, proved itself by experiment. The last of the Mohammedan leaders to unite all Moslem Spain against the Cross, the great Almanzor, had died in 1002. The interrupted but ever-rising tide of the Christian reconquest reached and held Toledo in 1085. All that long lifetime was filled with the spirit of a coming triumph against Mohammed. Adventurous squires from Normandy had gathered small strong bands in those same years to thrust the Saracen out of Sicily and to regain a Christian realm in the Mediterranean.

Then had come the change in Syria, the detested and sterile, torturing Turk, in the place of the old Arabian dignity; the bullying and worse of the pilgrims who continually streamed eastward to the Holy Places; the desecration of the Sepulchre of the Lord.

Further, the fruits of Manzikert were maturing. The Greek Island of high Christian civilization, lying in immediate fear of death by violence, called in paid adventurers even from those westerners who were quarrelling with it and attempting its conquest also.

St. Gregory VII, the greatest of the popes, he who had in the midst of the century reorganized and restored the Church, had, in the midst of his mortal anxieties and strains, dreamt of a universal Christian tide swelling out through the Levant and rescuing the Sacred Land. But the moment had not come. It came now ten years after Gregory's death. But the man who continued Gregory's work and confirmed the strength of the Papacy as Gregory had confirmed the structure of the Church, Urban II, ruled by no accident but with deliberate choice as of generalship. He gave the call.

The council had been summoned to Clermont to deal with very different things, largely with the condemnation of the King of France and his irregular divorce, more with the new details of ecclesiastical discipline. The abbots and bishops met there on November 18, 1095. For the first nine days not a word was heard of any matters other than those which the Great Assembly had been convened to debate. The tenth day, of set purpose, Urban rose to preach, not to his fellows of the hierarchy, but to the huge crowds of knights, adventurers and merchants, pilgrims and wandering folk, who filled the streets of Clermont. The story of what followed is famous. The loud cries of, "God wills it!" *Dieux le volt!* were taken up, repeated, swelling from the multitude below, roused by that impassioned oratory from the man who was the chief of Christian men. It was this speech which made, in a moment, the Crusade. It made not the material, but it set the material afire; and the fire was lit deliberately by Pope Urban. It spread throughout the West, and the air was filled with the name "Jerusalem."

Urban, having roused the world, continued: a month after Clermont he called a second Council at Limoges which filled the last days of the year—up to December 31, 1095, and thence onwards all winter, spring, and summer he spoke in the west of France and the south, from Carcassonne to Angers, from Tours to Bordeaux: one man doing one man's work.

What man was he? Was he as great as his occasion? Certainly

his effect was great, the thing he did.

He was French like those to whom he appealed. He was of Champagne, born at Chatillon of the Marne from a petty feudal family: the class of one-manor lords who descended from the old Roman estate holders, the owners of the *villae* with their slaves; the men who were called "Squires" in later England; in France, "small noblesse." It was the class whence half the creative minds of the Middle Ages came, as they came in modern times till yesterday from the professional upper-middle class, the men of liberal education. He had been trained at Rheims, a day's ride from his birthplace, and by the great St. Bruno, the soul of Cluny and of the Reform.

Urban summed up in himself that generation in the strong conflict of which his character had been annealed; the new Europe of the Middle Ages coming to birth: the wrestling between the anomaly of a clumsy nominal Empire in the hands of Germans and the high spiritual head of the West, the Pope, whose rule lay but in one sphere, ecclesiastical, but whose power there, unlike that of his lay rival, was indeed universal.

The first shock of Urban's cry raised tumults; confused mobs without a framework, wild with the zeal of enthusiasts first moved. The name of Peter the Hermit, the Picard, of Walter the German Knight, of Leisingen, of the Tubingen lord, and of Volkmar are best remembered among these incompetent robbers. Herds of some thousands already doomed, as must be all herds, straggled down the Danube way, were contemptuously ferried across to Asia by the Emperor, to whom such leaderless, hardly armed mobs were no threat, though their pillage and worse had made difficult the path the regular Crusaders were to follow.

For months after that creative speech at Clermont, such bands, mainly German, gathered at the spell and straggled off eastward. They massacred the Jews of the Rhine by way of send-off, storming or failing to storm the palaces of the bishops who would protect such victims, murdering in particular the Chief Rabbi of Mayence to prove their contempt for the special protection of him by the great lay rulers, the Emperor and the Duke of Lorraine.

Their anarchy filled all the spring of '96. They trailed off in successive mobs eastward to die well-merited deaths at the hands of the outraged peasants of the Danube whom they despoiled, or at the hands of the Turks in the salty dust of Anatolia. In the military story of the Crusades they count for nothing.

It is after the departure of these wastrels that the first true army sets out, feudal but organized so far as a feudal force could be organized. It was led by Godfrey, the Duke of Lower Lorraine, who took a second name from his long Ridge-Castle of Bouillon, in the Ardennes.

He set out with his ordered host, and with that the Crusade begins.

3

THE ARMIES

THE RECRUITING FIELD

The Crusading hosts and their fighting in the field cannot be understood unless we first understand the society of the eleventh century in Western Europe and particularly in Gaul. For it was Gaul, between the Rhine, the Atlantic, the Alps, and the Pyrenees, which furnished by far the greater part of the armies which attempted to restore the Christian Roman world and throw back the Mohammedan in the East. By seeing the thing as Gallic and feudal we understand in what its armies were at first so enormously effective, so suddenly ineffective: how they conquered like a flooding tide: why they were soon exhausted and failed.

The society of Western Christendom in the eleventh century was something so different from anything we know today that unless we learn what it was, we cannot understand any of its activities, still less a major activity such as the Great Crusade.

To see how true this is, let us imagine ourselves explaining modern Western Europe to a man of the late eleventh and early twelfth century. At the first sight of our modern condition he would be bewildered: "Where," he would say, "is the unity of Christendom? What is all this about 'Nations'? How are men got to work as craftsmen or on the soil without a communal village organization? Where does authority lie and how is it divided?—and, above all, *why* do you go on as you do go on in a fashion so utterly different from ours? *What are your spiritual motives?''*

We should have to explain to him that there is no common religion in Europe today and, for the mass of men, no religion at all; that the only motives at work are economic, that the way by which labor is enforced from unwilling men is the capitalist system. We should have to explain how property has been taken away from the masses and these reduced to wage slavery, and yet how the wage slave is not as yet technically a slave, but nominally a citizen, free and equal with his wealthy masters. It would all seem to make nonsense in his ears no doubt, but with patience one might explain the major outlines of the thing.

We should have to show him how our society was organized; the moral authority of the national idea, the theory of uniformity and equality among citizens in spite of the enormous contrasts in wealth, the absolute sovereignty of each nation, the lack of any common authority over the various nations, the immense power which a modern government can exercise, especially if it be allied with the central financial forces at work in its chief city; still more if allied with international finance. We should have to show him how the thing looked from below: most of men not peasants constrained to labor by destitution, living under the terror of insufficiency and insecurity, and therefore better content with a secure wage slavery or with communism than with insecure freedom. We should have to show him how, in our society, expression on any useful scale is possible only through the possession of newspapers; how these are either controlled by a handful of men in a plutocracy, or by a handful of men in a despotism.

We should have to explain how production is today undertaken for *profit*. We should have to explain how this profit was got hold of by shareholders in companies and by banks which lend money (both real and imaginary) at usury and upon whom the whole economic structure depended: how shares in property were kept secret and at the same time were fluid, saleable and purchaseable at a moment's notice: how no stability in hereditary property remained.

Then we should have to explain how religion had ceased to be universal and corporate among us: the unhappy descendants of that Christendom which *he* took for granted, and in which he saw a common morality and worship strengthened by a growing centralization under the age-long headship of the Western Patriarch who was also the universal religious chief, the pope. We should have to tell him how first, 400 years and more after his day, that unity had been broken by a religious revolution in which the corporate economy of the craftsmen disappeared and the already long-decaying village system disappeared with it. We should have to describe the gradual loss not only of common religious organization but of all doctrine, until today, seven hundred years after his time, there remained but a special body still holding to full doctrine: around it various fragments of that doctrine being vaguely held as opinions, and a much larger mass by which the whole system of doctrine was forgotten.

With such an outline before him our eleventh-century Christian man might in some dim fashion guess gropingly at what we have become: he would understand the absence of spontaneous movements, he would understand how it is that although modern Europe boasts a number of large, highly organized armed forces, which are fully disciplined units, working each as one body, it is yet incapable of common action by two or more national armies combined. He would perhaps half understand our political chaos as flowing from our moral chaos; why what remains of Christendom is terrified at the approach of war, but nonetheless advancing it.

A modern man trying to understand the Crusades must do the converse of all this. He will never understand their triumphs or their errors, least of all their failure, unless he has some vision of what the Western European world, the ground which today we call France, England, the Rhineland and Italy, meant to its inhabitants in the generations born between A.D. 1050 and A.D. 1070: men fighting in 1095-1100 when the hosts of the Great Crusade arose in a ground swell from Gaul and its adjacent lands, broke the old limits of the Dark Ages, surged forth foaming eastward, and for a moment submerged the Mohammedan world, nearly cutting it in two, and all but destroying its vital communications. These great hosts sprang from a certain Recruiting Field—a district and a society whence such forces could be drawn. What, then, was the Recruiting Field whence the Crusading armies proceeded?

Much of the detail of that society is lost. Not a few of its most common terms, intended to record social and economic relationships, no longer convey a precise meaning to us; on some of the most important there is still (and will, I think, always continue to be) unresolved debate. Thus the English record of Royal dues, commonly called Domesday Book (contemporary within ten years of the First Crusade), is a matter for unending controversy. Yet we know that society sufficiently to see how it contrasted with the recruiting field of the Byzantine forces on the one hand, and of the Mohammedan forces on the other, and how it conditioned the raising and working of armed forces drawn from every rank of the West.

The recruiting field whence the hosts of the First Crusade were drawn was that part of Christendom which included Italy, the Rhine valley with its tributaries, the upper Danube, England, and Southern Scotland, France and the Netherlands, Scandinavia and the northern part of the Spanish Peninsula. We must exclude Ireland, because Ireland did not contribute to the First Crusade; but we cannot exclude any other district mentioned because, although very few mustered from outside Gaul, although the effort as a whole was Gallic (or we should say today "French"), yet it was neither consciously nor actually attached to Gaul as a district, still less to any precise idea of a French nation.

National differences were already in existence and were recorded; the Byzantines, for instance, remarked the volubility and quick emotions of the "Gauls." When the native Saxon-speaking English appeared on the coast of Syria with their small contingent they were spoken of as something separate. But the ancient unity of the Roman Empire and of Christendom, its successor, was still too strong for provincial differentiation.

The great line of cleavage was between the Christian and the non-Christian. This is the main truth, and without a sense of

it no man has an idea of the generations between A.D. 500 and
A.D. 1000. No more grossly unhistorical error was ever
propagated than that which reads into these times our modern
preoccupations on language and on the more than half-imaginary
thing called "race." When Charlemagne raised his vast forces
for the expansion of civilization eastward to the Elbe and
beyond, most of his men must have spoken one or another Latin
dialect, a lesser number must have used various Germanic
dialects—for his recruiting field was most unevenly divided
between subjects of either speech. But no one troubled himself
on such a point. The Christian, civilized man from around
Cologne spoke German. So did the ruder pagan man from the
heaths of the Oder, but they felt no bond between themselves.
One was of the high imperial tradition, the other was an outer
fellow whom it was the business of the first to tame, order, and
instruct.

The German-speaking man from the eastern fringes of
Charlemagne's original realm, before the Saxon wars—from the
Rhine—was brother and kin to the man from the wide central
districts of the Seine, the Loire, and the Rhône. The man from
Aix was of one main sort with the man from Rouen or Orleans
or Narbonne; for they all had in common the same worship,
the same manner of thought, the same culture, letters, permanent
buildings, and laws, the same basis of Roman expression for
everything that counted—codes of justice, record, liturgy, and
above all, the Mass. As against that civilized traditional world
the barbaric pagan of Scandinavia or the Elbe was repugnant:
a thing to be resisted, overcome and absorbed. That task had
been accomplished long before the new awakening of Europe
and the Crusading March. The world whom Urban so stirred
had, for patriotism, an enthusiasm of religion, and for enemy,
not an opposing realm, but the pagan and the Mohammedan.

There was indeed, and had been for centuries, a second line
of cleavage of less importance between the Oriental Christians
who followed a Greek Liturgy in the Mass, and the Occidentals
who followed a Latin Liturgy: between the Christians who still
were or had been direct subjects of the Emperor at Constantino-

ple, and the Christians of the West over whom he had nothing but very vague claims, whom he could not order in anything, and from whom for centuries he had drawn no revenue—though he still thought of himself as the Emperor of the whole Christian world and was in a very tenuous way still so regarded, even by those who never behaved as his subjects and though the West had a nominal "Emperor" of its own.

This Western recruiting field, of which much the most important part, furnishing perhaps nine tenths of the whole Crusading army, was Gallic, depended in all its social structure upon what had once been the united and active Roman Empire. It was still governed as to its eastern part by one authority acting from one capital city, and had been so governed in its western part also until nearly the end of the fifth century.

That western part was separate not only in Liturgy but in political arrangement. The chief personage in the West was no longer an Emperor. He had come to be an ecclesiastic, the bishop of Rome. The primacy of his See over the rest of Christendom had always been admitted in the East as well as the West, but as the united civilization of Rome grew weak it acquired much stronger and more active power over its own western regions: North Italy and Gaul and Spain, Britain, the Rhine valley. What is called "the Medieval Papacy" existed in germ by the beginning of the fourth century, and was in active development by the sixth century. Mere custom had led to a difference in Liturgy between the East and West, not accompanied by any appreciable difference in doctrine, but the ecclesiastical authority in the West under the Pope of Rome had shaken off the civil authority of Constantinople three hundred years before the Crusade. The Emperor at Constantinople, affected by Mohammedan influence at his doors, had tried to enforce the destruction of images in the Italian churches and the cessation of liturgical service in connection with those images. Italy and the West had refused, and their refusal marked them off permanently from the Greek Eastern Christians.

But whereas the Greek East remained a centralized civil government under Constantinople, the Latin West under the

Roman bishop had no central civil rule. The Western world, with
its Latin Mass and the Pope as its center of unity and moral
authority, had fallen long ago into loosely divided districts, after
the decaying central political authority (from before A.D. 500
onwards) could no longer collect taxes or appoint officials in
the West as it *still* did in the East.

These divisions were the areas over which Roman generals
had, in the breakup of the central military authority, established
each his own rule, taking over the courts of justice and the taxation system and all the rest of it. Most of these generals and
their small armies of a few thousand men had been of German
stock, some apparently of Slav stock, because these districts on
the outer half-civilized borders of the Roman Empire had furnished cheap recruitment. The old Roman army upon which the
Roman State entirely reposed had come to be drawn from all
sorts of cheap labor; there were Celts in it also, Arabs, Moors,
and even Mongols from the northeast.

But the heads of the fighting groups which became more and
more independent of the central authority and were at last
wholly independent, were chieftains, mainly German, increasing
their authority over their half-civilized troops through family tradition. These chieftains would take on the names of the tribes
which they had originally ruled, though very early in the business these tribes had been absorbed in the general mass of
Roman society. Thus the title for a general of this kind being
Rex, there was a *Rex* of the little Frankish contingent, which
soon became like all the others, a mixed lot of Franks and Gallo-
Romans; there was a *Rex* of the Goths, both eastern and western;
there was a *Rex* of the Vandals, who may have been Slavonic
or may have been already largely German in speech, and so on.

These now independent generals, though all within the Roman
Empire, naturally warred one against the other, because victories
in this sort of game gave the victorious general a larger income
and a larger recruiting field. By the time of the First Crusade,
of course, all memory of this had long ago disappeared; but the
old names were still used, though they meant something quite
different from their original signification.

But as time went on, the officials appointed by these random generals, inheriting their power from the old Roman army and its half-barbaric recruitment, found that those to whom they delegated their authority over various districts could only be kept in a loose obedience. In the original Roman army there were high officials under the emperor called "companions"— *Comites*—(in the singular, *comes*, from which we get our word "count"). A general commanding-in-chief over a large area was called by the Latin title of *dux*, from whence we get our word "duke." The counts attached to the various cities or districts, having the duty of collecting much of the local revenue, began to keep much of it for themselves, and the *duces* [plural of *dux*], or generals over large districts, came to have so much local power that the whole thing (though the word "emperor" was revived in A.D. 800 by the king of the Franks for his own benefit) grew more and more decentralized. The commanders of territories great and small not only became virtually independent, but made their powers hereditary.

We must remember that all this time Christendom was being attacked violently by its enemies; by the northern pirates, by the hordes from Asia, and by the highly trained military forces fighting to extend Mohammedanism. Christendom was in danger of dissolution, and therefore each important military leader acted more and more on his own. You get districts which look at first sight like independent modern nations—the duchy of Normandy for instance, which was the old Roman division of the Second Lyonnese; or the county of Flanders—roughly the maritime Netherlands; the kingdom of Aragon in Spain; the kingdom of Castile; the kingdom of Navarre; the duchy of Brittany, and so on. But in each of them lesser lords had a power of their own, down to the petty lord of one village; so that the whole of Western Europe was a mosaic or medley of lordships large and small, with a bond sometimes very strict, as in Normandy, between the underlords and the overlords, sometimes much looser, as in central France.

Then again, a large group of more or less independent provinces would be held in a sort of loose unity under a *King*.

The title "king" meant that he had no overlord. He was the summit in a pyramid of overlordships and underlordships, but not necessarily as yet the most powerful or richest member of that pyramid. The King of France, for instance, was nominally the overlord of Brittany, Normandy, Flanders, Aquitaine, and the rest; but he was not a monarch in the full political sense of the word. He could summon his great vassals to help in the field for a few weeks, but he could not order them as soldiers. They in their turn could summon the lesser lords who held of them, but could not order them. They were bound only by loyalty and on special occasions for a short time.

The lords who were the superiors of one village only (the great majority of course), the greater lords (or barons who had separate rights over a whole group of villages, often widely scattered), had each a large measure of independence. The overlord who was virtually sovereign over a whole province (as was a Duke of Normandy or a Count of Flanders) held the allegiance of subordinate lords partly by the moral convention of the time, but also by the superior force he could bring into the field through having greater resources, but he had no true soldiers, no disciplined force, save what he might hire. The line of cleavage in society lay between those who received dues off the land as feudal superiors and all those below them. These receivers of dues formed a caste by the eleventh century. They were nobles. And all that noble class, from the lord of one village only to the commander of a whole province, formed a fighting class. Its trade was fighting. It had come to be that during the centuries of perpetual attack upon Christendom from the pagans and Mohammedans all around.

The main purpose of the fighting was the maintenance of Christendom against that attack, but subsidiary purposes ran that main purpose close. There was the purpose of maintaining claims against a rival; the purpose of increasing one's independence from a nominal superior, and even the purpose of earning a wage by hiring oneself out to fight for some bigger man engaged in a struggle of his own.

This feudal fighting class of armed and mounted gentlemen,

"nobles," fell roughly into three categories of income.

The very great majority were the lords of one village or two: not at any rate of so many villages as to make them important throughout any wide district. If they were lords of more than one village, the second or third would usually be in the neighborhood of the first. Nothing is more difficult in history than estimating the comparative value of income and revenue in different ages, but if we say that, in modern money, men of this group had each on the average some few hundreds of modern pounds a year but not a thousand, we should not be far wrong. Of course there were all manner of gradations, some quite poor for their rank, three or four hundred a year, others rich (two or three thousand), but that sort of average applies.

Next above these—not separated by any definite line, of course, but in bulk conspicuous—was a group of "many-village" lords: men gathering land dues from a dozen, or a score, or fifty village units, often widely separated, such widespread sources of income having come to them by descent from several feudal fortunes combining in one inheritance. These superior nobles often had dues from market towns and from mines and road tolls as well. They were on the scale of from say 3,000 to 10,000 or (exceptionally) 20,000 a year or more. It was to a family of this sort, but one of the more wealthy, that Tancred, Lord of Hauteville, the father of the Norman adventurers in South Italy belonged; and in later ages the Montforts, who became so famous, sprang from similar origins.

Lastly, far above all the rest in revenue, were the supreme lords of provinces—a Count of Toulouse, a Duke of Normandy or Brittany. These were not only virtual monarchs over great areas, but direct lords of very many villages and most towns therein. They drew revenue from the administration of law courts, from death duties paid them by great vassals, from "aids," that is, exceptional gifts offered by such vassals on special occasions, from the very large proportion of land *outside* the feudal system, called "Forest"; from harbor dues and road dues and market dues and the rest. They could also, and did, irregularly increase their incomes by selling posts of which they

had the patronage, and they had got hold of most of the public
goods which centuries before had belonged to the Imperial
Government. This group was on a vastly greater scale than the
one below them. They were few, and the greatest had incomes
of half a million upwards as we reckon such things today.

Throughout all these three groups reigned a common sentiment of noble blood, setting them apart from the mass of men.
It was a sentiment gradually developed since Roman times and
grown fully conscious in the generations before the Crusades.
Increase of income was aimed at and acquired by the marriage
of heiresses, women on whom a group of feudal revenues concentrated through failure of male heirs. There was no idea of
increasing by competition, as in modern commerce, still less
by force save in pursuit of a claim to inheritance by right. Such
claims were numerous and fiercely contested, but the conception
underlying them was always one of a just claim, not of
conquest—save over non-Christian land.

Lastly, and this is what most marks that time from ours, permanence of status and ownership was taken for granted. All—
from the small village lordship to the supreme feudal power over
a province—was thought of as hereditary, passing as a right from
father to son, or, lacking a surviving son, to a daughter.

Side by side with this fighting class, drawing land dues, was
a much smaller but most important religious or priestly class
which was also supported by portions of these dues on land.
They held these as endowments of their office. The parish priest
was endowed with dues on parcels of land; so was the bishop
above him, so were the convents and monasteries, large and
small. The endowment of these last came from gifts of land
which paid dues and had been made over by the founder, usually
a man of the noble class—especially the greater lords who commanded whole provinces. The Church thus organized was drawn
from all classes. It excluded the idea of a noble class and lived
its own life. Its members did not fight, but they taught in schools
and administered as public officers and decided many issues in
what came to be courts of their own using their own special
law. They also aided the government of a province or kingdom

with money, just as the fighting class aided it both with money and with arms.

So much for the two superior bodies in society, clerics and nobles, supported on land dues. Now if we look at all that from below and ask how the dues on land arose and were paid, what we see is the myriads of Christendom, perhaps thirty or forty times the total of the nobles and clerics, and occupied, as to far the greater part, in agriculture. There were towns, of course, some of them large, and a certain amount of commerce, and of course also a certain amount of necessary craftsmanship— smiths and carpenters and the rest—but it was work on the field that supported the community. The mass of men reaped and sowed and looked after flocks and herds.

They were organized in villages, each with its own territory; and the way in which work was got out of them and surplus values produced for the nobles and the Church can only be understood if we remember that the whole system had begun centuries before, under the active government of the Roman Empire when all Europe was one great civilization highly organized. The village of the eleventh century had slowly and imperceptibly developed from the Roman estate of the third, fourth and fifth centuries.

Now, these great Roman agricultural village estates were worked in the main by slave labor. That is the capital social fact at the root of the whole business—the thing which stands at the beginning of all our European development. We began as slaves under comparatively few masters, and we shall perhaps end by reverting to the same condition.

The great Roman estate had many other elements at work upon it, there were families of freedmen—people who had been slaves but were emancipated by their masters, but who owed on account of that emancipation some remaining service to their masters. There were also many small independent freemen owning farms greater or less. There were what we should call "ex-service men," that is retired soldiers, great numbers of whom, especially near the frontiers of the Empire, were of the semi-civilized tribes drawn from outside to form the bulk of the Roman armies. But the main division was the division between the master class and the slaves.

The old Roman slave master, living in the big house in the middle of his land or "Villa," had become, in the course of centuries, a noble and a feudal lord. The old village territory, most of which had been as a rule his private possession, had grown into a most complicated arrangement; the lord himself kept a considerable amount as his own directly administered property; often a quarter or even a third of the village land was so reserved. The rest was divided up among the villagers, descendants for the most part of the old slaves.

But by the time of the Crusades they were slaves no longer. The great bulk of them were both politically and economically free, they had hereditary right in the soil which they tilled, but they were unfree to this extent—that each parcel of land producing agricultural wealth in the village owed its dues, whether in labor or in kind, to the lord of the village. One family for instance would have, say, thirty acres, formed of a number of strips intermingled with the strips of others, for cultivation was largely cooperative. It would have to give so much produce to the lord at stated times, and it would have to furnish labor for the lord on certain specified days.

Of the total produce of the village much the greater part was owned by and consumed by the villagers; they had carefully protected rights in the village pasture, in the woodlands, and the common lands. On all this the villagers lived, each family continuing its little tenure by inheritance from father to son, but each little tenure bound to produce its quota for the lord as well as for itself. What it handed over thus to the lord and the amount produced on the lord's own land by the labor dues of the serfs (as the villagers in bulk may be called) formed the surplus values of the community; and those surplus values were the revenues which supported the noble class of every grade and the ecclesiastics.

Such was, very roughly, the scheme of that society. In practice there was an infinity of differentiation between the more and the less free, the small wholly independent man who was bound to no service and paid no dues; the often wealthier neighbor who was so bound to find forced labor or to pay dues. And the customs of the village, by which lord and serf were both bound, and freemen as well, differed infinitely from place to place; the observation of those customs was the chief social law of the time.

The bondmen of the "Villa"—as the village unit was still called, using the old original Roman name, or "Manor" as it was later called—were still in legal theory unfree. The lord could bind them to the soil, could claim their return if they moved away. He could forbid, by law, a serf from becoming a cleric, and so forth. Also, in mere theory, he could demand extra payment and extra labor indefinitely. But in practice the arrangement was elastic. The lord's active concern was to see that he got his fixed dues in goods and in labor. So long as the regular proportion of goods was delivered, and the work done at the stated times by the peasant family, a member of it, though legally unfree, would wander, would take holy orders, would engage in a craft or in traffic or hire himself out as servant or as soldier. Of the freeman's right to do any of these things there could be no question. Revolt against the regular dues was very rare, for they seemed part of the scheme of things. When such rare revolts occurred they were pitilessly suppressed by the noble, armed class. It was taken for granted by all that the government of the kingdom or province must put out all its strength to maintain the existing order of society, but that society had for its supreme authority in daily duty not force, but usage.

By a social structure such as this is explained the nature of those Crusading armies which it is so difficult for us of today to grasp. Such was the "Recruiting Field" present for the raising of troops in the adventure of the First Crusade.

THE STRUCTURE
OF THE CRUSADING FORCES

The structure of the great host which marched out eastward for the recovery of the Holy Sepulchre was determined by the form of that Western Christian feudal society which was their recruiting field. The fighting *mounted* class, the nobles, became of necessity the core of the fighting forces. The servants and retainers each could command or had hired, made up the armed infantry.

But its general character differed from that of older and other feudal armies in two ways; first, it was very much larger; second, it was intermixed with very many non-combatants.

The host was essentially a host of *pilgrims;* the armed as well as the unarmed thought of themselves as men engaged on a pilgrimage; a journey undertaken with a religious object for its goal and under a vow. That is why the unarmed formed a very large proportion of the whole: how large a proportion we do not know, but enough to surround the armed forces with a sort of *penumbra,* as it were, of civilians.

These were for the most part, of course, drawn from the poorest classes, those who were not bound to one particular sort of work in one particular place; those who were at liberty to go off. These came as much from the serf class of the day as from the free; and clearly the bulk of them had not the means to maintain themselves on a many months' march of 2,000 miles. How, then, were they provided with subsistence? Mainly by attaching themselves to particular leaders, but in part probably by arrangements for general provisionment made at the expense of the higher authorities.

We have no documents to guide us, we have not even a rough description of how the thing was done; all we know is that these first numbers did pour out, the first groups of them chaotically and almost unarmed, destined to destruction and yet able in some way to cover all the miles that separate the West from the East. The motive of almsgiving was a very strong one; there may have been support from this source. Anyhow, there certainly was attached to the original common effort of armed bands, many in large proportion unorganized, undisciplined, and for purposes of set battle unarmed folk, with many women and probably even children among them.

They were largely weeded out during the dreadful advance through the dog days over the salt tableland deserts of central

Asia Minor. By the time the main host appeared before Antioch it was reduced to perhaps one fifth, certainly to less than a third of what it had been in front of Nicaea; and in that surviving fragment the proportion of regularly equipped men organized, and as we should say today "embrigaded," was so much larger than it had been in the beginning of the expedition that it accounted for nearly the whole. The pilgrims who halted for so long before the walls of Antioch, and halted for so many months after the capture of the city through the disputes between the chiefs, were an army which had shed the bulk of its original surrounding mob. There were in the camp before the walls of Antioch, by the testimony of an eyewitness who was also the chief responsible officer for the political guidance of the Crusade—Adhemar—100,000 men; and we may be certain that the greater part of these were armed and obeying orders.

But what orders? We must not picture to ourselves anything like the strictly disciplined armies of antiquity and of modern times.

The forces were made up of two sorts, the second much larger than the first. The first sort formed one coherent body of a few hundred strictly attached to, partly paid by, one wealthy chieftain. The second was a crowd of feudal nobles, some with half a dozen dependents, some with scores.

Each of the great chieftains had a body of armed men strictly dependent upon himself; so many mounted knights, so many men on foot. For instance, we know (again by the testimony of contemporaries) that Baldwin of Boulogne, the younger brother of the great Godfrey, when he marched down into Cilicia with Tancred (each wishing to establish himself as local lord of that rich plain), had in his personal band 500 armed knights and 2,000 men on foot; and that Tancred had a much smaller body, a hundred knights and only quite a small body of men on foot, though there was a rather larger body of infantry following at Tancred's orders which came up with him later. These personal bands were kept at the expense of their lord; they were not free to leave him, they were of his household so to speak; but the great mass of the knights were not in that position.

There are various estimates as to the proportion of fully armed mounted knights to the rest of an armed force at that moment; some put it as low as 5 percent, others as high as 10 percent. It varied from one body to another, it varied also as to whom one might include in the term "armed men"—which might be extended from almost any of the half-equipped hangers-on to the regularly paid followers of a great provincial leader.

At any rate the knights, who were the main strength and meaning of an eleventh-century army, were a small minority of it. They were many of them small feudal lords—one-manor men. More were the younger sons and brothers thereof, who had set out with a certain capital in coin provided for them by the dues of their father's land, or borrowed from the Western moneylenders upon the security of those dues, to be paid during their absence.

The young nobles so provided were quasi-independent; they held themselves bound by allegiance, of course, to their feudal overlord; for instance, Raoul, the lord of Caen, followed the Duke of Normandy, as a matter of course; a man was bound in honor to his overlord. But still, the bond was loose especially in the course of a distant campaign. Feudal custom had arisen in limited and local conditions. The smaller feudal noble must keep the field for forty days with his overlord—but not longer.

A man who moved from one body to another, taking with him his immediate dependents (for even the poorest knight had some attendant, and most of them had several), was not a deserter in our sense; he was not even a deserter if he chose to ride away and have done with the whole business; the penalties which could attach to him for so acting were as a rule moral penalties only—if any.

Nor was the bond between the mass of the poorer men and the wealthier noble mounted men comparable to the modern bond of strict discipline. Gatherings of the common armed men to protest against some action of their leader's were not mutiny any more than gatherings of the populace in a medieval marketplace were sedition.

It is very difficult for the modern man to envisage an armed force of that day, principally because the bond of discipline as we understand it was absent. There was organization, and that organization must have run throughout the whole great body, otherwise it could not have moved at all; but it was an organization enforced on no rigid universal scheme such as controls a modern military instrument.

The reason that the numbers melted away continually during the advance was not only because many were lost through famine and disease and desertion, but also through men's preferring to attach themselves to this or that successful leader after each occupation of a post on the way to Jerusalem. Bohemond got Antioch, Baldwin of Flanders got Edessa; and to each successful head of the new colony (as we may call it) so many would come offering service, seeing an opportunity of betterment thereby.

There is one point often neglected in connection with this great eleventh-century expedition: its finance.

Such an effort—the moving of a body some half million or more strong and doing no productive work for one year and a half at least, many of them for two and a half—required *of necessity* the accumulation of a large fund: a large reserve power of demand—counting food for man and beast, remounts and repairs of equipment, at least 25 million pounds of our money.

Of instruments of credit in form sufficient for such a crisis there were none. The thing was done by the carrying of bullion in separate parcels: stores of coin were used. Money would be carried with them by the lords who went forward, great and small, for it could be then carried in small bulk to sufficient value for the purposes even of so long a voyage.

Weight for weight, money was worth anything from between twenty-five to fifty times what it is worth today. The effect of this will be easily conceived. Two sovereigns, as we should call them, were the wages of a sailor working on board a Crusading ship for a year. A man could buy a serviceable horse for a pound. It needed no very heavy bag for the younger son of a small village lord, starting from Flanders, to make a twelve months' journey, during which, or at the end of which, conquest would refurnish him or, more probably, a leader from whom he could claim new funds.

Finance was also at the bottom of the determination of the great leaders, Bohemond and Baldwin and the rest, when once they had got across the desert plateau of Asia Minor, to carve out new states for themselves in the Orient. For each of these meant a field of taxation, dues payable by the inhabitants to the conquerors who had replaced their old Mohammedan masters. Thus also the money of the main advance had been largely exhausted by the time the Crusaders reached Antioch, and one sign of this was the famine. Funds flowed again after the capture of the city.

After the feudal structure of the first Crusading armies, proceeding from the social structure of our Western society in the late eleventh century, we must next appreciate the armament of these bodies.

In this department of armament the first thing the modern reader has to do is to see the thing in terms of cavalry—and it is not an easy thing for the modern reader to do that.

Our generation can still see cavalry as an auxiliary arm, though under conditions of mechanized warfare it is rapidly ceasing to be even that; but it requires a strong effort of imagination to visualize almost every decisive tactical movement as a movement of horse. Yet those were the conditions of Syria in the Crusading centuries. They had been the conditions of warfare throughout Europe and the Asiatic world for centuries before the Crusades, and were to remain so for centuries afterwards. The mounted man continually dismounted; he dismounted for siege work, and not infrequently for battle. But a mounted man he remained throughout. Warfare was conducted by the armed rider, whether of Islam or Christendom, whether French or Greek. Great masses of men on foot would accompany an armed force; though most of them as mere followers, some of them as servants, some used for special forms of attack and defense. Of those on the Christian side (not on the Mohammedan) the archer was a man on foot: but battles were won and lost by cavalry, and campaigns were conducted in terms of cavalry.

In the antique pagan world, the high civilization of the Graeco-

Roman period, it had been the other way about. Infantry had decided the issue. And with the original Greek states, as with the early Roman state, the Macedonian phalanx and the Roman legion were both essentially infantry formations with cavalry only auxiliary and in comparatively small proportion. But at the time when the whole of the ancient world was changing, that is in the third century A.D., one of the main revolutions was the increasing preponderance of the mounted man in war. The main cause of this was the social degeneration which marked the last generations of paganism. All sorts of other causes have been imagined, and of course that worst of all bad history, the imaginary conquest of the Roman Empire by outer invading barbarians—a thing which never happened nor could have been within a thousand miles of happening—played its part in the group of false arguments. But, I repeat, the main cause is plain before one's eyes for anyone to judge; cavalry became increasingly important as the discipline and coherence of society grew less.

A man on foot cannot stand up to a horse at a gallop or even at a fast trot; but an organized number of men on foot trained to stand together, held closely as one body by a firm discipline, can be got to withstand the threatening impact of such momentum. Give them projecting arms, such that the horse will flinch at the approach, and the resistance of the footmen is easier; give them missile weapons which may check the horse at a distance, and it becomes easier still. In a high material civilization even where the range of missile weapons is short, trained infantry can always be counted on to resist cavalry if the society from which it is recruited *and officered* has the same excellence in the military art as in others. But unless a sufficient degree both of cohesion and training be present, then in the absence of obstacles or missile weapons at long range, the horse will defeat the foot. And that is what happened as the society of the old Roman Mediterranean world began to change from within during that pivotal lifetime marked by the reign of Aurelian. A lifetime later, by A.D. 300 to 350, the horse had won, and cavalry remained supreme for more than a thousand years. The change took place, of course, within the framework of the Roman army, which became more and more barbaric in recruitment; but the barbarians as a body gave it no new military knowledge—in this as in all else they had everything to learn and nothing to teach.

After the breakdown of central power in the *Western* half of the Roman Empire the nature of armies gradually changed. The legion disappeared. Rough temporary levies slowly replaced the old professional long-service soldier. Great landowners and high, wealthy officials raised groups of dependents and hired men, and these would be gathered together by the political superior of a district. By the eleventh century nothing was left of an army in the modern sense or in the sense which antiquity gave to that word. In its place were the feudal levies already described, of all sizes, each under its own lord. Within each of these units, large or small, were found the two highly different and contrasting elements: horse and foot.

The foot soldiers were in every case the more numerous. Often they were overwhelmingly the more numerous, especially in the very large units. In a small body raised by some petty local gentleman there might be on foot no more than double the mounted men: in the very large bodies the proportion might be as high as twenty-five times the horse or more. Of a general host some such proportion as one mounted man to 15 or 20 on foot seems indicated by the rough, often unreliable, and always scrappy, disconnected accounts which have come down to us.

But, whatever the proportion, the fully armed man on horseback was the essential of the force. Offensive power has always measured by the number of lances available, and the infantry, however numerous, were always subsidiary in function to the mounted arm. The footmen were, as a rule, irregularly equipped, some proportion were more or less trained archers using the short bow of the dark and early Middle Ages; these sometimes wore protective armor. Some had only a dagger or other close-quarter weapons: some had partial head protection, more had none; nearly all had some sort of body protection in leather or stuffed cloth—a protection commonly imperfect. But the fully armed mounted man, the knight, the *chevalier* (the

French for "man-on-a-horse") was elaborately and expensively furnished, standing out from the rest as a special social rank corresponding to the cost of his armor and steed which could only be used in connection with one or two servants, apart from the general infantry.

His head, when he went into action, was covered by a conical steel helmet with a piece projecting down in front to cover the nose and partially protect the face from sword cuts. His body was covered to the knees at least and often halfway down the calf by a "coat" of closely woven steel links—*mail* (which is the French for "a link"). Usually leg pieces of the same material were worn. He carried a sword and sheath slung from a belt about his middle, a long shield on his left arm, rounded at the top and tapering down to a point at the other end; but his principal weapon of offense was a lance. This, thrust forward in the charge, was the decisive arm of the first shock; after which, when the opposing body was shaken or broken, the sword would come into play.

To carry a Western man in such a weight of armor and equipment needed big and heavy horses. On the momentum of a charging line thus mounted and armed the Crusaders depended for their immediate early successes against the not shorter but more slightly built Orientals, Turk or Arab or Kurd, to whom they were opposed.

These used a much larger proportion of horse—sometimes *all* were mounted. Their mounts were less heavy and more rapid than those of the Christian knights, and the arrows on which the Turkish tactic depended were shot from the saddle. They trusted for victory to recurrent swift gallops in fairly open order, discharging a cloud of arrows when they got in range; wheeling round and opening for the next batch to gallop up and shoot in turn, to retire like the first and to be followed up by further waves. Also they continually extended their line at either end in order to envelop the enemy. If or when this tactic succeeded in throwing the Christian horse back in disarray, they would charge home all in a circling crowd together and close with the short, light, razor-bladed curved scimitar which was their subsidiary weapon. It was thus that they had won against the Greeks at Manzikert, and thus that they continued in actions of varying result during the active century of the Crusades, until their final triumph at Hattin.

At the outset, in the first encounters the Crusading charge of heavy-armed knights in line was crushing. But the charge needed infantry support to cover a retirement or to follow up an advance, and when such support was insufficient the knights might be overwhelmed by the counter-offensive of the lighter armed and much lighter mounted Mohammedan swarms.

It was at last the growing deficiency of solid Western infantry in Syria as the colonization took root that ruined the Crusades. The Christian colonists were remolded by the climate, became half Oriental themselves through intermarriage, and even as they became more native to Syrian soil grew less able to recruit the human material needed for meeting the mass of Islam which pinned them to a narrow strip of coast.

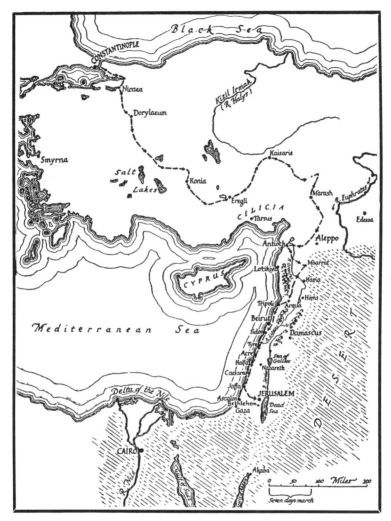

Map I. Line of March of the Crusade.

4

THE ADVANCE

The advance on Jerusalem is only interesting to military history in connection with the great feudal armies which did all the regular work and which founded the Christian Principalities in the Near East.

They took some time to organize; the greater and lesser nobility had to be summoned by their feudal chiefs, the mercenaries to be bargained for and gathered, and all the organization of a large force planned. They could not expect to be on the Bosphorus before quite the end of 1096, more than a year after the preaching of the Crusade; and the greater part of them arrived there several months later.

What may be called the regular armies of the first main Crusade, as distinguished from their large fringes of half-armed or unarmed pilgrims, were four in number.

The first in time as well as in distinction was the army mainly composed of French-speaking Walloons, which followed Godfrey of Bouillon,[2] the Duke of Lower Lorraine, who had with him his dark-haired, dead-pale, grave brother, Baldwin of Boulogne. It had a proportion of Flemish-speaking contingents and perhaps even a certain number of common men (and even

---

2. Bouillon was not a district conferring a title. It was a castle which was Godfrey's chief stronghold. It is not wholly in ruins today and stands conspicuously on a ridge which is the backbone of a small, narrow horseshoe peninsula on the river Semois, in the Ardennes, a few miles into Belgium, across the French frontier near Sedan. The family was that of the Counts y Boulogne, cadets of the great House of Flanders, which arose like all feudal local monarchies in the century after Charlemagne's empire broke up.

a few nobles) speaking other Teutonic dialects, for this half of
the old Duchy of Lorraine ran up eastward to the Rhine, and
in one place somewhat beyond it. But the bulk of the force spoke
a Gallic dialect of the Languedoc.

The numbers of regularly armed men following this leader,
but linked to his command in widely varying degrees of obedience, was something like seventy or eighty thousand.

The second army, following in similarly loose fashion Raymond IV, Count of Toulouse and Marquis of Provence,[3] was on
the same scale or larger still. It was joined, as were all these
Crusading armies, by volunteers who might come from anywhere in the West; but the bulk of it were what we should call
today southern Frenchmen and were generally alluded to by their
fellows as "Provençals": so it may be presumed that the effect
given by the host was the effect of that district, Provence, running from the Alps to the Rhine, and of its tongue. Raymond
of Toulouse (who was also called "of St. Gilles," just as Godfrey
is called "of Bouillon," from a particular lordship) had the
greatest authority within the expedition on account of his political status and of the wealth attached to it. He was monarch of
a much wider district than Lower Lorraine or Normandy, so
that his recruiting field was much the widest and its feudal dues
the largest; wherefore his resources for the hiring of mercenaries
were also the greatest among the chieftains.

He regarded himself during the whole advance on Jerusalem
as the chief figure and almost the leader, though technically the
central authority appointed by the pope was the Legate Adhemar,
the bishop of Puy in Auvergne. This great prelate was the moral
head of the whole Crusade, representing the pope who was the
creator of the movement. He was born on the borders of Raymond's territory as his family came from Valence.

---

3. That is, feudal monarch of the country between the mountains of France
and the Pyrenees as also of the country lying north of the coast between
the Rhine and the Alps. He commanded, one may say, all that is now southeastern France. He was technically vassal, for Toulouse and the Langue
d'oc, of the King of France in Paris, and for Provence, of the empire.

A third army might roughly be called "The Northern French." It had no single leader though it formed one loose body, of much the same size as the other two. The man of greatest power in it was the sovereign of Normandy, Duke Robert, the son of William, the Conqueror; he was perhaps also the one in that particular group who brought most money with him. At his side went his brother-in-law, Stephen of Blois, who had married the Conqueror's daughter, the son of the feudal lord of the Champagne country. The third notable of this group did not join it until it had come to Constantinople. This was Hugh, the younger brother of Philip, King of France. He was lord of Vermandois, called by that name and also "The Great"—for some reason unknown, perhaps his stature. He was in Constantinople months before the armies arrived and the Emperor kept guard over him as a sort of hostage—for reasons that will later be clear.

This third body, the least organized of all, was yet morally united because it was almost wholly officered by those northern French knights whose language and traditions were to characterize the new Christian State about to be founded in Syria, and its general recruitment spoke a common tongue, the *"Langue d'Oil,"* northern French. It was probably of much the same size as each of the first two groups, those from the Walloon country and from the south of France.

The fourth army demands particular attention for it was of a very special kind. It is generally called "Norman" because it was organized under those powerful men of Norman descent who had got hold of southern Italy and Sicily during the last two generations before the Holy War.

This is not the place in which to tell that story, however briefly, though it has a close connection with the Crusade. It must be enough to say that a small group of Norman gentlemen, who, like a few others of their kind, had wandered out to hire themselves as fighting men, chanced upon a chaotic state of affairs in the southern part of Italy including Sicily, coming there during the earlier part of the eleventh century, a lifetime before the Crusade.

The south of Italy and Sicily were then still held, by traditional right directly from Byzantium; they belonged, by traditional right, to the Greek Empire. The main towns followed the Greek Liturgy in their Mass, Greek was still spoken (though not universally) in their ports, when the Mohammedans largely overran those lands from the sea and rooted themselves especially firmly in Sicily.

The Norman adventurers, the sons of a middling noble from the district of Coutances, Tancred, the manorial lord of Hauteville,[4] brought small French-speaking bands with them from their native country. But these were nothing like numerous enough to form an army. As they occupied such and such a village or town they would use its revenues to buy up more recruits from the places around. With these they would gain yet more followers until they had a respectable force of southern Italian stuff organized under French commanders.

They next, with such native soldiers from south Italy, attacked the Mohammedans in Sicily. They there increased their bands with further recruitment as each success furnished them with funds wherewith to hire more fighting men, and so, going forward upon no very regular plan, they gradually became the leaders of the best force in the country where they were trying their fortunes.

No one in Christendom affirmed the right of conquest by force over other Christians; that doctrine is a purely modern one invented since the Reformation. There was always, in the old united Christendom, some pretext of *right* advanced for any contested claim; only in the case of victory over non-Christians could the victor simply take over the revenues of the vanquished.

Here in south Italy and Sicily the increasing Italian bands, led by a handful of Norman knights, could plead in moral support of their action that they were turning out the Infidel, the Mohammedan, who had got hold of Sicily and threatened to overrun the mainland. But at the same time they fought to get rid of the remnants of Greek government on the plea that the Greeks,

---

4. It is a little place on the slope of a hill overlooking the sea, ten miles south by east of Coutances. Go and see it, this origin of so much!

single-handed, had not proved competent to the task of ousting the Saracen, and also on another, more confused ground, connected with the papacy.

The papacy had possessed for centuries great landed estates in those parts and especially in Sicily. The presence of the Saracens had largely cut off that revenue; the presence of the schismatic Greeks had also largely threatened it, for there was unceasing friction (varying from temporary reconciliations to open war) between the Eastern and the Latin communions. It was not thought arbitrary to attempt the inclusion of former Greek cities within the unity of the Western Church. A combined effort in which the pope, with the aid of German troops, proposed the occupation of southern Italy, had clashed with the increasing power of the Norman adventurers; there had been a pitched battle, the Normans had won and the paradoxical result was that the papacy turned to rely upon this new force which it had just been fighting. The papacy gave legal status to the Norman efforts against the schismatical Eastern Christians, granted the first titles of government to the adventurers and their dependents, who became by formal deed the acknowledged feudal heads of Sicily and the southern Italian mainland. The masters of Sicily, though technically vassals of the pope, were henceforward called, on the authority of the pope, *Kings*. The name was adopted to show that they were independent of the Empire: that they had no lay, feudal, superior lord to whom they were accountable.

Now, of the family which had thus succeeded in establishing its new sovereignty, a remarkable cadet was the younger son of the original founder, the brother of the reigning King of Sicily, a man by the name of Bohemond, who at the time of the Crusade, 1096-99, was in early middle age: a grandson of the original ancestor in Normandy.

Prince Bohemond was a man not only of high military capacity, but of continuous and careful political talent. He was famous for his fluent French eloquence and suspect for his Norman guile. But both these characters went with great physical strength and an imposing presence, for he was a tall man: something remarkable among the Normans, who were a short, stocky race.

Bohemond had carried the fighting against the Greeks across the Adriatic. He had designed a deep invasion of the Greek Emperor's territory beyond the Adriatic and found himself unable to carry it out; but he had maintained a first-rate fighting force, more closely knit than the three much larger armies which had prepared to march for Jerusalem.

The news of the Crusade which was stirring all western Europe came to Bohemond as an opportunity, not as an enthusiasm. He at once conceived a clear plan, statesmanlike and therefore full of duplicity, and ultimately, after all manner of ups and downs, successful. He would join the other Crusaders with his well-handled, disciplined body of Sicilians and southern Italians, working under the cadres of these few northern Frenchmen of whom he was one; he would then make it his special business to arrange matters with his former enemy, the Greek Emperor, through whose territory they would have to march; he would support that Emperor's own ultimate and vague sovereignty over whatever the Crusade might recover from the Mohammedan in Asia and so would get for himself a principality really independent under the nominal legal headship of Constantinople; not the Holy Sepulchre, not Jerusalem, was his secret objective, but some realm of his own to be occupied and settled on the way to the Holy Land.

That was clearly the well thought-out and secret plan of the man who was the most subtle, the most tenacious captain of his time.

That strong, welded, united contingent with which Bohemond crossed the Adriatic and [which he] offered to use in support of the other great chiefs, Raymond and Godfrey and Hugh and Robert and Stephen, was much the smallest of the four groups, as it was also much the most compact; and we must never forget throughout all its coming adventures that the human material of which it was composed was southern Italian. It is called Norman in the history books through its leadership, but it was no more Norman in substance than Hannibal's Army at Trasimene was

Carthaginian or Marlborough's at Ramillies, English.

These four bodies were to converge by way of rendezvous upon Constantinople.

Godfrey, Duke of Lorraine and his northeastern Frenchmen, Walloons, and some few Flemings and Rhinelanders, went by the Roman way down the Danube; the newly Christian and civilized government of Hungary had had an evil experience from the first unorganized mobs and might have made difficulties, but there was a sufficient general discipline under Godfrey's command to keep the peace, and they carried on that very long advance almost to the end without clash, were accepted at the frontier posts of the Greek Emperor, and after only one bad episode of indiscipline of pillage, came in due course before the Imperial City. It was in the Christmas week of 1096 that the Greeks of Constantinople saw this first great contingent of the West under their walls.

The Emperor in Constantinople, Alexius, had two political objects of the first importance before him when this first great host came in sight. His chief object was, of course, to *use* these large bodies of Western men who would follow on, corps after corps, until their total would be five or six times as great as any Byzantine army yet gathered.

This matter of *scale* is of great importance to our understanding of the first Crusades. The loose Western armies of those adventurers were huge hordes in the eyes of the Greeks. The highly civilized Greeks had a strict military organization, elaborate tactics, and had a whole school of strategy. To them the Western feudal levies with their lack of cohesion and learning seemed barbaric. The courage and still more the drive of the Western nobles impressed Byzantium, and most of all their numbers, the like of which had not been seen in the East—even in the Moslem attack; but morally and intellectually Byzantium despised them.

Byzantine armies, regularly levied and carefully framed, were restricted even before Manzikert: they were lessened after it by the loss of the Anatolian recruiting field. Those vast numbers pouring in from the West, Alexius would use as allies and instruments for the recovery of the territories which the Greek Empire had so recently lost to the Infidel.

Manzikert, the initial disaster which had put all Asia Minor into the hands of the Turks, was still recent in the memory of all Byzantines not in their first youth; it was only 25 years since the Mongol hordes had overrun the provinces which gave Byzantium the bulk of its soldiers and the bulk of its revenue. There had been a later reaction, at least in the southern part of the lost territory, and when the first Crusaders arrived on the Sea of Marmora in the middle of December, 1096, it was only fifteen years since the southern provinces of Asia Minor had been recaptured by the Turks and only nine years since Edessa had been overrun; the bulwark of Christendom on the eastern borders of Asia Minor in the mountains of the upper Euphrates.

But the memory which was most vivid in Byzantine minds, even perhaps more vivid than that of Manzikert, was the memory of Antioch. That town was still the great capital of Syria, it was still Christian, still full of traditions binding it to the Greek monarchy through centuries; still the symbol of Greek and Christian dominion upon the Mohammedan frontiers, when it had fallen to the Turks, only ten years before Pope Urban had preached at Clermont. It was barely eleven years that Antioch had been under the domination of a Moslem garrison when the Duke of Lorraine appeared upon the Bosphorus with his sixty thousand.

Clearly the main use the Emperor must make of such vast reinforcement—enormous in proportion to all that he could himself levy and arm—was the recovery of Antioch.

The bulk of the Crusaders were not marching with Antioch in view, nor fixed as yet upon the occupation of any territory save that of Jerusalem and the Holy Places. Antioch was on the way to the Holy Land; Syria would certainly fall more or less into the power of such allies; but still those allies might be persuaded to admit the ultimate sovereignty of the Byzantine Emperor should they recover Antioch and hold it of Alexius as his liege men, and he might feel himself re-established in something of the old majesty of those whom he succeeded on the imperial throne. The frontiers of Christendom would have been recovered, and though Greek dominion might at first be indirect, it would at least be legally admitted.

So much for the first branch of the Emperor's policy. The second branch was difficult to reconcile with the first. For this second branch was the prevention at all costs of a junction between the various Crusading armies under the walls of Constantinople, or still worse, within the city. Their enormous size would have completely dominated the Imperial Government.

Alexius, therefore, was burning to get each contingent as it arrived across the Straits and into Asia: to pass each successively on to the further shore and put the water between them and his capital, so that they should be beyond doing harm to Constantinople or imposing their will upon the city and himself. But he could not pass even this first contingent over until he had got some promise of what they would do concerning his claims to lordship over whatever reconquest they might make—and especially over Antioch. To get them to swear allegiance to himself would take time. He had already got Hugh to swear allegiance. But then Hugh had no army, and was a sort of prisoner. Baldwin and Godfrey would be reluctant to bind themselves, there would be delay—and delay might be fatal. Yet it was unavoidable. That was the political dilemma in which Alexius found himself during the Christmas season of 1096.

All the end of that winter, and on into the spring of 1097 that delay continued. The thing had grown to an open quarrel. Godfrey and Baldwin were blockaded in Pera beyond the Golden Horn where the Emperor had lodged them. He thought to coerce them by famine. They broke out, attacked the walls of the city, nearly took the Palace, but failed to do so; and their failure led to their surrender on the point of principle. Godfrey and his feudal lords accepted the overlordship of the Emperor; and it was understood that whatever they reconquered should have the Emperor for ultimate monarch.

The date of that agreement was the second week of April, 1097. The moment it was made the Emperor hastened to provide craft for the ferrying of the Lorraine army over to the Asiatic side.

He only did so just in time. Immediately on their heels came the southern Italians under Bohemond. They had crossed the southern Adriatic at Durazzo and come up by the Roman road through the Balkans.

Bohemond himself had come to the capital in advance of his army: he swore allegiance to Alexius almost with enthusiasm, having made it his secret plan to use a nominal dependence upon the Emperor as a weapon against the rivalry of his fellow commanders, so that he might enter into secure possession of Antioch with a sort of legal title to it when it should be reconquered. He obtained from Alexius the promise that he should be lord of Antioch when the time came.

Then arrived, almost coincidently with Bohemond's army, the great force of Raymond—the men of the Languedoc and of Provence. These had marched by way of north Italy and then through the wild mountainland, filled with half-barbarous Slavs who had now for some generations held Illyria. These southern Frenchmen had with them Adhemar, the Papal Legate, and his presence gave them a sort of pre-eminence over the other groups. From the Adriatic they in their turns came across the Balkan country to Constantinople, and the last army, the northern French under Robert of Normandy and his colleagues, did the same.

Thus the first very great and victorious march of the Crusade was made entirely by land save for the ferrying across the Bosphorus and the short crossing of the Straits of the Adriatic by but a portion of the Crusading armies. The rest of the work was foot slogging and horse mastership. It is remarkable that the one main Crusading effort, the earliest one, which was alone really successful, thus neglected, or was unable, to use sea power. It is the more remarkable because the distances involved were so great. A manorial lord taking the Cross in lower Normandy—as we know so many of them did—covered well over 2,500 miles first and last before he reached Jerusalem, if he had the good fortune to be among the few that did achieve that avowed object of their advance. A man from one of Godfrey's central districts, say from Bouillon itself, in the Ardennes, covered perhaps some 200 miles less. Even the nearest group, the men from Sicily and southern Italy, covered well over 1,500 miles. The effort was greater than that of the Grand Army (in 1812), only the furthest units of which had marched near 1,500 miles before they reached Moscow; while the nearest units, drawn from the Napoleonic garrisons in Germany, covered only from 800 to 1,000 miles.

That the first successful effort was made by land while the later unsuccessful efforts were made in part by sea and at last mainly by sea is an illustration of something which you find running all through military history, to wit, that dependence upon sea power in military affairs is a lure, leading to ultimate disappointment. In the final and decisive main duels of history the party which begins with high sea power is defeated by the land power: whether that sea power be called Carthage, or Athens, or the Phoenician fleet of the great King, it loses in the long run; the land wins.

The point has often been discussed why this should be so, but at any rate so it is. Transport by sea, especially over great distances, has three glaring advantages: it is more rapid, it is less in danger (for those who are superior at sea), and it is far freer in choice of objective. The force commanding the sea can "switch off" from one plan to another; it can feint on widely distant points also. One might add a fourth advantage: sea transport is *commonly* less exhausting to the numbers and to the health of the advance.

The main reasons for the neglect of the sea by the First Crusade were as follows:

1. *Numbers.* Very large bodies of men have been transported by sea throughout history, the only necessary condition being that the navy should be civilized. Uncivilized men cannot go in large numbers save by land; that is why the North Sea pirates often called "Anglo-Saxons" were so few, as were the Scandinavian pirates called "Danes" centuries later. But highly civilized men have been able to transport large armies over comparatively

short stretches of water. The Carthaginians could act thus between Africa and Sicily. William the Conqueror in the Hastings campaign handled 50,000 men with their due proportion of cavalry brought across 60 to 70 miles of water in one voyage.

But when you have to deal with great distances it is another matter: you need provisioning, high organization, and a mass of supply: the coefficient of tonnage per man, per horse and per ton multiplies far more rapidly than the numbers to be transported and the distances. The tonnage that carried the Conqueror's 50,000 with perhaps 14,000 horses or less in one night across the Channel would not have carried a quarter of that number from the western to the eastern Mediterranean. And could enough shipping have been found for half a million?

2. *Dispersion.* The Crusading contingents, being of all sorts and sizes, could not be organized for one form of transport by sea. They came in at all times and in all dimensions. By land they could ultimately converge and cohere: by sea they would have arrived haphazard.

3. *Finance.* Who could have hired the shipping, if indeed so huge a fleet of transport could have been gathered? A land advance might partly pay for itself by conquest and partly live off the country—not so an advance by sea.

4. *Reluctance.* Lastly, there was the reluctance of the half-organized or unorganized mass attached to the regular bodies to venture on an adventure by water—especially in great numbers. Later the thing could be done and was done by trained and disciplined bodies. In 1096-1099 it could not have been done save by the small central groups which followed the chief leaders, and the mass of the pilgrims would have been abandoned.

Therefore it was that, beyond Constantinople, the advance continued by land.

All the great leaders had ultimately taken the oath of allegiance to Alexius before the march into Asia began. The last and most reluctant was the Count of Toulouse. He was more of an independent monarch than any of his colleagues except Robert of Normandy, and Robert was but one of many northern

French leaders, while Raymond was true head of his very large southern French army. But there was another reason for Raymond refusing this oath to Alexius: a rivalry between himself and Bohemond had already begun, and with Bohemond working as the Emperor's man, Raymond was for standing off. At last, however, he also yielded—just before the last crossing of the straits, in April—and when the march began only one of the chiefs, Tancred, Bohemond's nephew, remained inflexible. He refused the oath to the end.

But Alexius accepted the position, offered a Greek contingent, and had the opportunity to put his claims to a test almost at once, in the case of Nicaea, close at hand.

Let us ask, as the advance into Asia begins in this late spring of 1097, what true military effectives the leaders had at their disposal. It is unfortunate that we can only make an estimate within a very wide margin of error. In judging the military character of a campaign some estimate of trained numbers is essential, but for very few (even in the least documented times) have we less precise evidence than for this great expedition.

This is not due to the inaccuracy of medieval numbers as a whole. There is nothing commoner than accusing the Middle Ages of inaccuracy. The truth is that medieval numbers are either very precise when there is occasion to be precise, or else mere popular rumors and rhetorical statements. The latter can never be expected in any period to have statistical value save within wide limits of error. But for the former there is no period of the past for which we have so great a mass of exact and detailed numerical statement as for the Middle Ages. This is particularly true, for instance, in money matters. Accurate and detailed accounts were kept of which, for the later centuries at least, a large bulk has come down to us. But in the case of the First Crusade, as with so many of the medieval campaigns, a good basis for the judgment of total numbers is lacking. Some few of these campaigns do furnish reliable evidence; we have first-rate evidence, for instance, on the numbers just quoted as commanded by William in his invasion of England in 1066; a contemporary and a man who acted as his secretary, who witnessed the summoning of the host, gives us the figures. But for the numbers that mustered beyond the Bosphorus in April to May, 1097, we have to rely on vague, exaggerated rumor and inference.

We begin, of course, by eliminating all that was not effective fighting material. When we are told that the Christians surrounding Nicaea for instance, at the very beginning of the campaign, were two thirds of a million men, that statement has always been treated by modern critics as wild. It need not be so if it is applied to every human being present in the vast congregation outside the walls of the besieged city, but it was certainly enormously larger than the numbers of effective fighting men under any form of organization, however loose.

We have about a dozen bases for information apart from this general statement, which even if it be approximately right gives us no knowledge of the proportion of effectives in the human herd that spread in its myriads round the twelve to fifteen square miles of swarming ground outside Nicaea.

We know how many more or less organized army corps there were following the main leaders: there were four, or, counting subdivisions, six. We know what a contemporary estimated to be Godfrey de Bouillon's own section: 80,000 men. But we also know that that witness was a royal princess, with no good judgment in such matters. We know that the same witness says each division she saw was larger than the Byzantine army: but that is no unit for measurement. The Byzantine army which had been defeated just before her own birth had gathered 60,000 men into one field, while others employed in actions of high political importance were hardly one tenth of that number. We know that some contemporaries of a single Western force—Godfrey's—put it at 20,000 and others at 40,000. We know that Urban II, the Pope, writing to the Emperor of Byzantium before the army started, tells his correspondent that one third of a million had taken the Cross in that spring: but "taking the Cross" is a vague term and covers unarmed pilgrims as well as soldiers.

The enemy accounts do not help us; they are purely rhetorical—for if Christian rumor in the early Middle Ages was vague, Moslem rumor was even vaguer. We know that the personal band of the Norman leader, Bohemond, counted 500 knights, and to multiply the number of knights by ten in order to find the total of an effective fighting force is a good average coefficient. But Bohemond was followed by a much larger body than the special group under his own direct, personal, feudal allegiance. His *total* of knights alone was said by one contemporary to be 7,000. Those under Raymond of Toulouse are called in one place 30,000 men, in another 40,000.

All this is very vague and lies between far too wide limits; but for reasons which will be presented below I think it a fair guess to call the number of effective fighting men under leaders, obeying regular orders and capable of action in regular conflict, to have been at the beginning of the Crusading march in front of the first obstacle—the walled city of Nicaea—some 300,000 men. That is about half the huge numbers of the complete total affirmed by one contemporary; because that complete total must have included such masses of broken remnants from the first popular movements, so many local Christians, and so many hangers-on of the camps and columns, that half the vague number would not be too small an estimate for what was of any military effect.

This figure of about 300,000 generally corresponds with Urban's letter to the Emperor, though it is a great deal more than could be made up by adding up the limited figures of the men directly controlled in each section by the feudal leader thereof. If the average of each section was, say, that of Raymond of Toulouse, the total would have been less than 200,000 men. If we take a middle figure in the case of Godfrey's section, and call it 40,000 men (halving the 80,000 of the Byzantine princess), we get a quarter of a million rather than a third of a million for the total of partly trained and organized men at the beginning of the march.

But the best check on these vague estimates, with their vast limits of error (between a sixth and a third of a million), is the more precise evidence apparent towards the end of the march. You are then dealing with much smaller numbers, because the host has dwindled enormously through disease, hunger, thirst, casualties in action, and desertion. The Papal Legate, who was certainly accustomed to accounts and figures, tells us that there were in front of Antioch, after the terrible march through the ruined land of Asia Minor and after the deduction of the body which had gone off to Edessa, 100,000 fighting men.

Such a remaining body fits in fairly well, considering the heavy work at Nicaea and much heavier work at Dorylaeum, with an original estimate of 300,000. That about one third of those who left Nicaea should have remained effective in front of Antioch is a reasonable conclusion.

We have another more particular check. About a month before the fall of Jerusalem, at the very end of the campaign (July, 1099), more than two years after the assembly of the host upon the Bosphorus, Tancred said that about one in ten of the original fighting men were left for the final assault upon the Holy City. At the same time we know within fairly narrow limits how large that final army in front of Jerusalem was; it had 1,500 knights, which on a rough multiple of 20 would mean perhaps 30,000 men; those present, estimating the numbers vaguely and including perhaps noneffectives, gives 40,000. If about one tenth of the original numbers survived to attack the walls of Jerusalem, and if that approximate tenth were a little over 30,000 but less than 40,000, that is not far from a general estimate of 300,000 to a third of a million, in front of Nicaea.

It is, then, perhaps best for history to say that the Crusading march began at the Bosphorus with some third of a million effectives, but allowing, in such a very general estimate, for a margin of at least one sixth either way.

Such a military force, then, with as much again accompanying it as noncombatants of every kind, lay round the first obstacle to their advance, Nicaea, which the conquering Turks had made their capital, in the very neighborhood of Constantinople.

Like all the inhabited towns the Crusaders came across till they had passed Antioch, Nicaea held a population mainly Christian. It was Mohammedan and Turkish only in the sense that its armed garrison was such. But throughout these wars it was the armed men only who had to be reckoned with. A great majority of unarmed citizens or even the entirety of them differing from the armed garrison in religion, speech, and culture were negligible however numerous, save for the slight aid they might give as spies. So long as the armed men, Christian or Mohammedan, within the walls of a city were of a strength sufficient to hold the place and overawe the population, this place counted as Christian or Mohammedan for the purposes of the war, irrespective of the civilians.

Nicaea was a very large place, its towered walls ran miles in circuit, and were on one side protected by a wide mere [pool]. The Crusading host did not at the beginning of the siege in the first week of May, 1097, cover the whole circuit. It was not until the last contingent, the northern French with Robert of Normandy, came up that all the gates were blocked: nor would blockade alone reduce it: it could be revictualled by water from the lake. But for the Byzantines with their siege train and the boats they put upon the mere, Nicaea would not have fallen, and as it was six weeks were spent in vain upon the attack. Yet to take it was essential if the march were to proceed. The Sultan of the Seljuk Turks was not within the walls. He had been absent on an expedition against a rival and was surprised by the newcomers—a good example of that incoherence in command from which both the Crusaders and the Turks suffered but from which the highly trained Byzantine army was free. There had been months in which the Turkish Sultan might have gathered full intelligence on the invaders; he failed to do so. He had left within Nicaea his treasure and his court. Its fall would disorganize all his hold on Asia Minor—yet he did not prevent it.

They had six weeks of broiling weather before the garrison offered terms of surrender, and when they did, they approached not the French but the Emperor. When therefore, at the end of June, 1097, the last assault was preparing, the chiefs of the Crusades saw the imperial flags already planted on the walls. They had but recovered Nicaea for Byzantium after a Turkish occupation of sixteen years, and had to be content with knowing that the first stronghold barring their way east was now reduced. Bohemond understood the position: the others raged. But all accepted it. It was on June 26 that the city fell and three days later the immense camps before Nicaea broke up and the march into the unknown began.

* * *

To reach Antioch and enter Syria, the leaders of the Crusade proposed to follow the great Roman road which cut the plateau of Asia Minor transversely from northwest to southeast.

It is probable that although they must have obtained sufficient information in Constantinople, the leaders did not realize the task before them. It is nearly always so when great distances, new country, and very large numbers combine to make formidable a military adventure. The last major example was Napoleon's Russian disaster. Alexander's advance to the Indus narrowly escaped the same fate as Napoleon's to Moscow.

Here, on leaving Nicaea, all seemed well: a fertile country, water, and a civilization which, unlike that of the interior, was not as yet badly hurt by the Turkish invasion. Further inland they would find increasingly a succession of ruined towns and fields gone back to waste: also lack of water. Within a week's marching they would be fully engaged on the salt deserts of the central tableland.

For, in advancing by land on Syria from Constantinople, there is no choice save one of two ways. You may try and work along the broken and mountainous coastal lands, very difficult going indeed, but at least watered; or you may go by the direct road which cuts diagonally through Asia Minor from northeast to southwest and was designed by the Roman engineers to give the most rapid access from New Rome to Syria and the all-important Persian frontier.

But the Roman engineers had surveyed and built that great highway in a time of high and organized civilization. They had built posthouses at regular intervals, cisterns for fresh water where such might be needed, stores for provisions, etc. Now, in the year 1097, not only had all that long disappeared but the land had been, for fifteen years past, ravaged and destroyed by the vile destructive spirit of the Asiatic nomads. At the best all the middle part of this way was terrible, and in the height of summer—the season when the advance was made—doubly terrible. The heat is infernal, the glare blinding, and through all the middle part of the way they would be condemned to advance through land where such rare water as they could find was brackish—the land of salt lakes without issue.

But all this was to come. They went forward the first three days after Nicaea along the road which is today the trace of the railway, leading from Europe to Syria. They passed through the gap between the two mountain ranges and made for the open plain called after the ruined city of Dorylaeum.

Today that plain takes its name from the Turkish town, Eskishehir, already on the edges of the highland; for although it is fairly well watered by the river now called Pursaqchai, this plain is the antechamber to the deadly desert plateau beyond.

The enormous body, still presumably all told (counting the women and children and camp followers and everything) over half a million human beings, straggled along in two columns, some few miles apart and each containing its large nucleus of more or less trained soldiery; the bulk of that soldiery were footmen, but the core and life of it all were the mounted knights.

The first echelon was composed of the Normans, of the southern Italians and of the northern French and Normans, and was the smaller of the two; its leaders being, of course, Bohemond and Tancred and Robert, the Duke of Normandy, the son of the Conqueror. It marched through the mountains by the northern of two alternative tracks. About two hours' march to the south, or right of the advance, and starting later, followed the rest of the army, with Godfrey of Bouillon and his Lorrainers and Flemings, Raymond of Toulouse with the men of Languedoc and Provence, and Hugh the Great. This double formation was adopted presumably in order to facilitate provisioning, but there were those who blamed the Normans for their rashness and getting too far ahead, seeing what was to follow.

The vanguard, then, came out onto the Dorylaeum plain upon the last day of the month of June, three days' march from the city which they had stormed and given back to the Emperor.

The pace was not bad considering the climatic conditions, fearful for men of northern Europe. They were covering between ten and fifteen miles a day.

Of intelligence work there was, of course, none. It is remarkable how slowly the A, B, C of organized warfare was relearnt as Europe emerged from the Dark Ages. Having thus no idea of what was in front of them this Italian Norman and northern French vanguard stumbled unexpectedly, in the open land beyond the mountain gap, upon an enormous concentration of all the Turkish forces assembled for the defense of what had so recently been a main Turkish conquest—the fruits of Manzikert.

Here, so early in the great adventure, was to come a test of life or death, and the Crusade came within an ace of extinction, a thousand miles short of its objective. The commander of the victorious Turks who had overrun Asia Minor and almost reached the gates of Constantinople, had, during the siege of Nicaea, gathered every man he could to destroy the Western effort while yet it could be destroyed. Oilij Arslan, he the Seljuk, had in the presence of this peril made his peace with his rivals (Turkish also), and upon what was to follow depended the fate of Europe perhaps quite as much as upon any of the other battles fought between East and West.

The Western men, our people, had never yet met the light-armed, swift-riding Nomadic hordes from the steppes of Asia which had so recently all but destroyed Eastern Christendom. They had no experience of the Turkish tactic, which had destroyed the Emperor's army those few years before at Manzikert. The Norman vanguard was taken completely by surprise, and outnumbered altogether by the swarms of mounted Turkish archers.

These came in by every issue of that hill country in clouds upon the plain, dust rising from their gallopade over the far left and north and round all the half circle and more to the right and south of the Christians who suffered a complete surprise. They were very nearly surrounded at once by this mass of horse dashing forward in small groups, shooting from the saddle with their light short bows, killing the horses of the heavy armed knights, and then galloping back at top speed to be replaced by fresh levies, one after the other; each wave harassing and weakening more and more the heavy Western figures in their mail, under the fierce heat of the rising morning.

The shock was taken before nine, it was pressed till far beyond noon, and the knights attempting to charge again and again could never get home against that hail of arrows and the perpetually repeated lightning advances and retirement. The Christians fell back between the repeated charges, still seeking to avoid the envelopment that seemed inevitable and beginning to bunch and lose formation.

Bohemond in the morning, at the first sight of the great concentration appearing before him, had sent urgent messengers to bring up the rear guard, with Godfrey and Raymond from the second column seven miles to the south; they came up only just in time. Of these Godfrey of Bouillon was on the field first, with fifty knights only about him. The rest of his command—the mounted part of it—coming on at a gallop.

Immediately afterwards Hugh with the rear guard and the men of Provence came up in support. But it was almost midafternoon, between two and three o'clock, before the reinforcement—far superior in number to the original forward column—could make its weight felt; and already that advanced body had been pushed back against its baggage train and was defending itself as best it could, partly covered by the vehicles. The Turks were already outflanking either end of the original Christian line, now hardly a line any longer but rather a scrum; they would have surrounded and annihilated it in another hour or less, when the large second echelon began to arrive.

These sufficed to turn the tide of the battle. It would seem from the confused accounts which remain to us that they succeeded in doing so by extending rapidly upon the left wing of the enemy until the Turks themselves were exhausted by their six-hour fight. At last, as more and more of the southern French came up the Turks were threatened with envelopment in their turn, and gave way. Once they had given way, it was a rout.

The immense concentration of Turkish forces (which their enemies estimated as a force as large as all the Crusaders and Pilgrims together) turned into isolated mounted bands flying eastward and northward through the hills.

Though there was no destruction of the enemy force, Dorylaeum, as the sun sank somewhat lower in the bronze and dusty sky of that broiling afternoon, had proved to be a complete decision. The Seljuk Turks could attack no more: the long way to Syria was open, and, what was more, the West had proved, after so many generations, its superiority over the East. Loosely knit as these Crusading bands were, they had discovered sufficient energy in action to throw back the Seljuk menace to Christendom; they proved themselves capable of advance against Mohammedan armies in an ordeal to which the two religions had each summoned all the force at its disposal. The victory was won.

The Christians here camped by the riverside for two days and then took the road forward. Dorylaeum had been fought upon the first of July. Through the second and third there was no movement; on the fourth the long and now united column set out once more.

The thing that was coming was a trial so severe that we can hardly explain even the partial survival of that army. The Turks had devastated everything along the road which the Crusaders must follow, though there was little enough to devastate in that increasingly salt world. Still, what there was to take had been taken and what there was to burn and pull down had been destroyed. The Crusaders came on no crops. They passed, and that but rarely, villages that were heaps of rubble and isolated unroofed walls, occasional blackened stumps of what had been fruit trees, and wells filled up and dry. Water gave out, men died of thirst in multitudes and of exhaustion: most of the horses were lost. The animals driven for food, the kine and even dogs, were pressed into the service to carry such essential provisionment as the army, and its still remaining bands of unarmed followers, had to take with it.

At last they came through the mountain gates into the fertility of the Iconian plain.

Iconium (Turkish Konich?) is 150 miles as the crow flies from Dorylaeum; by the road the host had taken, skirting the mountains, the distance was half as much again, and it is a testimony to the nature of that march of death that the advance averaged less than eight miles per day.

The policy of devastation had been carried out thoroughly here at Iconium also; the city was found utterly deserted and gutted of every form of provisionment. But before they set out again certain chance Armenians (Christians, of course) dribbled in and gave them good counsel; they were advised to take provision of water with them because there was yet another desert to come, curling round the Black Mountain, the Kara Dagh, with no water course in the whole of it at that season save the one stream of Tsharshambe—a true desert stream which soon lost itself in the sands. Just at the end of this desert passage, about a month after leaving Iconium, when their pace had got still slower—they took 30 days to cover a little under 120 miles—they reached Heraclea, of which the Turks have made "Eregli."

The worst of their trial was over. They were at the foot of the Taurus range, and were approaching that cleft which was called the "Cilician Gate." Before them and below, when they should have passed through, would lie the Cilician Plain, its wealth, its Christian people and its welcome—the antechamber of Syria.

Even here at Heraclea the Turk made one last effort to stand. Knowing how heavily his enemy had lost in numbers and energy during this business of the salt deserts, he attempted an action to delay them, but he was swept away.

After Heraclea (Eregli) there comes a change over the Crusading march. It takes on another character, and unless we understand how that change took place all the remainder of the movement, the occupation of Syria and the character of Latin Christendom in the Levant—the whole Crusading establishment as distinguished from the original advance—remains inexplicable. For after Eregli, the Crusading march, which had been almost wholly and directly a religious thing, becomes a thing political as well as religious. The chiefs of the Crusade, the great territorial princes, Tancred, the Count of Toulouse, Baldwin of Flanders, Godfrey's younger brother—all of them except Godfrey himself—began to remember their private fortunes alongside with the recovery and holding of the Holy Sepulchre. They began to think of the Crusade as a feudal thing. They began to think of settlement, of revenue, of taking root after feudal fashion in the soil. Bohemond had thought of little else since first he had crossed the Adriatic; but now all the others, or nearly all, were about to feel the temptation. Instead of holding Cilicia, and Syria beyond, as the avenue of advance to Jerusalem, garrisoning it point by point, and pressing on, they would each in turn establish himself in a lordship on that road and leave to a last remnant the long business of reaching Sion and redeeming the Sepulchre.

Each of the leaders could count upon a more or less organized army under his own orders, with its nucleus of fully armed mounted knights and a larger body of infantry; and these forces had the power to attach to themselves larger, less strictly organized groups from the mass of the Crusaders around. Each, therefore, had the opportunity of making himself an independent prince in the East such as his relatives who remained in the West had been for centuries.

Tancred makes the effort to establish himself in a lordship of Cilicia. His uncle Bohemond ends, after a long and somewhat obscure but desperate wrangle, in establishing himself as Prince of Antioch and all the fertile land around it. Baldwin of Flanders has the astonishing adventure of penetrating to the mountains of the Upper Euphrates, crossing the great river and establishing himself as master of Edessa.

Later, when Palestine itself was occupied, though there was a stricter order of hierarchy, the whole thing remained feudal. The kingdom of Jerusalem can only continue on condition that it is supported by vassals; the long maritime strip of central Syrian coast called the county of Tripoli is independent of the royal capital, Jerusalem, save for the feudal bond, and even the great lords directly holding of the king himself in Palestine have their measure of feudal independence, notably (after the first generation) the lord of that great key castle just beyond the Dead Sea—Kerak of Moab.

The crude explanation often given to this new character in the Crusade, which begins to show itself after Eregli, is to ascribe it to avarice. We are told that the great Western chieftains were incapable of agreement among themselves because each was grasping as much territory and revenue as possible, and that this swamped in them the Crusading spirit: that they had so far lost the soul of the great expedition, that they had destroyed its unity and made it impossible to attain the original objectives.

But to talk thus is bad history. The great feudal chiefs of the day acted as great feudal chiefs because they could act in no other fashion; they were of a feudal society, and the Western government they were to establish in the Levant could not have been established in any other fashion. They must recruit their revenues in order to carry on, they must hold territory in order to gather such revenue, and these territories must command and guarantee the approaches to Jerusalem by sea and by land.

Moreover, the wider the area the feudal western European class could master, the more was Islam weakened and the greater the chance of maintaining permanent mastery over the Holy Places. The feudal motive was mixed with the love of personal gain, but it is a misreading of the time to think that the love of gain was the driving power of these men. It had its place in their thought and actions, debasing Bohemond most and Godfrey of Bouillon least. The others in between were affected by it in varying degrees; but even Bohemond continued to the end a Crusader, and there was not one of them, not even Bohemond, who did not feel the inspiration of the Cross. The Christian name is perpetually invoked, it is the rescue of the Christian populations in the East which fills the story, and for the common purpose there is always to be discovered, in spite of fierce rivalries, a common action.

Nor did the Crusaders wreck their own effort. This loosely organized military society did, after all, take and hold Jerusalem, and triumphantly maintained, for nearly a century, the mastery of Christendom over the Holy Places. Bethlehem, Nazareth, the hills of Galilee, the Holy Lake, the shore of the waters which heard the predication [preaching] of Our Lord—all these were recovered from the Unbeliever. The Crusading effort failed at last, but it did not fail from being feudal; the European feudal system was a more solid thing than the Mohammedan world. The Crusading effort failed because distance and climate were too much for it, reinforcement too scanty and inferior.

From this point of Eregli the direct road to Syria should have led the main body of the Crusade through the gap in the Taurus down to the Cilician plain, round the Gulf of Alexandretta, and so to Antioch and the Syrian coast.

That has always been the main road (for it is the shortest and easiest) between maritime Syria and the West. Alexander followed it. But this road was not taken by the bulk of the forces. These turned the tangled mass of the Anti-Taurus range by the north, marching for the ancient Caesarea of Cappadocia, thence they turned southeast into the very heart of the Armenian mountains, thence south through the gorges of the Djihar (which is the Pyramus of the ancients) until they came out upon the plain of Marasch, from which town ran the road southwest again to Antioch. Through all this line of march they were everywhere rescuing the Christian population from their new Turkish masters, and though the further they advanced the greater was their temptation to establish independent feudal states, they still kept their word to the Emperor, even at Marasch, and handed over that town to the Byzantine authority. There remained strongly fixed in the Crusading mind the conception of a feudal link between whatever lands they should occupy and the Imperial City, the chief of all Christendom in the East.

Had the Emperor at Constantinople, Alexius Comnenus, acted with energy and sent sufficient Greek reinforcement to the aid of the French, all Syria might have been ultimately attached, though only in feudal fashion, to the Imperial Crown. It would have "held" under Byzantium. But for some reason, probably a defect in character but never fully explained, Alexius hesitated. He took advantage of Dorylaeum to re-establish imperial authority over western Asia Minor, but he never pushed a suffi-

cient force eastward to march side by side with the Crusading
host and affirm the ancient rights which the leaders of that host
would have granted him—for nearly all of them had sworn fidelity to the Emperor and the bond of such an oath was in those
days a strong one. Even Bohemond, the best tactician and least
loyal of the band, would have consented to govern his principate
under tenure of Constantinople.

But Alexius failed. Cilicia, of which Tancred had hoped to
make a feudal state for himself, was indeed soon reoccupied by
the Greeks, and then, after alternating fortunes, was ultimately
held more solidly by the Armenians. But further south than that
or further east the effort of Byzantium did not extend. All the
reconquest of the Levant, from the Gulf of Alexandretta to the
Egyptian desert, fell wholly to the men of the West. It is due
to Alexius' hesitation that the first great Crusading Christian
State in the East was established, becoming for the better part
of a lifetime the northern rampart of the Crusading conquest—
the Countship of Edessa, under Baldwin of Boulogne.

Baldwin left his brother, Godfrey of Bouillon, and the main
Crusading host, in the middle of the month of October, 1097,
just before they started on their last stage on Antioch. He went
off eastward, got adopted by the Armenian chief of Edessa after
having recovered for the Christians certain outlying towns which
the Turks still held. He and his men appeared, therefore (when
he had been thus adopted), as the saviors of the Armenian Christians of the district.

He took advantage of a local revolution against the power of
Thoros, the elderly Armenian chief, who had adopted him. In
March of the next year (1098), he completely took over the
government of the stronghold of Edessa and its dependent country, and consolidated his power throughout those hills, and east
and west of the upper Euphrates.

What made Baldwin's act possible was what runs throughout
the early Crusading time, the military superiority of the northern
French knights over Orientals. Not only had they overthrown
the Seljuk Turkish garrisons and armies in the field, but the
Armenian mountain chiefs, and still more the Armenian town

merchants, recognized them as leaders. The names of the French towns from whom these families were drawn sufficiently testifies to the qualities of the garrison. You get such names as the lord of Toul in Lorraine, the lord of Nesle, and one from as far away as Chartres.

While Baldwin was establishing himself thus as lord of Edessa and all its hill country—an independent Christian Crusading State, a northern bulwark against the Turk, and a corner bastion against Mesopotamia to the south and east—the mass of the army marched on from Marasch, making for Antioch.

The columns passed within striking distance of Aleppo, but the Turkish Governor of Aleppo did not move, for the Moslem world was fallen into a dust of divisions and he who governed Aleppo, the head of the garrison there, did not govern as the servant of his superior in Mesopotamia but as an independent chieftain—Ridwan by name. He was the brother of the corresponding Turkish Governor in Damascus, but also his fierce rival; and the man in command of the Turkish garrison in Antioch itself played the one brother against the other, pretending to support each alternately, and alternately betraying each.

In such a condition, how could Islam rally against the men who had proved their power at Dorylaeum? No attempt was made to cut or even to harass the long column of the Crusade as it approached the Orontes and came within its last march upon Antioch.

5

ANTIOCH

Passing Aleppo unvisited to their left and east, leaving Aleppo undisturbed in Mohammedan hands, the captains of the great column now making south and west for the Orontes began the final failure of the Crusades. The neglect of Aleppo in 1097 was the root of all their future weakness, their increasing difficulties in holding Syria for the next two lifetimes, and their breakdown at Hattin after ninety years of desperately maintaining a doomed and falling cause.

Three successive steps mark the progress and result of this grand strategical error upon which the fate of the East was to depend.

The first step was this original neglect of Aleppo in 1097.

The second was the neglect of Damascus in the following year 1098.

The third was the insufficiency and blunder in front of Damascus fifty years on—1148—when, at long last, an effort *was* made to seize that key of the Syrian land. But the effort was made too late. It was understaffed and bungled; and when the trumpet sounded the last retreat from before Damascus there could be no return. Henceforward ruin menaced, and the blow fell at Hattin in 1187.

In order to understand why the neglect of Aleppo, and after that of Damascus, was fatal to the Crusades we must understand how the maritime belt of Syria lay in the Mohammedan world.

If we reduce to a simple scheme the shape of that world, we can at once see why the Syrian belt was vital to all Islam. If we consider the Syrian belt in detail, we discover the all-importance of Damascus therein.

After the battle of Manzikert, the land of the Near East subject to the Mohammedan control consisted of one great bulk stretching out eastward indefinitely from the Aegean Sea, covering Asia Minor and going on to the steppes of Asia, to Persia, and to the confines of India. This may be called one half of the Mohammedan territory, though it was, of course, in actual size much more than half. To the south of this body of territory controlled by the arms of Islam lay another. It covered the Valley of the Nile, a narrow belt between the Mediterranean Sea and the Sahara Desert and went on westward to include what are today Tunis, Algiers, and Morocco, and nearly half of Spain.

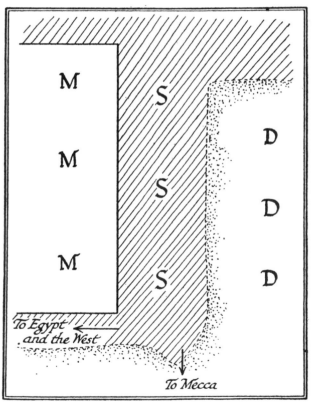

Map II. Diagram of "The Neck."

It will be observed that uniting these two parts of the Mohammedan domination there runs a perpendicular neck marked on the diagram with the letters S S S. On the one side of it, at D D D, is a desert across which armies cannot march. On the other side of it at M M M is the Mediterranean Sea. General communication, therefore, between the two parts of the Mohammedan world, the passage of armies from one to the other, of administrative orders, even of secure commerce and all inter-Islamic travel must pass up or down this neck S S S. If that neck were cut, the body of Islam would be divided. Now, this narrow belt, S S S, lying between the desert and the Mediterranean Sea and vital to the whole body of Mohammedan power, happened to contain the Holy Places of Christendom. In order to approach these, to master them, and to hold them, the Crusaders could not but march through and attempt to control permanently this narrow Syrian belt. Had they succeeded in holding it permanently and completely they would have so weakened the power of Islam that it could not but have retreated during the ensuing centuries.

The Crusaders had no such general intention. It was only a coincidence that the Holy Places which they had come to rescue from the infidel were geographically necessary to the continued strength of Islam in its duel with Christendom; but that coincidence gave the Crusades an opportunity of which the Middle Ages grew more conscious as time went on—but by that time it was too late. The belt of maritime Syria, the neck or corridor, S S S, was never fully held, and therefore it was that ultimately the Crusading effort failed; therefore it was that the united force of Islam could be brought to bear, at last, by Saladin to overwhelm the Crusading garrison of Jerusalem itself.

What was the nature of this failure to hold the all-important Syrian belt? In order to answer that question we must make a diagram of that belt in more detail.

The essential to all military operations in maritime Syria is water. The absence of sufficient rainfall renders desert the wide territory lying to the east of the Syrian belt, also renders desert all North Africa and makes life, the founding of towns, and the passage of armies and commercial traffic impossible save upon certain conditions of water supply. Either there must be a sufficient rainfall, or there must be enough wells, or there must be watercourses fed from distant sources of snow or good rainfall and therefore running all the year round through lands not sufficiently watered by rain. Such a watercourse is the Nile, which creates Egypt, drawing its supply from the rainfall south of the desert and the highlands of Ethiopia. Such a watercourse is also the Euphrates, running along the eastern side of the Syrian desert and in the middle of its course cutting right through the uninhabited sand and stony waste.

In Syria itself there are two conditions which permit of a water supply even in the summer season when no rain, or very little, falls. The first of these conditions is a continuous run of highlands parallel to the seacoast of the Mediterranean and standing between that coast and the desert. The second condition is the limestone formation of these highlands. The seacoast range intercepts the moist air from the Mediterranean, and causes a good winter rainfall, and, on the higher slopes, stores part of it in the shape of frozen snow. The limestone rock of this same seacoast range absorbs the winter rains, holding them like a sponge or cistern, so that they provide springs, some of them perennial, and all of them flowing long after the rainy season has ended. Moreover the upland snows feed, as they melt under the summer sun, torrents descending from the mountains on either side. Those falling on the desert side are soon absorbed in the sand and only in one narrow sector are they large enough to fertilize any considerable district. But before the sands of the desert swallow them up they serve, especially by artificial irrigation, to produce crops and to support, as we shall see in a moment, at least one large town.

But the long chain of highlands which runs all down the Syrian belt parallel to the seacoast is not a single range: it is double. Immediately against the coast there is one succession of heights running throughout the 400 miles and pierced only by two gaps, one in the middle, and one to the north. To the east of this coast range lies a profound valley, from which to the east again rise a separate set of heights between that valley and the desert. This valley which runs for so many hundred miles north to south provides a bed for three rivers, the Orontes on the north, the Litany in the middle, and the Jordan on the south. The Orontes escapes to the Mediterranean through the northern gap in the maritime range, the Litany through the middle gap, while the Jordan does not get out at all. Its bed falls deeper and deeper below the level of the Mediterranean and falls at last into the very deep depression of the Dead Sea, hundreds of feet below the coast.

The general scheme of the maritime belt of Syria, is, then, a corridor sufficiently well watered in one fashion or another for men to live and armies to march within a certain distance of the Mediterranean seacoast. Cities can stand and men can travel in large numbers from north to south through the Syrian belt until it merges into the desert. The breadth of that habitable belt between the waters of the Mediterranean and the sands of the desert varies from 50 or 60 to under 40 miles, stretching in places to nearly 80, but the belt is everywhere narrow compared with its length.

To this simple scheme there is a very important exception. On the eastern or desert side the melting snows of the mountains irrigate to some extent lands which, save for them, would be sterile. The result is that there runs in a sort of fringe round the great desert between the Euphrates and Syria, land which is fully habitable near the sources of the mountain streams and grows less and less habitable as those streams die away in the burning waste. There are mountains to the north of Syria whence streams come down south, the largest of which, of course, is the Euphrates. From the mountains of Syria itself there is a barely sufficient water supply running down towards the desert in the northeast, and further down south along the inland range and on the edge of the desert there continues a fringe, part of which is habitable and bears crops. The whole thing may be represented diagrammatically as follows:

M M M is the Mediterranean coast, H H H are highlands along that coast; O is the Orontes; L the Litany; J the Jordan; the line K K K K is the highland east of the central valley, east, that is, of the watercourses, the Orontes, the Litany, and the Jordan. The desert which extends beyond the highlands east of the river is modified by the presence of water coming down from the hills or soaking through the limestone during the winter rainfall and supplying wells. Also, so far as the winter rainfall extends eastward there is a belt of more or less fertile land which gradually fades into desert. This strip of fertile land F F F F

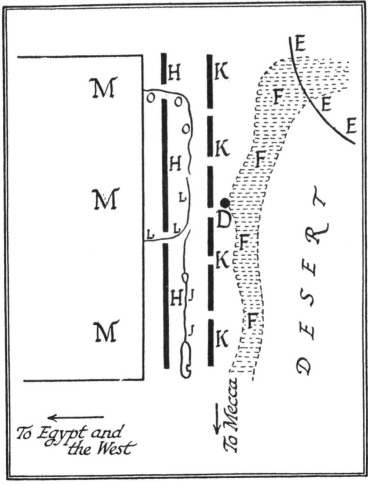

Map III. Diagram Showing Key Position of Damascus.

broadens to the north but gets thinner as you go south till you get to a sort of waist near D, which is Damascus.

At this point D which lies right under the highest part of the eastern highlands, the Anti-Lebanon, there is but a very narrow space, a few miles broad, upon which men can live. On the other hand it is watered by a plentiful supply from the snows of the Anti-Lebanon. When all the other lesser watercourses of the eastern highlands are dried up in summer (and they are all very small and short), these torrents, the "rivers of Damascus," may be seen pouring under the summer heat as full and unfailing as might be rivers of western Europe. It is true they are almost immediately swallowed up when they get east of Damascus and lost in the desert sand, but during their very short course from the mountain slope to the desert they are able to support a large population. Damascus is the flourishing and large city it is, surrounded by fruitful gardens on three sides, because this water supply irrigates its land.

Southwards after Damascus the belt of fairly fertile land broadens, men can live in the Druse hills though they are forbidding and sterile; corn grows further south in what the Greeks called the Ten Cities and all along the plateau of Moab.

We have seen how the Mohammedan world to the north and east of the Syrian belt needed that belt as a passage in order to communicate with that other Mohammedan world to the south and west—Egypt, the lands on the Mediterranean as far as Morocco, and Spain beyond. There was needed a free passage for Moslem armies from north to south and south to north along the Syrian belt if Islam was to escape being cut in two: if Mesopotamia and all that lay beyond it eastward, Persia and away to the Indus, was to remain in touch with the great pilgrim and caravan road down the west of Arabia to Mecca and Medina, and with the southern Mediterranean coast and with the wealth and dense population of the delta and the Nile valley.

Now from the arrangement of the Syrian corridor in three parallel belts—the coast range and plain, the interior Rift valley, the highland on the edge of the desert—it follows that there were three main ways by which Mohammedan forces could freely

march to and fro between the two halves of the Mohammedan
world.

The first road would follow close to the shore between the
Mediterranean and the coast belt; it would link up the ports of
that coast. The frequent torrents from the hills and the ample
winter rainfall stored in wells made it possible for great bodies
of men to advance and to rely upon towns and villages everywhere, with stores of provisions.

The second road would naturally follow the central valley, getting plentiful water from the Orontes and the Jordan.

The third road would follow the fringe of the desert: the narrow easternmost strip watered by short streams and wells and
having habitation all the way along, towns and villages, the chief
of which by far was Damascus.

By each of these three avenues Egypt and the West, as also
Mecca, could be reached from the semi-fertile ribbon which ran
under the Armenian mountains and linked up Mesopotamia with
the northern end of the Syrian coast.

Of these three ways the first or western one along the seacoast
is very difficult in its earlier northern part from the mouth of the
Orontes down to Latakia (the ancient Laodicea), for the whole
of that country is a wild tangle of hills. From Latakia southward
to Mt. Carmel it is much more easy to use, but it remains interrupted by the spurs of the mountains which thrust out into the
sea, enclosing between them fertile but comparatively small
plains. These spurs form headlands upon the coast, sometimes
so high and abrupt as to make the road perilous even under good
modern engineering. After Carmel the going is easy all the way
to the beginning of the Egyptian sand; it carries along the broad
sea plain between the Mediterranean and the hills of Judea, flat
all the way, and is the ancient country of the Philistines.

The second or central way, that by the inner valley and the
line of rivers, is not as continuous as it seems to be on the map.
All the northern part is easy and thoroughly well-watered, sup-
porting two quite considerable towns, Hama and Homs. Centuries ago it was equally possible for large bodies to continue along
the Litany valley until they reached the watershed between that

valley and the sources of the Jordan; but since the Mohammedan conquest this middle section along the Litany has been allowed to fall back into a marshy state and is in places impassable.

The southern end of the line after one leaves the Litany, that is, the course of the Jordan, is unsuitable for travel. At first, indeed, on the upper Jordan, above the sea of Galilee under the slopes of Hermon, an army or a large caravan can pass, and all the country round the sea of Galilee is open and able to support a large population; but beyond that lake, southward, the Jordan, though it provides water, does not provide an easy passage. It runs through a narrow, very deep and hot gorge full of rank vegetation. Small parties can go along it, and in old days Galileans would use it when they made the annual pilgrimage to Jerusalem; but it had no large settlement until one got to Jericho at the very end and was not passable as a highway for large columns of merchandise or armed troops.

In practice, during the last fifteen hundred years and more, men have used a combination of the coastal and the river way; they have gone up the Orontes a certain distance, then cut across to Latakia and then down the coast. Alternatively they have used the upper part of the eastern road to beyond Damascus, and then cut across by the neighborhood of the sea of Galilee to the seacoast; or alternatively from the hills of Galilee over the line of Judean hills to Jerusalem. By either way the northern and eastern part of the Mohammedan world communicated with the southern and western part.

The third, eastern, or fringe-of-the-desert road is everywhere an excellent and open track. Its northern part, from Aleppo, runs through fairly fertile land. From above Hama to Homs it is merged with the Orontes road. South of Homs it bifurcates: one track leaves the river valley to make for Damascus, skirting the desert side of Anti-Lebanon: the other follows up the Orontes, down the upper Litany and then crosses the pass to Damascus. They join at Damascus to become one road again. Beyond Damascus it goes along the heights of Moab and so southward until one comes to Akaba or forks to the left and follows the track leading to Medina and Mecca.

The ultimate failure of the Crusades lay in this: that Christendom got hold of the first or seacoast road, kept only a doubtful or disputed grasp on parts of the second or river road, *and altogether failed to hold the third road along the edge of the desert.*

After the First Crusade no large Mohammedan armed body could use the coast road: Egypt and Mecca and the west were cut off from Mesopotamia and the Mohammedan north and east so far as the coast road was concerned. The second way, that along the rivers, less important for the reasons we have already seen, was discontinuous and could not be permanently used; moreover, it was in dispute between the Christians and Islam. *But the third road, that along the eastern side near the desert, remained open to Islam the whole time.* Aleppo at its northern end, where the approach from Mesopotamia curls round southward, was never held by a Christian garrison. Between there and Hama there were but rare and occasional seizures of land by the Christians. Through Hama and Homs on to Damascus the Christians had no hold, and south of Damascus Islam continued to hold the eastern road throughout the Crusades. By that road a Mohammedan power could concentrate forces from Mesopotamia, communicate with Egypt, and always menace the Christian garrisons to the west of them, towards the Mediterranean.

Had the eastern road been held from the beginning or captured later, all that lay to the west of it—that is, all the habitable Syrian corridor—would have been permanently in the hands of us Westerners, and the Eastern culture, our opponent, would have been so wounded as never again seriously to menace Europe; for it would have been severed at the waist. Mohammedan Africa, including Egypt, would have decayed and been recaptured; there would have been no Empire of Saladin to ruin our cause.

The first thing that ought to have been done for the capture of the eastern road was to seize Aleppo so as to cut off Antioch from succor and to block any Mohammedan advance from Mesopotamia; then to take the string of towns south of Aleppo along the eastern road, then to seize and garrison the great city of Damascus. After that, Jerusalem would have fallen of itself and our people would have held the whole belt. The opportunity was missed, perhaps inevitably missed, for reasons that will appear in a moment; and therefore from the beginning the Crusading effort was doomed. It was concentrated upon Antioch. It did not proceed from Antioch to Damascus, which might have sufficed even if Aleppo was neglected; it switched off to the seacoast road, approached Jerusalem in that fashion, and gave up the eastern road for good. The effect of this error dominates the whole story.

It is not arguable that the active army, the efficients, numbering even a little later as much as a hundred thousand men, could not have dealt with Aleppo. It is arguable that after having wasted a year in taking Antioch and then quarrelling as to who should retain it, the actual force remaining was not sufficient to seize Damascus. It is arguable I say, but not certain. But that they could have seized Aleppo at the beginning *is* certain; and had they seized and garrisoned Aleppo and gone immediately down the Damascus road, Damascus, which is the master point of Syria, would have fallen.

The reason that Aleppo was not attacked was that the feudal chiefs of the Crusades had no general strategic plan, and perhaps could not, considering their time and place, have had one. Their large army was not coherent; individual chiefs had to be satisfied; and Aleppo did not provide anything like the revenue which Antioch still provided. Antioch was the immediate rich prize— therefore was Antioch alone their goal.

To carry out so general a strategic plan as the seizure of Aleppo, the subsequent advance along the eastern road, the taking of Damascus and the following up thence to Jerusalem would have needed not only the strategical conceptions of a more instructed society than that of western Europe in the twelfth century; it would have needed also an exact discipline and a united command permanently obeyed by the whole force. Both these were necessarily lacking to a feudal body of such magnitude. But the taking of Aleppo, though important to the final success of the Crusades, was secondary to the permanent holding of Damascus. If the Crusaders after Antioch had marched immediately upon Damascus and taken and garrisoned that great town, they could still have remained the masters of Syria. The idea occurred to them too late, in what is called "The Second Crusade"; Damascus never fell, and because Damascus remained in the hands of Islam, Jerusalem sooner or later was bound to follow.

What gives Damascus this capital value in the strategics of all that land is the position it occupies, coupled with the size of the city and its resources. Damascus is the point that can be reached most quickly from the extremes of the Syrian belt. It is central to them all. Messengers dispatched thence to Aleppo, to the seaports, to Jerusalem, to the edges of the Egyptian desert, by Gaza, take in the aggregate less time on their journey than they would from any point upon the coastal western boundary such as Beyrouth, from any point on the north, such as Antioch, from any point on the south such as Jerusalem. Armed forces could be concentrated on Damascus from the north, from the south, and from the seacoast, with greater rapidity than on any other point. This truth does not appear immediately upon a map, especially upon the map without contours, but it appears immediately in actual travel. When the King of Jerusalem desired to rally the Christian forces he was so far from Antioch that it could hardly be reached. Even from the county of Tripoli he could receive only tardy aid. When Edessa in the north was menaced it could not easily be succored because it lay too far off. But with Damascus as the headquarters, so to speak, of the military Crusading effort, all Syria would have been in hand.

Apart from this central quality—central in time and opportunity of access—there was the defensive character of the place. It was so well watered as to have permanent large provisionment of its own; it was so populous as to give permanent support in numbers and in wealth to any garrison fixed therein; it was the chief port of the desert commanding the main caravan route direct through Palmiera from Mesopotamia. It got news of all that was passing in Syria in less time than the average time taken for news to reach any other place. The mountain range at its back, the desert conditions immediately in front of it and half around it served as a further protection.

On account of all this it is Damascus throughout the ages that has determined the fate of Syria. It was Damascus on which the Assyrian power had concentrated centuries earlier and had found so difficult to grasp; it was from Damascus that Pompey gave orders which made the Roman soldiers the possessors of the whole land; it was the fall of Damascus to the first Mohammedan invasion which determined the success of that invasion and made it permanent—and now it was Damascus that would have confirmed the Crusading effort.

But of all this the leaders of the First Crusade were ignorant. Bohemond in particular had fixed in his mind the name not of Aleppo or of Damascus but of Antioch; the conversations of the Emperor and all that they had heard in Constantinople fixed his mind on Antioch; Antioch was taken as a matter of course to be the only immediate goal. Thither, therefore, did they march from the neighborhood of Aleppo, turning down south and westwards towards the Orontes.

*   *   *

To know what that was upon which the Crusading host came when they at last saw Antioch, a man must himself have seen the strange small relic of what Antioch once was, standing now today upon its river bank: that little shrivelled present town, the huge precipitous mountainside towering above it, miles and miles of fortified wall with curtain and tower climbing up and down the mountain slopes, crossing the profound gorge and encircling like a vast arm all that now wasteland whereon the mighty city once stood.

It is more than a mile from the banks of the Orontes southward and upward to the crest which the topmost of the wall still follows; it is two miles at least from the western extremity of those defenses downstream, to the eastern extremity, along the Aleppo road. All that great space had been filled for a thousand years with clamor and life. Antioch had been the third city of the Eastern world; it had been crowded with every kind of movement, officialdom, and wealth, a mass of temples and palaces, with colonnades that stretch from end to end. Today it is something larger than a village but not much larger, with not one stone of its antique grandeur remaining to stand against the sky as such things stand in profusion throughout the ruins of antiquity elsewhere, from Mesopotamia to the Channel, from the Sahara to the Rhine.

Of that ancient splendor, how much remained for the Crusaders to see? How much could the Crusading myriads see as their still prodigious column wound down the road from the Orontes crossing towards the walls, with the wide, very large shallow lake upon their right and the dark mountain with its line of towers frowning above them, much as Cader Idris frowns over its abrupt southern steep. What they saw as they approached was certainly something very much more than remains for us today after so many centuries of Mongol barbarism and general Mohammedan neglect.

It was barely a dozen years since Islam had again garrisoned Antioch in the last of its attacks, only those few years since the Greek order and discipline had been thrust out. In 1087 the bulk of those now empty fields within the walls where today you may not even find the trace of a foundation, were still covered. Great structures were still apparent and great numbers at work therein.

The town had been shaken by earthquakes more than once; it had suffered, as did all the East, the decay of the middle centuries, and, as had especially all Syria, the decay consequent upon the instability of Islam at its gates. It had certainly decayed badly by the time the Crusade approached it but it was still a great city, though how great we do not know. If we venture on a guess at 100,000 inhabitants still remaining we shall perhaps not be far wrong; there may even have been more. In the height of her power Antioch had been many times as populous: it had rivalled a modern capital.

Against its walls came up from the north and east the long defile of the 100,000 fighting men remaining from the original third of a million or more which had set out from Nicaea. What was the military task before them, in the presence of so huge a thing—a thing still so huge after centuries of slow decline?

Very numerous as the Crusading host was—it had to the restricted Mohammedan garrisons of the towns the aspect of a deluge—it was not numerous enough to establish a blockade against a circumference of this magnitude.

They had crossed the Orontes by the fortified bridge called "The Iron Bridge," which is on that road whereof one branch goes to Aleppo eastward, and the other, coming from into the mountains, was that along which the great Crusading column had come.

The Crusaders carried the bridge, with its fortified towers and their garrisons of crossbowmen; some could have crossed by a ford had they known or had they cared, but the carrying of the bridge was needed if it were to be used for great numbers and especially for vehicles. They had gone on along the few miles to the flat at the foot of the mountain, where the northern sector of the wall of Antioch touches the plain and runs up to the Orontes; and there they had pitched their three camps, each under one of the chief leaders.

But those camps did not at first cover more than a small fraction of the armed circumference of Antioch. All that two miles' length along which one can still see the ruins of the wall and towers standing on the ridge they did not approach; the greater part of the two miles between their emplacements and the southern end of the city—the plain beyond the river whence ran the western wall everywhere following the river bank—they left at first untouched.

From the day on which the Iron Bridge was forced (October 20, 1097) and the morrow (October 21), on which the camps were pitched, there was for some little time no attempt at a true siege. The main bridge out of the town where the walls run right along the river, a bridge on the site of the one that is still used today, was left open for the Turkish garrison within to use as it would. The road to the sea where, at the mouth of the river, the port of St. Simeon stood, was equally open: one might have wondered how the issue could be determined or how a conflict could be joined.

The first thing that occurs to a modern man reading the confused and sometimes contradictory accounts of contemporaries is this question: Why was not an effort made to seize a sector of the wall, and having such an advantage in numbers, to pour through the town and destroy the garrison or at least compel it to take refuge in the small citadel high up on the summit of the mountain, where it could have been closely blockaded and was ultimately bound to fall?

A sudden stroke of this kind would probably have been successful. The Turkish garrison within was but one-eighth of the besiegers. The population was mainly Christian and would have been hard to hold. The Turkish garrison feared to take any action for a whole fortnight and kept strictly behind the shelter of the walls. Could it not have been rushed?

One of the leaders, Raymond, had advised such a surprise attack. His advice was not followed—as like as not because the chieftains were already watching each other, each jealous lest ultimately one of them should alone possess the great prize. Their camps lay in a string along the northeast corner of the walls, from the gate called "The Gate of St. Paul" (whence starts the road to Aleppo), past the next gate, round the corner on the eastern side ("The Gate of the Dog"), and extended across the little brook which flows from a deep ravine in the mountains: a trifling thing, but a sufficient obstacle to form a boundary for some little time.

The Moslem garrison had built a bridge over this brook; the Crusaders took that bridge, and just beyond the point where the brook falls into the Orontes they threw a bridge of boats across that main stream to give them communication with the wide and fertile plain beyond.

Not quite a month after their arrival in front of the walls, a small fleet from Genoa appeared at the mouth of the Orontes with scanty provisions, insufficient for any length of time. The Western sailors had already begun to establish themselves tentatively along the Syrian coast. Among them was an independent sort of half-pirate from Boulogne who had landed at Laodicea during the past summer. Henceforward throughout the Crusading epoch the sea was to be the open road for such intermittent reinforcement as could reach this very distant enterprise of the western Europeans.

During the first three months, that is, over Christmas and the turn of the year, the stalemate continued. The line was gradually extended; a blockhouse was built to command the main bridge out of the city. By the end of three months one may say that the whole of the western side whereby most of the provisionment of the garrison could arrive was covered by the Christian line of tents.

There had been one considerable effort just after Christmas to force the main river gate of the town by night; it had failed with some loss. Instead of forming a true siege, which even such numbers as theirs could not accomplish, they dispersed from time to time to forage, especially up the Orontes valley. But meanwhile, as the new year proceeded, want appeared in the Christian camp. Food began to fail. The famine took a heavy toll, not only in numbers but in morale, and still a true siege could not be laid nor a sufficient assault delivered against those very strong walls. Yet such was the dispersion of Mohammedan force through the rivalries and quarrels of the individual chiefs that the opportunity for a general concentration against the Christian camp was missed, and the relief of Antioch was delayed. It was not till February 8, 1198, that anything serious was attempted against the Crusaders from the outside.

The Emir of Aleppo, having settled his long quarrel with the commander of the garrison in Antioch, made the effort: Bohemond was the chief agent of that effort's failure, and it was his success on that occasion, day and night, which indicated him later for a momentary and most important supreme command. He occupied the narrow neck between the lake of Antioch and the Orontes, it was the only passage by which the enemy could attack, and though there were only 700 knights (the mass of the infantry having been left to guard the camps), the men of Aleppo were thrown back.

While the struggle was proceeding the garrison of Antioch made a sortie, but they made it too late: the victorious Christian cavalry reappeared and the garrison retired again behind its walls.

Thenceforward the siege took a more regular turn. Not quite a month later was built the blockhouse just mentioned, which commanded the main bridge; it was Raymond of Toulouse who set it up and garrisoned it; and already another more serious sortie of the besieged had been thrown back with very heavy loss—or, at least, loss heavy for the desultory fighting which had so far marked the operations outside the walls of the huge city. The Turkish garrison left behind them, drowned in the river of corpses upon the plain, fifteen hundred men, and a dozen of their higher officers.

But the deadlock might have gone on forever, or more probably been solved to the destruction of the whole Crusading effort by a tardy rally among the hitherto hopelessly divided petty chieftains of Mohammedan inland Syria, when an accident of treason determined the issue.

It is remarkable that treason seemed necessary to decide the fate of Antioch in all times. It may have been treason that permitted the Persian rush upon the city just before the Mohammedans had appeared between four and five hundred years before. It was certainly treason which had lost Antioch to the Emperor of Byzantium twelve years before. This time it was a disaffected commander within the Turkish garrison who decided the fate of the city. He was a certain Firuz, by one account an Armenian, that is, a renegade in the service of the Turks, and placed by the Turkish governor of the garrison in command of the strong five-sided tower which stood on the south of the city, just where the mountain comes down to the plain. It was called "The Tower of the Two Sisters." Firuz nourished a grudge against his superior officer, who had confiscated certain goods of his— perhaps a store of food during that time of famine. Whatever the cause was, he entered into secret negotiation with Bohemond.

Bohemond had been intriguing and waiting for his chance all

that winter long and through the spring; he had a certain right to expect primacy, during the siege at least, on account of his victory near the lake, and now there had already begun to arise rumors of united command among the Christian leaders. It was a necessity; for the prospect of a Mohammedan concentration was beginning to take shape, the Mohammedan concentration which had tarried so long. A very large army was on the march, under the Turkish chieftain of Mosul, who had swept into it every Mohammedan element he could gather for a decision. This chieftain, Kerbogha, to spell the name as the Christians spelled it (Kurbuga is nearer the original pronunciation), was said to be leading 200,000 men.

The Christian leaders in that peril promised Bohemond a united supreme command; they even promised him, if he could establish himself in Antioch, the possession of that great place—but only on condition that he should hold it under the Emperor of Byzantium, whose undoubted right they had promised not to violate; and if that monarch should arrive to the succor of the Crusaders, Bohemond was to hand back the city to him.

There has not often been in history so close a conjunction of dates. The great host of Islam was approaching. Bohemond had achieved his temporary ambition and was to be given supreme command on May 29, 1098. In the night between the second and third of June, Firuz sent word to Bohemond that he would, during that darkness, betray the Tower of the Two Sisters. About four o'clock in the morning Bohemond himself climbed up to the lowest window, and all along the wall to the left the escalade of a few began. Sixty Christian knights occupied the Tower of the Two Sisters itself, and garrisoned the place. In the dusk of the morning all the towers on the south one after the other were thus seized, since the key tower had been betrayed—the great pentagonal "Two Sisters."

The Christian population of Antioch, quite unwarlike, but the vast majority of the town, took advantage of the breach in the defense and opened the gates, beginning with the gate of the bridge. The Turkish garrison (or what was left of it after the surprise fighting) took refuge in the citadel on the very summit of the mountain; but as full day broke, their commander, the Emir, who had thought himself secure until the new great host of Islam should arrive to relieve the town, saw the purple standard of Bohemond floating from one of the towers close at hand. He fled, and fell, far off, into the hands of Christian workmen in the woods, who killed him as his companions escaped.

That was on the third of June. And the very next day, the fourth, the advance guard of the huge relieving army forced the Iron Bridge across the Orontes, coming down the Aleppo road, killed off its Crusading garrison and appeared before the walls of the city.

The battle of Antioch for the relief of the Moslem world repeated the experience of Dorylaeum—the experience that all these wars were to confirm over and over again.

The French mounted knights when sufficiently supported by the infantry were certain of victory against the light-armed and light-mounted swarm of Moslem bowmen. Bohemond was in command because he was recognized by all as the best tactician among them, but the tactics were of a simple kind and were to be frequently repeated with similar success in battle after battle of the Crusades. To ensure victory, all that was required was a sufficient number of heavy armed Western gentlemen on heavy horses to deploy and charge in a line too long for the cloud of light-mounted enemy bowmen to envelop it by the right and the left. Weight for weight, stroke for stroke, energy for energy, the Oriental could not stand up to the Western man. The danger would come years on when Western numbers were so depleted and Western blood so diluted that conditions between the opponents would be more equal; and even then the final defeat that fell at Hattin was due not only to inferior numbers but to the sheer incapacity of the infantry from the exhaustion of an ill-conceived march to act in support of the knights.

Here before Antioch on June 4, 1098, the Christian victory was immediate and certain. The hail of arrows from the Turkish archers, reinforced by fresh bands which galloped up, retired, were replaced by other bands, as we have seen was the universal tactic of their people, lasted for a much shorter time than at Dorylaeum because the Christian host was much larger in proportions and better prepared. After the first few discharges of arrows the heavily mounted and heavily armed mail-clad French knights swept the light Turkish cavalry back as a wind sweeps back mist.

When the Turks of Kerbogha rallied they attempted here again to use that tactic which they invariably used against the more disciplined and solid ranks of the Christian soldiery—a tactic well suited to the rapidity of their mounts and excellent horsemanship. They tried to spread out on either wing and to envelop. There was not much room for a turning movement, for though the plain between the river and the hills of Mt. Amanus gets wider the further one goes westward from the lake, yet the width is not sufficient for a large sweep round.

Bohemond easily met the enveloping maneuver by detaching a reserve force and sending it out to extend his left. From the six "battles," that is, deployed lines of mounted knights, he withdrew a certain proportion of Godfrey's command and of the Duke of Normandy's, forming them into a seventh corps which he put under the command of Reginald of Toul, one of the lords from Lorraine. The Turkish turning movement was thus blocked, and even as it failed the mass of the Christian mounted knights delivered their second main charge.

The enemy began to break up. Some of them as they retired set fire to the dry summer grass that the smoke might interrupt the pursuit—whereby we know that there was a wind from the north on that day—but the obstacle was not sufficient, the whole Christian line got home and on the enemy's side there was a general breakdown.

Kerbogha's rout was pursued relentlessly right up to the Iron Bridge and even beyond. Kerbogha himself got away with a few followers to Aleppo; then went back, a broken man, to Mosul. The Emir of Damascus also went back to his own, and no further army on this scale could be gathered from the divided and jealous Mohammedan leaders.

The citadel of Antioch surrendered. Its capture was the

occasion of a renewed quarrel between Bohemond and the Count of Toulouse. But Bohemond, having been in command on that victorious day, had his way in the matter and planted his banner on the height of the mountain.

This second great battle of the Crusading march decided the fate of maritime Syria, as Dorylaeum had decided the fate of the Turkish occupation of Asia Minor. What was still the great city of Antioch, still mainly Christian in population, was acquired permanently for the new Christian state that was about to be founded. From the day of Antioch, June 4, 1098, Islam did not lift up its head in Syria for half a lifetime. Kerbogha had been but the representative of the central Seljuk power; the Atabeg of Mosul stood for the Sultan; the defeat of the Atabeg was the defeat of the Sultan. That defeat was complete and for the moment final.

6

JERUSALEM

The taking of Antioch and the securing of that town by the complete overthrow of the army coming to its relief should have been but an episode in the full Crusade. In a modern regular war, or in a war such as those which antiquity undertook in the height of its civilization, Antioch would have been only a first step to the full conquest of Syria.

It is true that the Crusaders, having already neglected Aleppo and switched off all their forces onto Antioch had committed a strategic error, but that could still have been remedied had there been one united force under one command working towards one military object. But the Crusaders were not that; they were a feudal force, incoherent, enjoying no united command and having no definite strategic object. Indeed their advance had only one definable objective, and that objective not military. They had set out to secure the Holy Places, and especially the Sepulchre of the Lord in Jerusalem. They had no plan save—such as persevered—to go forward. Nor could they even go forward continuously.

Suffering from these disabilities the Crusading effort, instead of garrisoning Antioch and going on at once to grasp Damascus or at least to attain Jerusalem, was wasted in nearly half a year's delay: from late June, 1098, to mid-January, 1099. This delay was due to Bohemond's determination that he should be independent lord of Antioch and all its district. His ambition, even more than that of all those about him, was personal and feudal. He had taken the oath of allegiance to the Emperor at Byzantium with the idea that under some vague feudal tie to this Emperor he should enjoy the sovereignty and revenues of Antioch, and to this end he directed his sly but determined and tenacious mind. Against him stood the other great leader, the Count of Toulouse. *He* had not sworn allegiance. He was the wealthiest and politically the most important of the great French feudatories now on the march; it irked him bitterly that he should be sent off on a mission to the Holy Places while the enormous prize of Antioch fell to a rival.

If the Greek Emperor had marched side by side with the Crusaders and taken his full part in the effort, the quarrel would hardly have arisen; Alexius—or his general—might have left Bohemond lord of Antioch under his allegiance but not as an independent prince; and the Greeks would have been a full support to the remainder of the Crusading army on their way to the Holy City. But the Emperor of Byzantium was one of those men who will risk nothing. The Crusaders had given him Nicaea; they had relieved the pressure on his capital; Dorylaeum had enabled him to retake the western part of Asia Minor. He preferred to consolidate himself there and left the Crusade to go its way unaided.

The critical moment, the turning point in the relations between the Emperor and the Crusaders, had come as early as January, 1098, two months after the host had first appeared under the walls of Antioch.

Bohemond had, until that moment, desired that the Emperor of Constantinople should make him, after Antioch was taken, its local lord, under a feudal tie to Byzantium. He had already declared himself in Constantinople the vassal of the Emperor, he had already taken an oath to hand back to the Byzantine authority whatever he conquered. He began by threatening to retire from the Crusade altogether, but he made this threat not to the Byzantine emissary who was with the army, but to the Christian leaders of the host. His threat had the effect he expected: they all but *one* promised that when Antioch should be taken Bohemond should be made the lord of it. But that one who stood out was the most powerful of them—Raymond. Next Bohemond terrified the Byzantine Emissary, Tactikeos, but he was careful not to make it a personal threat. What he did was to persuade the Greek that the other leaders of the Crusade thought the Byzantines were working with the Turks and betraying them. Tactikeos fled, and with him disappeared the last hope of Byzantine control over the movement. When he had gone, Bohemond loudly denounced his treason. After this piece of trickery, typical of that excellent general, great soldier, and bad character, the counterclaim of Toulouse to Antioch was outflanked. Bohemond could make certain of the reversion of the town, although (as we shall see) Toulouse held out to the last moment. Bohemond had grievously weakened the Crusade by his selfishness; Raymond of Toulouse by his jealousy. Still, the main fault lay with Alexius. Bohemond could not have played his trick nor Raymond have angered against it if Alexius had sent a sufficiently strong contingent to support the Crusaders, and affirm his regular right. Alexius hesitated to do so from timidity. He had left Christendom in the lurch, and it was right that he should pay the penalty.

When later the great Moslem rally had been defeated in the main battle of Antioch, the council of the Crusading leaders just after the victory were still willing to keep their word if the Emperor would take advantage of their offer. They sent Hugh, the French King's brother, back to Constantinople as their ambassador, to say that if the Emperor would bring or send up an army, even after this long delay, to help them in their advance through Syria and stand with them in the last object of their march, the deliverance of Jerusalem, they would hand over Antioch to him. If he had come with his army, he would have had not only Antioch but probably Jerusalem as well. Byzantium would have appeared again as Queen of the East. The Emperor would not, indeed, have been the absolute master of the Levant as his predecessors had been for centuries; he would only have held its authority through the aid of the Crusaders; still, the Crusade would have fallen within the orbit of the Eastern Emperor, his empire would have been restored; probably Egypt also in the long run would have been recovered. Above all, there would have been sufficient Christian strength in Syria to master Islam for good.

The Emperor did not march: no Greek army came. I have said that his failure was a failure of timidity; but it was perhaps also in some part a failure of means. He may have doubted whether he had sufficient forces to detach for such a march—and we must remember that the request was made in the height of summer. Later on, after the Crusaders had wasted the whole autumn and half the winter, in possession of Antioch, indeed, but delaying to go forward, the Emperor, in the April of the following year, 1099, did propose to send a contingent and join the Crusaders in their march on Jerusalem. But it was too late, Bohemond by that time had consolidated his power, and there was no ousting him. All the forces remaining with him in Antioch were lost to the Crusade.

The quarrel between Raymond of Toulouse and the Norman Bohemond with his contingent of highly trained soldiery might have been put right by the authority of the Papal Legate, Adhemar. He was the one man in the Crusading host to whom the masses looked as possessing lawful right of decision in great matters. But an epidemic fell upon the remains of the army during the torrid heat of that Syrian summer, and Adhemar had died in August. Raymond would not give way to Bohemond, yet Bohemond remained in practical possession. There was a deadlock. The army wasted away and did not move.

There was in all this another element which plays a very great part in the picturesque story of the Crusade but which in a military explanation of the great adventure and its failure need only be mentioned to explain the tenacity with which Raymond held out in his tussle with Bohemond. After Kerbogha had come up outside the walls of the city just too late to prevent its occupation by the Crusaders, there had been three weeks in which it seemed as though the whole business of the Crusade would break down. The Christian besiegers of Antioch, now possessed of the town, were besieged in their turn by Kerbogha; they suffered a severe famine, and their morale sank to the lowest.

At that moment, about a fortnight after the blockade of Antioch by Kerbogha had begun, a man connected with the forces of Raymond of Toulouse came forward saying that he had

had a vision: the Holy Lance which had pierced the side of Our Lord on Calvary, the lance of the centurion Longinus, was, he said, buried in the Church of St. Peter; and he had a mission to recover it.

The floor of the Church was dug, and the lance was discovered. It may well have been the true relic buried there during the Moslem occupation: or the thing may have been a coincidence. Antioch, the earliest of the Christian settlements, would certainly have preserved what it could of the relics of the Passion. On the other hand, we have no former account of such a relic. Anyhow, the lance head was found, and it worked a moral miracle. That same French temperament which we must always keep in mind when studying the fortunes of the Crusade, lit a sudden enthusiasm through the army. It was roused from its lethargy, even from the consequences of the famine, it was filled with the certitude of victory, and in that mood it had sallied out by the bridge gate and won its great triumph over the besieging Mohammedan host.

But for our purposes, what we have to notice is that the finding of the Holy Lance being connected with the forces of Raymond of Toulouse strengthened his position against Bohemond. Although it was Bohemond who commanded as we have seen in the battle which followed, Raymond and all his contingent, and all who sympathized with him against Bohemond, and all who now so bitterly complained of Bohemond's holding up the Crusading march by his ambition and greed, made of the discovery of the Holy Lance a sort of rallying cry. Perhaps if the Holy Lance had not been discovered and if the enthusiasm following its discovery had not helped to win the great battle against Kerbogha, Raymond would not have had sufficient support to stand out against Bohemond. As it was, he had that support and the wrangle went on all through the summer with the army still diminishing and melting away. The main advance and object of the Crusade was checked and perhaps frustrated.

Knowing this, we can understand the details of the halt between the battle of Antioch and the resumption six months later of the march on Jerusalem.

Immediately after the victory over Kerbogha a formal council of the great leaders was convened. On the decision of that council—had they known it—depended the whole future of the Crusades in their largest meaning; that is, the whole future of the effort suddenly and enthusiastically undertaken by western Europe to thrust back Mohammed. Had the conditions of that day permitted so much as the idea of grand strategy, the decision would have been taken to march not on Jerusalem, but on Damascus. In that phrase you hold in your hand the central strategic truth of the situation.

To march on Damascus and to march at once, to take and garrison that nodal point of all the Levant, would have guaranteed the secure and permanent holding not only of Jerusalem in due course but of everything between the desert and the Mediterranean.

Why, then, was the march on Damascus not undertaken? The losses in the recent battle had not been very heavy on the Christian side, whatever they may have been on the other. A garrison would have had to be left in Antioch, but even so, we may reckon that in that summer of 1198, a column of some 70,000 men, of whom, say, five or six thousand would have been fully armed knights, could have undertaken the essential task.

The distance by the road the Crusaders would have had to take, that is, by the Orontes valley as far as Homs, and then under the slopes of the Anti-Lebanon, by the main track which leads from north to south, joining up all the ports of the desert, would have been no more than 120 miles. The direct distance from Antioch to Damascus is not much more than half the distance from Antioch to Jerusalem. The seizing of Damascus would have been all the easier at that moment from the disunion among the Turkish commanders, which had become worse than ever through the complete defeat of the only leader who had hitherto been able to bring them together. Kerbogha had lost all prestige. Aleppo certainly would not have moved. Further, a direct advance along the Orontes and so up to Damascus, thence on to Jerusalem, would have been by far the easiest route. What, in the long run, the remnant of the Crusading host did was to take the road which branches off westward from the Orontes valley to the sea and so along the coast; and it was most arduous, going through one defile after another, where the passage was crowded between the steep limestone hills and the shore, compelled in some places to climb to the heights, and all cut up from beginning to end into isolated plains separated by the spurs of the mountains.

The right thing was not done, the plain strategic decision was not taken, Damascus was left intact beyond its mountain barrier; the eastern way up and down Syria which united Islam in Egypt to Islam in Mesopotamia was left open, and the Crusading effort was doomed for as long as it might endure to stand on a difficult defensive; it had to hang on precariously to no more than the fringes of the wide belt which it might have occupied entirely at a blow.

Why was this error committed? Mainly, as I have said, because the time was not one of which a general strategic scheme could be expected. Not that the twelfth century was incapable of strategy on main lines—after all, these are only common sense, and the twelfth century had as much common sense as we have, or more; but they did not think in terms of a united command, still less in terms of an indirect objective. The host was, so far as military operations were concerned, a federation rather than an army; each of the various major military chieftains would have had to feel some personal interest in the attack on Damascus to cause a combination of all for the purposes of that attack.

Jerusalem as an ultimate objective they understood—and all understood it, even those who did not join in the final effort and were therefore not present at the capture of the Holy City. Every man in the great concentration before Antioch (which still counted, remember, close on 100,000 men) had Jerusalem in mind as an inspiration and a name. None so had Damascus in mind. Had the march on Damascus been undertaken the mass of the troops, most of them but half under discipline, only a minority fully organized, would not have understood the nature of the maneuver; and you could not order a feudal host against its will.

It is true that the approach on Jerusalem by way of Damascus was an alternative not unknown to the leaders; even the chroniclers, most of whom were not soldiers but clerics, had heard of this alternative. That it was an easier way than that by the seacoast those acquainted with the geography of the region had told them. Acting onwards from Damascus an army is impeded by nothing, as it makes southward for Jerusalem; there are no defiles, no narrows to cause congestion or give opportunity for a check at the hands of a smaller force, unless perhaps it be the valley approach through the district of Samaria and the pass in which Nablus stands. Even this, however, is nothing like so difficult as a dozen at least of the strangled corniches and torrent bridges along the tortuous coast road.

But the effort, if it was to be undertaken at all, must be undertaken without delay. The army might need some repose for a few days, the advance would be painful in the height of a Syrian summer, but it would at least have been well watered till within the last approach to its objective. Such rapidity of action demanded by military rules was rendered politically impossible; and what rendered it impossible was the combination of two things: first, the Emperor of Byzantium who might have come up in aid and might still have claimed Antioch for his own, continually hesitated and delayed. Second, there was this violent division between the Crusading leaders and particularly between Bohemond and the Count of Toulouse as to who should remain in possession of the revenues, the great population, the whole new fief of Antioch.

The Crusading council were still loyal, even after their victory over Kerbogha, to the oaths they had sworn at Constantinople; even Bohemond rallied to the general decision that the Emperor must have his original territories restored to him, though no doubt upon terms. Bohemond would have been willing enough to have remained at Antioch in a feudal dependence upon the Emperor, he would still have been the master of the town and its taxes, he would still have held a position which the great feudatories of western Europe understood and could work. But the Emperor did not come; no great Byzantine force arrived to strengthen the Crusaders and make certain of their final triumph at Jerusalem. The causes of this glaring political error have been described; Alexius had hesitated and left the task undone.

In his absence the quarrel for the possession of Antioch had a free field to develop and prolong the delay indefinitely. Bohemond had his men in the citadel and his banner on the towers thereof; his men were also quartered over a large section of the city, perhaps the greater part of it. From his prestige after the victory, in which he had been for a day commander-in-chief, from the fact that it was he who had first benefitted by the treason of the Tower of the Two Sisters, and he whose men with himself leading them had first passed the walls; from the right of possession in which he stood, dominating the whole town from the mountain fortress of the ridge above it, his claim was stronger than that of any rival.

Most of his colleagues supported him. The Count of Flanders did so, so did Godfrey; but the Count of Toulouse held on to his castle beyond the river which commanded the bridge out of Antioch westward. He continued to maintain in a negative sort of way his claim against Bohemond.

In respect to the attitude of either of these main rivals towards the Emperor in distant Constantinople, there was a paradoxical turnover. Bohemond, who had taken the oath to the Emperor and hoped to be master of Antioch as the Emperor's vassal, now declared that the Emperor's failure to arrive put an end to all such bonds, and declared himself hostile to the Byzantine connection: while Raymond of Toulouse, who had refused to take any oath to the Emperor and had stood for independence from Byzantium, now proclaimed the Emperor's right to the city. He not only kept the bridge gate and the fort which commanded it, but occupied the governmental palace in the lower town where the Turkish commander had lain during the siege. That occupation gave him a certain hold, just as the occupation of the citadel a mile away on the heights of the mountain gave Bohemond a hold.

There was an attempted solution of this deadlock by establishing a dual control; Bohemond should have the city on condition that he consented to march with the others on Jerusalem, and the group from Provence, that is, the army of the Count of Toulouse, would on that condition accept the ultimate decision of their colleagues. But Bohemond reserved the point of fidelity to the Emperor and all duty to accept Byzantium and its suzerainty over their conquests.

The upshot of all this was that the great body of armed men stood useless for the purposes of the Crusade that summer and on into the beginning of the winter months.

Of the men of Provence, one comparatively small group went off on its own to try and get a lordship beyond the Orontes. Their leader, for whose benefit this was to have been done, had been in touch with the Christian population of that region, and particularly with those of the town of Maarrat, which lay in the highland plateau on the edge of the desert, itself ill-provided with water and in the midst of half-barren land. The town was poor, but as a point of attack not ill-chosen, for if Maarrat could have been held it cut the great road from Aleppo to Damascus, and there could be no going round it by the enemy through the desert to the east. The Crusaders, leaving a garrison in Maarrat, could have advanced on Damascus at their leisure. I suggest that since the expedition was made up of the men of Provence it was not haphazard, but had been privately suggested by Raymond of Toulouse—an experiment as it were. Should it succeed he might have planned for a further advance up the Orontes and so towards Damascus. But this is only a guess: we have no documents. Raymond could not, of course, make such a decision openly, it would have been equivalent to abandoning his claims on Antioch which, through his rivalry with Bohemond, he had to watch, and so dally in the city.

Anyhow, this *coup de main* in Maarrat with a small detached force failed. The Mohammedan garrison of Aleppo, which would have been unable to stir against the main Crusading force, drove the Maarrat detachment back. But it is remarkable that even so, the superiority of the Western cavalry over the Oriental was strongly marked. It was but a handful of knights that rode against Maarrat: when the local Christian foot levies broke, the knights were compelled to retire, but they retired intact.

So fixed in their stationary delay at Antioch had the Crusaders become that after the failure of the little expedition against Maarrat, Raymond went off on his own to Edessa to pay a visit to Baldwin in the new lordship there; and Bohemond went off on his own also to the Cilician plain, to make sure of the loyalty of the garrisons in Tarsus and Adana. Then in September there was another excursion, in no way concerned with the main purpose of the Crusade. The Count of Toulouse went off to capture the town of Bara, on the way to Aleppo, to turn out the Mohammedans, free the Christians there and set up a bishopric, choosing for that office one of his own clerics from Narbonne.

The worst of the summer had passed, and though they could certainly have advanced (with difficulty and some loss) during August and September, they could advance without difficulty of any kind now that the cooler autumn had come. Yet still they delayed.

On November 5th, the leaders met in council in the old and most venerated Church of St. Peter; but nothing followed.

Towards the end of the month Raymond of Toulouse, leading a second far more serious attack on Maarrat, underwent more than a fortnight's desperate fighting along the walls to capture the city. They got it before the middle of September; but the diversion, though it was strategically useful, cutting, as I have explained, the main road from Aleppo to Damascus, was no solution to the quarrel which was still holding up the Crusaders after all these months, and preventing the advance southwards. Indeed the capture of Maarrat was the occasion for further subsidiary quarrels among the lords, upon the question of dividing the booty.

The longer the delay lasted, the stronger became Bohemond's position in Antioch; he favored therefore every kind of postponement. Raymond determined upon taking the Jerusalem road at last. He summoned yet another council, and offered a subsidy to compel a general advance: ten thousand pieces of gold for Godfrey, another ten thousand for the Duke of Normandy, six thousand for the Count of Flanders, five thousand for Tancred, if they would give the support of their troops. But even so the quarrel went on, because Bohemond, now that Raymond was solidly established at Bara and Maarrat, was more determined than ever upon being recognized as the full lord of Antioch.

What put an end to this wretched paralysis was a mutiny on the part of the great mass of the armed forces. Perhaps mutiny is not quite the right word to apply to any feudal body, so free were the elements of it to go each their own way. The mass of the foot soldiers, joined perhaps by many of the knights, rose against their leaders and clamored for the Jerusalem road.

In the enthusiasm of that half revolution they most foolishly dismantled the newly conquered town of Maarrat, saying that thus they could prevent its being a bone of contention between the princes. But the rising had its effect, the Count of Toulouse put himself at the head of the column organized for the southern march; he went out by the southern gate of Maarrat, barefoot as a symbol that he was once more a pilgrim, and though the Count of Flanders and Godfrey still hesitated, they joined him soon afterwards—within three days. Raymond was awaiting them at the end of his first day's march, twelve miles along the southern road out of Maarrat.

The Christian force thus going forward at last was far weaker than it might have been had it started all those months before from Antioch. It lacked the masses who followed Bohemond, it lacked those who had fallen in the various conflicts during the delays, especially the two attacks on Maarrat; it had been diminished by epidemic during the preceding summer, and it was to dwindle still further before the objective was reached.

Would they have been still in sufficient force to attack Damascus? The thing may be doubted: at any rate they ceased to follow the Damascus road. They did not even follow the Orontes line; they made for the sea, and in that decision they were no doubt supported by the advantage of getting into touch with the Christian ships.

In this new march they had different enemies to meet from those Turks who had fought them hitherto without success, but with repeated energy. They came from Maarrat southward towards the sea, into districts where, since the partial breakdown of the Turkish rule, little Arab chiefs of towns and villages and independent castles had set up their independence. These had not the strength nor had they the desire to challenge the column on its march. Even when one of the principal strongholds of the Orontes valley was met, the fortress called "The Castle of the Kurds," no resistance was offered.

The march was very slow. Halts for days at a time were frequent. Meanwhile the Governor of Homs, the town which, had they gone straight for Damascus, would have lain right in their route, treated them as friends, sending them horses and a sort of tribute, signing a treaty in which he promised to treat his Christian subjects with favor. It was Candlemas, February 2, 1099, and by the time they were holding feast in the empty castle it was nearly another fortnight before the whole body of them were fully established on the sea plains, within sight of the Mediterranean. The Arab lord of Tripoli had met their advance by a submission comparable to that of Homs; he sent them horses and gold and allowed the banners of the Count of Toulouse to be set up upon the walls of his port.

One place resisted: Arqua, just northeast of Tripoli. The camp was pitched before the walls of that fortress on St. Valentine's day, the 14th. Three days later the port of Tortosa, which had thought of resisting, was carried without a struggle, and henceforward was an excellent point for the Christian ships to land their provisionment. The siege of Arqua, small as the place was, dragged on too long; there were rumors of a general attack coming from the mass of Moslems in the interior, but they remained rumors only. Those who had compelled the delayed movement from Antioch, that is, the bulk of the remaining army, were not to be kept waiting longer in the effort to acquire new towns for their leaders; the host knew by this time that it would be fairly welcome down the Lebanon coast, with its large proportion of Christian population, and the march was resumed.

Here it is worth pointing out that in this advance there was no necessity for maintaining land communications in regular fashion by the establishment of a chain of garrisoned posts—

which would have weakened the already gravely depleted strength of the few thousands left for the final attack on Jerusalem. Those few thousands were provisioned in part by purchase from the population of the coast, in part by requisitionment, in part by the Christian shipping which followed them and which now, since the capture of Tortosa, had a good port of call.

The man most influential in persuading his colleagues to accept a popular demand for resuming the march was Godfrey of Bouillon, and it is from this point onwards (the siege of Arqua was raised on May 13, 1099) that Godfrey's name gets a new prominence, which was of course raised to a summit when he was later elected "Defender of the Holy Sepulchre." He, the Duke of Lower Lorraine, may be said henceforward to replace the Count of Toulouse as leader; but even so, there was no commander-in-chief as there should have been. The Crusading effort continued to lack unity of command, even beyond the ordinary for a feudal body. And there was another point of importance in connection with this change of primacy. This was the beginning of that colonial policy which later was to bear great fruit—a policy of compromising with the petty independent Mohammedan town governors and making friends or subjects of them.

Thus Toulouse wanted to seize Tripoli by force; but Godfrey accepted the offers of Banu Ammar, the local Mohammedan lord of the place. Banu Ammar was willing to pay fifteen thousand gold pieces if the Crusaders would abandon the siege of Arqua, and as willing to fill up their complement of horses and mules—even to pay them a regular tribute. The little local Moslem lord of Byblos did the same thing on a smaller scale; further, guides were provided by the new allies, and this was important, for the coast road is tricky enough even in its present modern well-engineered condition—in the twelfth century it must have been perilous at intervals of every few miles. The whole line down as far as Mt. Carmel is a series of enclosed plains divided by spurs from the mountains, and the track had to take these spurs as best it could, sometimes overhanging the way by some hundreds of feet. At each of these bottlenecks they dreaded a check at the hands of a hostile force, but none appeared.

It must be remembered that, to this day, a great part of the Lebanon coast is Christian, and in the twelfth century of course, a much larger proportion of the people were Christian. The local lordships were in the hands of Mohammedans, but the populace followed the Greek or Syriac liturgies, and were left in peace.

The march, therefore, became more normally rapid; it took them three days to get to Beyrouth from Tripoli, and another four to get to Tyre: a very good pace under the conditions, indeed the regular marching rate of more than 12 but less than 15 miles a day. They reached Caesarea, beyond Mt. Carmel, after something like a forced march—averages of 20 miles a day and more—though why they were so pressed we have no evidence remaining to explain. They had been reinforced somewhat by knights coming in from the north to take part in the final adventure, the last stage of which was now upon them. They kept Whitsuntide during a fairly long halt of several days in Caesarea; then having reached Arsouf, 25 miles on, they turned inland to mount the slopes of the Judean highlands, which had followed them along their eastern horizon during all the last days.

Jerusalem, with its large Egyptian Fatimite garrison, was close at hand; by the time they got to Ramleh it was only one day's riding away—say 25 miles by the shorter of the two roads. They therefore broke the rule they had hitherto followed of keeping all together; they left a small garrison in Ramleh to guard against surprise and made for the uplands and the Holy City.

For three days they stood at Ramleh, at the foot of the final ascent. They had found it evacuated by the enemy; they set up a bishop (a Norman from Rouen), gave him the feudal lordship of Ramleh and Lydda close at hand, and dedicated the See to St. George, who had become the patron of all the later part of this march since a vision or dream of him had been told throughout the camp.

This halt at Ramleh was used for a last council of war. It is interesting that one of its members boldly proposed to neglect Jerusalem for the moment and march straight on Egypt, arguing that if they could hold Cairo they would hold all Palestine as well; for it was the heretic Mohammedans of Egypt who now held Jerusalem and the Holy Land.

Strategically the idea was sound, but there were not the means for carrying it out. The army was reduced to some fifteen thousand fighting men at the most, and of these only one in ten were knights. It was a risk even to attempt Jerusalem with such a force, for the vizier of Egypt had garrisoned Jerusalem with a large body of trained troops, including Sudanese blacks. The walls had been repaired, and from what follows it seems clear that the Moslems thought the Holy City impregnable—at any rate, to such forces as this last remnant of the Crusades could bring to bear.

While the host thus stood at Ramleh there came a deputation from the native Christians of Bethlehem urging them to press forward, as every day aided the preparations of the Fatimite garrisons in Jerusalem. That garrison had not only strengthened the defenses, but built new engines of war—notably catapults for the counter-bombardment. They were poisoning the wells and filling up the pools all round the district, and there was no time to be lost.

On Monday, June 6th, the little column—we may call it little for the task it had undertaken and in comparison with the great body of which it was the last poor survivor—set out upon the riding road. On the morning of the next day, Tuesday, the 7th, they at last saw their goal, dark against the morning sun—the flat domes, the few towers, and the long line of the western wall, standing sharply against what was then bare, stony, and empty land, a slight lift of which hides the Holy City from the sea.

As they came nearer to the object of all that terrible journey, the end of those two years of marching through enemy land, of continual combat, famine, desertion, and waste of every kind, this elect, this sacred band which had endured to the end, was filled with glamour. They were illuminated, entranced, moved by one of those enthusiasms which breed triumph. Already, outriders had visited Bethlehem, and in the rare words of those who witnessed the thing you feel the vibration of their souls. Here are those words:

"In procession did they [that is, the Christians of Bethlehem] lead them [the hundred Christian knights led by Tancred, who had galloped all night to reach Bethlehem] to the Church built on the place where the Glorious Mother brought forth the Saviour of the world: there did they set eyes on that cradle where lay the Beloved Child who was also the Maker of Heaven and of Earth; and the people of the town for joy and for proof that God and their leader would give our people victory, took Tancred's banner and set it high over the Church before the Mother of God."

The encirclement of Jerusalem was accomplished within a week; to the Norman tents on the north side opposite the Damascus gate were added in their order the men following Robert of Flanders, who pitched camp at the corner of the walls, where they turn down southward towards the citadel at the Jaffa gate. In front of that citadel and the Jaffa gate itself Godfrey and Tancred stood guard. The very steep eastern and southeastern sides where assault was thought impossible were left unguarded.

On the Monday, the sixth day after the first sight of the city, all was thought ready for attack and a final assault was made; but it just failed, for lack of leaders. And naturally, seeing the failure of the assault, that failure cost the besiegers dearly in lives. Further, it meant the necessity for a fully ordered formal siege, and the peril of this lay in the lack of water. Once more the test had come, as at Dorylaeum, as at Antioch, in the torrid heat of an Eastern summer. Skins had to be filled even as far off as the Jordan, and brought on camels from over twenty miles away and up more than 3,000 feet. The few stagnant pools remaining were quite insufficient for the 15,000 armed men and as many pilgrims and followers.

It was further necessary to build. Engines, catapults, and high moving towers were all that was required for the attack on the walls.

The besieged within, under the Fatimite commander of the garrison, Iftikkar Al Dawla, had plenty of supply, and plenty of material to construct their great machines for hurling stones.

The besiegers, in that denuded country, wherein so many centuries of Mohammedan rule had already destroyed nearly all the trees, had to send far and wide for the scanty wood they needed. The council of war, two days after the first assault, decided on the immediate building of the movable towers, ladders, and catapults. Whether there were sufficient local supplies of material is doubtful, but happily the day after the morrow two galleys from Genoa anchored before Jaffa, bringing not only cargoes of food, but timber as well.

A hundred knights of Provence rode down to make contact with the Genoese, and the move was made only just in time; a body of Moslem ships from Ascalon attacked just after the cargoes had been landed, and the Genoese barely escaped—but escaped with their task accomplished. The energy and rapidity of the Crusaders, even after such a march and in such a foreign burning air, amazes the reader of those chronicles today. Within twenty-four hours the whole mass of material had been transferred to the camps of the besiegers, north, west, and south of the city. And still the enthusiasm rose, and still that exaltation, in which all things seem possible and the miracles of history are accomplished, continued. The passing of the days, the increasingly impossible heat, did not check this rising mood. Adhemar, the Legate, long dead, he who had lent that unity of command to the host (which had since been so grievously lacking, but was now for a moment recovered), appeared in a dream to one who then preached the marvel throughout the ranks. He who had imposed unity and in whose absence that unity had dissolved would now know that though no leader had reimposed it, the intensity of the Crusading flame in these last hours supplied the lack.

A general fast was ordered. When the completion of the engines approached, the army marched in procession round the walls (it was upon the 8th of July). They went in solemn train, chanting the holy chants, from the Mount of Olives, dominating the town, round by the north and west to Zion hill; and all the walls were crowded with the Negroes and the Saracens, jeering at them and their chanting—planting crosses in full sight of the

Christians, which they spat upon and otherwise defiled, until the warriors singing in columns below cried out that they would soon avenge this dishonor done to Jesus Christ.

It was the Friday, the day of the Passion of the Lord, that these things were done.

Under cover of the Saturday night, Godfrey and Robert of Flanders and the Duke of Normandy brought up the wooden wheeled castles against that part of the north wall which lies east of the Damascus gate, standing on a traditional spot where St. Stephen was stoned. Further west they could not attack, for the defenses were too strong. On the Sunday morning the garrison in the first dawn were astonished to see the high wooden stages topping the wall and threatening escalade.

On that same day, upon the further southern side of the city, Toulouse had brought up his tower in turn, and his catapults, "where the good carpenters and sailors of Genoa had known well how to build the mangonels and other engines of war."

The main assault was not delivered until the third night, the night of the Wednesday, July 13 to 14. On the 14th the hammering at the walls continued and the counter-hurling of great stones from within and the rain of Greek fire with which the garrison sought to destroy the wheeled towers, in spite of their covering of horse skins. So all that day the furious attempt blazed on; but they never got a foothold on the wall, thrown back perpetually by the flame-bearing arrows, the Greek fire, and the hot oil poured upon every effort to scale. It was not till the morning of the Friday, the 15th, that the first of the besiegers forced his way in, bursting forward along the gangways from the towers to the summits of the wall.

Who was the first man into the city we shall never know: local legend is not to be despised, and I have always hoped that it was indeed that lord of Sourdeval, the Norman from the Cotentin. But those who were with Godfrey and his brother, Eustace of Boulogne, on the high wooden tower will have it that when about noon two Flemings pushed a gangway forward, these were the first in Jerusalem, Godfrey and Eustace themselves immediately following. But no eye-witness can tell us to whom this honor should fall, for simultaneously by the north and south the eager armed groups were mounting the scaling ladders and holding the wall upon either side. The gate of St. Stephen, that is the gate which looks towards Damascus, was also taken. The host poured in, the garrison fell back upon the height of the Temple enclosure—where a violent resistance ended in general massacre.

That massacre spread from the great Mosque throughout the city. Tancred had attempted to check it, but the madness of the successful attack coming after the violent insults and provocations was too strong for any orders to be heard. The wholesale killing went on all that Friday afternoon; it continued on the Saturday; at last, before night it was ended. The garrison of the Fatimite Caliphs of Egypt, their black soldiers and their trained Arab bands had perished together. Such few as survived paid ransom, and it makes us understand what the temper of the moment was that when the Count of Toulouse accepted such ransom from one unhappy victim, hardly spared, the cry of avarice arose against him.

This carnage—a thing of uncalculated fury—was politically an error. It was claimed by some of those from whom we have the tale that the terror of that Friday broke down all resistance and made certain of victory throughout the land. It is the very plea of those who defend Cromwell and his massacres in Drogheda and Wexford.

But there is another side to the question, and a more important one. Ever since the Crusaders had come down towards the sea from Maarrat the policy of conciliation, of tolerance, which was politically a policy of alliance between the petty Moslem chiefs and the Crusaders, had been fruitful. The awful story of what happened at Jerusalem would make the pursuit of such a policy for the future more difficult. It is true that those who had fallen in the Holy City (holy to the besieged as to the besiegers) were not the amenable and free chiefs of the Lebanon, but of a very different sort, mercenaries of the Egyptian Caliph who had turned from a proposed alliance and had become an enemy to the death. It is also true that when the shock of the news came to Baghdad it stunned and paralyzed that capital of Islam, instead of provoking reaction and a holy war. Whether it were politically serviceable or not (and it was not serviceable), the massacre was an ill ending.

But the great march had been accomplished, the objective had been reached—just barely reached—by one fragment left from the half million that had set their faces first from Nicaea towards the east. Of those who had cried "Jerusalem! Jerusalem!" throughout two years and a thousand miles of way, not one in twenty came up at last to the town.

7

MONARCHY

What followed upon the taking of Jerusalem was an episode most remarkable in the story of Christendom. An isolated Christian State was established, against all likelihood, in the heart of the Moslem world, and astraddle of its vital point: the "Bridge" uniting Eastern and Western Islam.

It seemed not possible that the new intruding Western experiment should survive.

It was of fantastic shape, apparently indefensible, strung out for hundreds of miles along a stretch of coastal land which was rarely more than one long day's journey wide from the seacoast on horseback and in some cases hardly a day's march. Even had it been fully occupied it would have been of such a shape as to be apparently doomed to be broken almost at once. But it was not even fully occupied: no, not even at the highest moment of the Crusading power. There were always patches where a Moslem community, or a city or castle under a Moslem chief, formed an island on territory nominally subject to the new Christian rulers.

The population was chaotically mixed in race as well as in religion. There were the native Syrians, there were the descendants of the Turkish garrisons and their recent recruitment, there were Arabs from the desert. There were local leaders who were adventurers from the northern mountains, or the remnants of a former Egyptian rule. The Christians, in most places a minority, were divided into the Western Catholics following the Latin Mass (which was that, of course, of the Crusaders themselves); the Eastern Christians of the Greek Mass; and these again

117

divided among themselves. There were even men of Syriac Liturgy.

The Mohammedans were both orthodox and schismatic and politically attached to chiefs whose authority varied and whose boundaries fluctuated. It was in no way an organized state either, with frontiers; it was rather a series of strongholds and walled cities holding what they could of the countrysides around them.

Then, again, this new attempted, invading Western State had, even among the established governing Crusaders, sharp divisions of interest. Edessa in the northern mountains was supported by a large local Christian Armenian population. It was therefore well suited to act as a buttress for all to the south of it. But it was so far away from Jerusalem that the union between the two was difficult indeed to maintain. Antioch was in perpetual rivalry with Tripoli and Byzantium, Tripoli jealous of its independence, at any rate of independence in the feudal sense of the word, of a separate district governed by its own chief lord. And Tripoli was the more difficult to fit in to any general scheme because, of all the divisions, it was the most unnatural in shape, the thinnest and the most strung out.

The new Crusading State being of such a kind was continually pressed upon and continually penetrated and raided by the Moslem myriads of the interior on the fringe of which it precariously lay. Add to all this the growth, soon after the Christian establishment, of separate and jealous military orders, of strong and wealthy Italian commercial self-governing quarters in the harbor towns; add the unorganized influx of pilgrim masses who came in their thousands and then as rapidly ebbed away—unarmed and yet requiring armed defense; add the vast distance of that Levantine seaboard even from the Italian cities and its still greater distance from France, which was the main source of Crusading armies and governing men. Consider all these disabilities and see how heavy were the odds against even an unstable and tottering maintenance of the Latin world in the Holy Land, that is, of this French adventure. It was further handicapped by the Gallic temperament whose energy is coupled with disruptive forces so that the same power which had driven the charge home and seized the Holy Places half across the world, yet was perpetually at issue within itself, subject to the violence, the jealousies and rivalries and rebellions of its blood: "Civil War, the vice of the Gauls."

Yet for one active lifetime of forty-five years the garrisons remained and were even extended; Edessa was apparently impregnable in the north, so were Antioch, Tripoli, Jerusalem, as one went southward, on to the confines of Egypt. The strange experiment stood firm all that while. Though it could rarely muster an army of twenty thousand men in one field, though it often fought its battles with not a quarter that number, it strongly survived and even seemed permanent.

This miracle was achieved by one main force: Monarchy.

There was much else, as we shall see; but Kingship was the basis of that life and why it was thus essential we must first know before we attempt to understand its achievement.

At first sight the presence of kingship at all in the midst of a feudal state seems a self-contradiction. We know as a fact that kingship did develop strongly during the feudal generations, but a comprehension of that paradox is rarely attempted. Since the very essence of feudalism is a number of local, almost independent powers, giving even to the lord of one village a sort of absolute position, how could the general principle of kingship arise and flourish in such a conglomeration of lordships, each formed of noble blood? How, especially, could it rise and flourish in the Holy Land which began its career as a state at the moment when feudalism was at its strongest, when all men thought in terms of local independent lordships bound together only by customs of vassalage and loyalty? Crusading Syria and Palestine were the typical feudal States of the Middle Ages. It is characteristic of this Syrian State that it has left us, in what are called the "Assize of Jerusalem," the most perfect model of a feudal constitution. In practice it was composed of military forces entirely feudal, following local lords and ignorant of that organized central command which the ancient civilization had taken as a matter of course in its armies and which our modern civilization takes as a matter of course also. How, then, did feudalism breed kingship? Especially here in the Orient?

Feudalism bred kingship everywhere as a corrective to itself and had the power to do so through the traditions inherited from the Roman Empire.

Remember that feudalism was not aristocratic. Every feudal lord was, as it were, a little king in his own sphere. Feudalism did not work by committees (which is the mark of aristocracy); it had not that placid cohesion which is the strength of a governing class. No: it was derived from the original Roman landowners who, in the decay of the Empire, had become more and more absolute each over his own land, his own slaves, his own freed men and his retainers.

Even the greatest of the feudal leaders, men like the counts of Flanders or the dukes of Normandy, were essentially owners of a great number of individual estates before they were rulers of the provinces wherein those estates lay. This sense of personal power in the units which built up a feudal society was reflected in the acceptance by those units of one central head who should preserve the principle of unity for great bodies who all felt something in common. Such kings were limited indeed in their authority—but they *were* kings, and they represented in the eyes of all men the principle of authority itself.

On account of all this, the effect of monarchy in a feudal state was decisive. The great example of it was the Capetian Monarchy in France. Local monarchy in a feudal State represented the tradition of Rome. A universal empire was no longer possible, but allegiance to one of the feudal families as representing some one large province, France, England, Castile, continued the tradition of rule. It prevented chaos, it restored political discipline. It was very imperfect compared with what we expect of a strong modern national government. Each great vassal was a true sovereign in his own principality or county; the Duke of Normandy, the Count of Toulouse, the Duke of Lower Lorraine, the Count of Brittany, and the Count of Champagne—these held real authority when the King of France could not exercise similar authority save over his own personal lordship round Paris. In the same way, when monarchy was instinctively developed in the Crusading Holy Land, Antioch, Tripoli, Edessa still remained separate states under a very loose feudal bond with Jerusalem. And even the lesser lordships within each of these main districts—for instance, Galilee under Jerusalem—had a life of their own.

That was of the very nature of feudalism. Nothing more centralized would have been possible, because the Feudal Society took for granted the independence of each lord in its hierarchy and only existed as a federation of lordships. Still, the name of King and the very lively sense of the allegiance due from a vassal to his royal superiority informed that society and gave it a sufficient unity to withstand the pressure of the Moslem.

Among the weaknesses of medieval monarchy was the great part played by personality in it. A king who was personally courageous, clear-headed, rapid in thought, made more of monarchy than one lacking those qualities; also personal popularity with vassals counted. But even medieval, feudal monarchy had a strength of its own apart from the personality of the monarch. It was continuous, even when it was elective; and even when it was elective there remained a sense of heredity about it. It was passed on, if possible, from father to son. If there were no son, then from brother to brother, or cousin to cousin. If there were an heiress only, then to her husband. The principle of succession was maintained and unity in the dimension of time thereby accrued to monarchy just as its territorial dominion made for unity in the dimension of space. The feudal king was not complete master save in his own private estates. He was not occupied directly in governing and appointing officials save in the province over which he was immediate lord. But he not only *could* intervene when there was dispute on the succession of his main feudatories, but was necessarily called upon to intervene. He was the natural guardian during the minority of an heir to the half-independent states attached to his throne and the arbiter between rivals. He alone could summon the feudal court before which rival claims appeared and hear and, in great part, decide.

A feudal monarch had also a special financial power. He held all the land called "Forest," that is, land not included in the feudal organization. In European feudalism this was consider-able—in England, for instance, about one third of the whole area. Palestine afforded apparently no large revenue of this sort. But the King of Jerusalem had, like all other feudal kings, the right to ask exceptional aid from his half-independent inferiors when he went to war, and he could summon them to his armies—though he might not be able to compel them to come when summoned, or to prevent their leaving the host after join-ing it. He also got revenue from his royal courts of justice, over and above the judicial revenues of the local courts; and he could ask for levies of money from the merchants of the towns.

This royal office was a further strength to the Christian State in that its Mohammedan enemies possessed no such center of unity. Monarchy is inherited from Rome. Islam knows nothing of it. Within the religious unity of the Moslem world was a fluid mass, the vague authority over which was vested in the "Head of the Faithful," while actual government was exercised by individual masters of troops or garrisons: mostly Turkish, but some Arab. A great military leader would arise, men would attach themselves to him in the hope of adventure and profit. Some, as his power increased, he would draw into his armies by force. When in full power he would appoint, over cities and districts, officers of his own. But these would rebel and conspire. The successful Moslem commander held his place by a personal tenure of courage and intrigue and talent in leadership. His grasp was individual and might be relaxed in a moment by illness, death, or successful rebellion. Of a permanent kingly office there was none.

The Moslem unity which formed at last against the Crusading State, and destroyed it at Hattin, was an accident due to the suc-cession, by no rule or custom but by hazard, of two determined, energetic, and ambitious men. Zengi began it. After the interlude of Zengi's son, Saladin—who was no connection in blood or even in race with his predecessors—took it up and increased it. But hardly was Saladin dead when the men of his blood fought over his inheritance, divided, and ruined it. Unfortunately Saladin's individual power had lasted long enough to do the trick. He had managed before he died—the ephemeral unity of command died with him—to pull down the Crusading State and to expel the Cross from Jerusalem.

It is capital to the understanding of the position to know that the strength of monarchy was not intended. It grew. The original Crusaders had no permanent head. The great leaders would not brook the presidency of anyone among them over the rest, and when de Bouillon refused to call himself King it was not only, as posterity believed, from the refusal of such a title in so holy a place, but more because both the authorities of the Church and his fellow companions ill favored the name of king. But the necessity for kingship appeared when Godfrey died such a few months after the sack of the Holy City. When the nobles from Jerusalem, reaching Edessa, asked Godfrey's brother, Baldwin, to come down south and rule them, the invitation was an invitation not only to be the feudal head of the Jerusalem division, but titular king of all the conquered land. And when Baldwin was crowned on Christmas Day, 1100, in the Basilica of the Nativity at Bethlehem, the French principle of monarchy had proved too strong for the claims of the Church to direct the rival crusading leaders, and too strong for allowing the overlordship of Byzantium.

There had to be a king, and though that king only exercised his power occasionally outside the province of Jerusalem itself, though he had even less direct control over his feudatories than had the King of France over his, yet the name and the title and the office of king had their effect, not the least of which was what the word "King" connoted: independence of any temporal superior and therefore no definite connection with the Emperor of Constantinople—although the Crusaders at the outset of their march had promised to recognize the suzerainty of the Emperor over anything they might conquer.

When we ask ourselves what else beside monarchy made the new State to take root and, after a fashion, flourish in spite of the very great numbers opposed to it locally, the vast reserve numbers, behind these again, in Mesopotamia and eastwards throughout the Moslem world, in spite of its absence of frontier and in spite of Mohammedan raids perpetually reaching in between the points of Christian occupation, in spite of maintenance on the coast, of one point after another in Mohammedan hands, we find the answer in three forces.

These three forces are the Italian merchants at the ports, the military orders, and a third factor, that odd Gallic power of assimilation which, after centuries, has reappeared in the relations between modern French and the Mohammedan world.

This third factor is less remarked by historians than the first two because it is not defined or conspicuous, but it was perhaps of more effect than the others, because it was ubiquitous. It entered into the social stuff of the new State everywhere. It is a racial or cultural asset, against which must be set the heavy debt of Gallic instability in policy. The same qualities which make the French of today understand, and largely be understood by, the Mohammedan population whom they with difficulty administer, were apparent in their ancestors all those centuries ago: but so also were apparent then as now the changes in policy, the internal dissensions, the consequent instability which at all ages weakens Gallic effort in its activities overseas.

The support given by the new commerce which followed up the Crusade was a factor of a totally different kind, but quite as valuable in preserving the experiment of a Crusading State, as its Monarchy. Venice, Pisa and Genoa, the three main maritime cities of Italy, seized the opportunity. They lent the aid of their ships for the blockade of ports held by Moslem rulers whom the Crusaders besieged by land; they transported material and men and the perpetual recruitment of the war; they supplied money from the funds which their rapidly growing trade gave them. But for the Italian merchant cities and their fleets the seaboard would never have been conquered and the Crusaders inland would have been strangled and starved out in a few years.

For such help the Italians asked and obtained their price. The trading cities had quarters of their own in the Crusading ports. They made their own regulations in these quarters and governed them as though they were part of the parent state. Venice even had its quarter in Jerusalem, the capital. Genoa was strong in

Tripoli and Antioch; Pisa, less important, had a few establishments; even Marseilles had its own established quarter in Jerusalem.

Christian power, thus stretching along the eastern seaboard of the Mediterranean, tapped all the exchanges between the East and the West. Aleppo and Damascus and Homs and Hama were the ports of the desert, but the silks and the ivories and the spices which they handled they could not now pass on to Europe save through the medium of the ports wherein the Italian towns and merchants had established themselves. These merchants, mainly Italian but also southern French and even sometimes Flemish and German, continually increased their fortunes.

Apart from the exchanges from the interior they dealt with the glasswork of Tyre and with the mass of agricultural produce. They formed a separate establishment here in the new Kingdom of Jerusalem just as they did in every feudal realm of their homeland in western Europe. They had their guilds and all their machinery of self-government. They appeared, in the Assize of Jerusalem (the document wherein were registered towards the end of the second generation the feudal customs of the new kingdom), as a bourgeois caste, below the governing nobles socially, but often individually their equals in wealth and collectively richer than the noble class as a whole, save, of course, those few who handled provincial revenues in the mass, the heads of states.

All this middle-class, mainly Italian, contingent was based on the sea, although the opportunities of approach to Syria by sea were insufficient. We know as a matter of historical fact that the Crusades opened up a mass of new traffic by sea with the Levant. They founded the Venetian commercial control of the eastern Mediterranean. The Second Crusade and still more the Third Crusade were expeditions which at the end depended upon the sea. Yet when he looks at the Syrian coast, it is difficult for a modern man to understand how the approach from the sea could have played so great a part—increasing throughout the Crusading century from the first to the last.

The landing places are either open roadsteads, or ports

seeming to us absurdly small and shallow. One can hardly call them rare, seeing that in not much more than three hundred miles of uninterrupted straight coastline there are nearly a dozen of them, but they seem wholly inadequate to the task of supplying an army and its communications.

The solution to the problem lies in the following considerations:

First, the harbors were deeper, and some of them larger, in the twelfth century than they are today. Next, the vessels of the twelfth century and especially those built on the Western model, were of light draught, depending for their carrying capacity upon breadth of beam, and for their holding of the sea and checking of leeway (which always remained imperfect) upon the steepness of their long flat sides. Thirdly (and most important), even the transports did not depend upon harbors, but could use beaches—and as for shelter from weather they were accustomed on the Syrian coast to ride at anchor in the open roads. The very important point of Jaffa is an example.

As to the first point, it forms part of a general problem— among the most fascinating in history—the fate of enclosed havens, particularly of havens at river mouths.

In all parts of the world these tend to grow shallower and to silt up, save where they are originally of great depth—what are called "drowned valleys." Much the greater part of havens useful to man have, in the course of history, grown shallower and shallower, and a great number have disappeared. This is due not only to the alluvium brought down by the rivers, but to the way in which the marshy land which you commonly find on the edges of an enclosed natural harbor tends to add to itself yard by yard with the growth of aquatic vegetation. This tendency is called on the south coast of England the "innings" of a marshland, and it has been particularly noticeable in the case of Pevensey Harbor, which was as large as that of Portsmouth at the time of the Conquest, though it is true that in the case of Pevensey the process was hastened by a rise of level in the whole of that part of the coast, reaching a maximum of eleven or twelve feet by the time one gets to the Isle of Thanet.

In the case of the Syrian harbors, from the Gulf of Alexandretta to the Egyptian boundary, there does not seem to have been any marked change of level in historical times; but the silting up of the harbor has been rapid, and both ancient tradition and modern observations show that it is due to the Nile mud brought up along that coast by the northern current.

Such a process at once suggests the conclusion that the life of harbors anywhere must be limited in historic time. We have record of Syrian harbors in use for 4,000 years, but it is difficult to understand why in the immensely longer period of earlier time during which they have been subject to the deposits of the Nile they did not wholly disappear.

More useful than natural small harbors along the Syrian coastline was the shelter of island groups, or clusters of rock. It was in the calm water between such and the mainland that Tyre and Sidon gave shelter to their commercial fleets, and you have an instance of the same kind of thing as far west as Algiers—the name of which means "islets."

Medieval craft, as has been said, was, like the general run of Arabic craft today, shallow. Direct evidence is not easy to obtain; you get no accurate representation of a sea-going vessel in miniature or sculpture until the last generations of the Middle Ages; the early representations of ships are conventional and symbolic. However, we know something of what their section must have been from the way in which they were handled, the rivers up which they were able to sail and the few remaining relics of their structure—which, oddly enough, survive more from the very early periods than the later.

We can estimate with some accuracy, for instance, the dimensions a boat must have had to come up the canal from the sea to Aigues Mortes even as late as the thirteenth century; and we may conclude that a draught of even twelve feet would have been thought considerable. The sea-going ships provisioning Rome came up as far as the island of the Tiber; the galleys of antiquity reached Tarsus; and in our own northern waters, outside tidal limits, sea-going ships went up as far as Cologne on the Rhine, and as far as Arles on the Rhône. In other words, dealing with channels which keep naturally dredged by the force of a current, far above the bar at the mouth, two fathoms of water or a little more was enough to take ships that had come in from the outside.

But the third point is by far the most important. The Middle Ages, until at least the twelfth century, and, in a dwindling fashion on into the thirteenth century, used beaches alternatively with closed harbors. Antiquity had always done so, and the custom disappeared only with the later Middle Ages.

How this use of open beaches by large vessels (capable of carrying horses and all kinds of heavy baggage and provisions as well as troops) was managed we do not know. It is one of those many mysteries of history on which modern writers prefer to be silent.

Of course the beaching of small craft has been universal since men first used the sea; but how did they beach considerable transports? We do not know: we only know that they did so. The great concourse of ships which brought over William the Conqueror's 50,000 fighting men and thousands of horses was beached on the northern, landward side of the shingle bank protecting Old Pevensey Harbor. Caesar's fleet had been beached on the open seaside of the shore near Deal a thousand years before. It went on till about six hundred years ago—and then suddenly ceased. Some use of instruments to which we have no clue got the big ships up above high-water mark. When they neither used an enclosed haven nor were beached, ships rode it out in the open.

It was in connection with this practice that so many of the Mediterranean harbors, especially the eastern Mediterranean, when they are not closed havens but half-open roadsteads, are double. Alexandria was of this kind and Sidon was of this kind. The seasonal winds are fairly constant, the mariner knew more or less when he had to take shelter from the northern wind and when from the southern; in the season when the danger was of gales from the north he would come round the southernmost of the two points of the hammer-headed land on which, say, the later Sidon was built, and anchor in the horseshoe between it and the coast; and when it might come on to blow from the southward he would enter the northern port beyond the isthmus. But it is remarkable that Tyre, the most important of the Phoenician seaports, seems to have had at first no such double basin. It never developed, as did the original island of Sidon, into a hammer-headed peninsula by being joined up to the mainland, but remained as island rock to Alexander's day.

The knights and the noble class of the new kingdom in general got their revenue in Syria much as they had done at home. It was made up of manorial dues from villages of which they were lords and from the proceeds of their courts of justice; but to these the knights and barons of Palestine added pillaging of Moslem goods and the ransom of Moslem prisoners. They and the merchants between them directed the state. There could be no question of popular admixture in that government such as was native to men of European blood in their own countries, for here the populace, even where it was Christian (and most of it was Christian still in Antioch and between the mountains and the sea on the Lebanon coast, and much in Palestine itself), was mixed in character and differed in language as in customs, at first at least, from the new arrivals.

The strength given by the military orders was a more particular and definable gain. It was peculiar to Palestine and was the special fruit of the Crusades. We associate the names of the Hospitallers, the Templars and even that of the Teutonic knights with the Holy Land and the Crusading time.

They rose thus:

There had been, long before the First Crusade was launched, an organization of Christian volunteers who looked after pilgrims coming from the West to worship at the shrines of the Holy Land and particularly, of course, at the Holy Sepulchre. They organized guest houses and hospitals in the modern sense, that is, centers in which the wounded and the sick could be healed. These, shortly after the capture of Jerusalem, began to take a more regular form. They had vastly more to do than before, and they had a correspondingly greater revenue. They organized themselves as an order with regular rules, they took the three vows of the monk: poverty, chastity and obedience; they were therefore celibate and had the advantage of wielding their capital in mass and as a whole. They wore a distinctive dress as monks, which might almost be called a habit, and this was worn over armor, a black coat of arms to cover the mail, and a white cross sewn thereon. The individual member of the corporation had no private fortune, but all was massed in central hands to devote to pilgrims, to rid the roads of robbers and to help where necessary side by side with the mounted nobility and the footmen in the fighting. Later another body branched out from these original "hospitallers." Within a quarter of a century of the capture of Jerusalem these obtained regular endowment and status, spread from the original body and, as the King of Jerusalem gave them the Temple enclosure for their special quarter, they became known as the "Templars" or "Knights Templar." Their surcoat was white with a red cross. The fact that they were combatant from the beginning gave them a superiority over the original stock of the Hospitallers, whence they sprang.

The power of these two orders increased. Large endowments were left them by will or given them in the lifetime of the donors. They arranged for the disembarkation at the ports of those great numbers who perpetually came into the Holy Land. They made also the arrangements for their return. They handled money continually, apart from their great wealth from feudal dues of their lands. They began to play the part of bankers. Later on they purchased the lordships over sundry great castles, notably Markab in the north. It was on the scale of a thousand men to garrison it, with stores of food calculated for five years' consumption. And they purchased that most splendid pile of all, Kerak of the Knights, on twice the scale of Markab, guarding the road from the interior to the main port of Tripoli.

The military orders were the most highly organized thing in the Holy Land. Add to this that, unlike the noble class from which they were drawn and side by side with which they worked for the administration of the country, they were an undying corporation. They outlasted the Crusading century for generations.

Their spirit and the tradition of their discipline inspired successors, notably those who, first in Rhodes, then in Malta, defended Christendom against the Mohammedans. Finally it must be remembered that they were responsible only to the Papacy. They were not feudatories of the kings of Jerusalem nor the ecclesiastical subordinates of the bishops. They were alone. That isolation was a great element of strength.

Much later than the others, obtaining corporate power only after the fall of Jerusalem itself, came a third order formed from the Germans who had followed the Third Crusade. They were known as the Teutonic Order. Later on their principal role in history was the maintenance of the Christian German frontier against the heathen Lithuanians to the east. We should remember, not without irony, that it was from these last and their estates that Prussia developed. At the time of the Reformation the Hohenzollern at the head of the Teutonic Knights seized the goods of their corporation, sent them packing, and established himself as master over their former lands. Hence Prussia.

Other elements were added to the main political element of *Monarchy* in support of the Crusading venture. The first of these was the superiority of the Western fully armed gentleman on horseback to any type of fighter the Oriental could bring against him. The charge of the heavier armed and heavier bodied Westerner on his heavier mount decided one major engagement after another. First, in spite of surprise, at Dorylaeum, then in front of Heraclea, then in front of Antioch. Though the numbers perpetually dwindled and though there remained for the last effort not one man in twenty of those who had crossed the Bosphorus, the Western chivalry had proved itself apparently invincible, even when there was brought against it a concentration for the moment numerically far superior. Then Jerusalem having been taken, the remnant of the Christian forces occupying that town were to win another great victory against superior Mohammedan forces at Ascalon. So it continued to the end. Arsouf was fought and won by a charge of heavy cavalry, as Dorylaeum had been a century before.

In general there seemed to be established a tactical superiority of Western chivalry over Orientals which was almost like the discovery of a new weapon. So far so good.

But that tactical superiority, the repeated success of the heavy armored Christian charge, could not be repeated indefinitely. Shortly after the capture of Jerusalem the bulk of those present sailed back to their homes. The effort at reinforcement later on mainly failed. The forces remaining seemed quite insufficient for their task. Tancred had only eighty mounted companions when he rode into and occupied Galilee. Godfrey, at the head of the forces at Jerusalem, commanded only three hundred horse and one thousand foot after the rest of the southern Crusaders had sailed home. There was the same depletion everywhere, and the starting point for what was to follow was a basis absurdly narrow. Thus in the south, apart from Jerusalem itself, the only armed Christian bodies, and those small, were in Bethlehem, Lydda, Ramleh and Jaffa. Tortosa, occupied during the advance, had had to be abandoned from lack of men to garrison it. There were larger forces to the north, but even those were exiguous.

When Baldwin came down from Edessa to the south he could leave only five hundred men in his walled town of the north, and he himself had no more than a thousand foot and a hundred horse wherewith to ride out. Things, then, were on that scale and yet they succeeded. One after another the towns on the sea-coast were taken and received a Christian garrison. In a few years the kingdom of Jerusalem as a whole was effectively occupied, from Hebron in the south to the Gulf of Alexandretta, yet while this was going on there was not sufficient unity binding the Christian leaders. They were at issue with the others, some-times nursing personal quarrels like the standing quarrel between Baldwin and Tancred which had begun in Cilicia and went on for years, or the quarrel between the Count of Toulouse and the followers of Godfrey as to who should retain Jerusalem. There were chiefs who returned home capriciously like Hugh, the Great, and Stephen of Blois.

The heavy handicap in numbers could only be met in one way: by depending on fortification: and this second element, very well-designed castle building, was decisive in permitting the

Christian hold upon the Syrian seaboard. The Crusaders met magnificently the desperate conditions imposed on them. Using masses of local conscripted labor, ordering all with rapidity and developing prodigiously the arts of defense which they had learned at home, they set up in their first generation those huge strongholds which are their chief monuments today. There is nothing like them for "frozen energy" to be discovered in our world. The castles of Syria, the Christian castles, made possible during those 88 years the continuous though precarious tenure of Christendom in the face of all Islam. Though crushed in there and harried between the desert with its eastern road and the Mediterranean, the French chivalry with its huge castles to support it held fast.

In order to understand what fortification meant in the heart of the Middle Ages, and especially what was the use and significance of its chief example, the medieval castle, we have to begin with a conception of which modern European warfare knows nothing, so that the very memory of it has decayed—and yet it seems in a fashion about to reappear—the conception of a necessarily *superior* arm which is also necessarily highly limited in numbers.

Europeans have in the past done astonishing things against non-Europeans through the superiority of firearms over more primitive weapons; the chief example of this was the Spanish conquest of the Americas, though that was due as much to the iron Spanish character as to superior armament. But of superior armament *necessarily limited* we have had no example in the warfare between the various parts of Christendom since the introduction of artillery.

Artillery on the one side meeting its absence on the other made victory almost certain; the loss of the last Plantagenet districts in France (especially the battle of Chatillon, where the great Talbot fell) are examples. But artillery is not a necessarily limited arm. Anyone could have as much of it as he was able to pay for. The Western mounted armed gentlemen of the twelfth and the thirteenth centuries were at once a superior arm *and a necessarily limited one.* Such men were provided by a limited class, and in the case of the French in Syria their numbers were further limited by local conditions—the distance from Europe and the insufficiency of their recruitment and maintenance. Where in a particular field there could be found a sufficient number of units drawn from this limited supply, in that field Christian chivalry (a "heavy cavalry") always won. But for this superiority to be permanently available it was necessary to provide sustenance and security for the few knights during the intervals between battles. A Crusading army in Syria could only survive artificially as it were, sheltered behind made defenses until the moment when it should be called into use.

We might get a modern parallel to that state of affairs if we should imagine an occupying force to be restricted in the number of its aircraft possessing only a short radius of action. A force well equipped with aircraft will certainly be the master of a larger force deprived of aircraft; a force possessed of much swifter aircraft than another and much heavier, capable of attacking ground troops with machine gun fire, would commonly be the master of a force possessing slower machines and less fire power, whether of machine guns or bombs. Aircraft is a new form of artillery at long range, and superiority in aircraft may be compared to the superiority of a force with heavy guns over a force with none.

Now suppose aircraft for some reason to be limited to flights of 40 to 50 miles at the most in a day, and commonly to not more than 20 or 25 miles; you would then have the situation of the Christian knights in Palestine.

The fully armed mounted man, the knight, had a reach of 50 miles a day at the very most, half that distance as a rule, in daily practice, less than half that distance. Where he *could* present himself on the field at his own chosen moment against forces perhaps numerically superior (but not overwhelmingly so), he was master. The lighter-armed, less muscular, and lighter-mounted man, the Moslem, could not stand up to him. The Mohammedans had been driven before the charge of the Christian knights over and over and over again, and the Christian knights were confident of repeating such successes, even against considerable odds. But there were so few of them, and their radius of action was so limited, that any one group of the many groups scattered over so large a territory would have been doomed without fortification.

We have seen how Tancred took over Galilee and made himself securely lord of that fairly large district. And yet Tancred had ridden into Galilee from the south with only a handful of knights. The army that took Jerusalem, though it was a concentration of all that could be spared south of Antioch, had not more than fifteen hundred knights. Even such numbers could establish themselves, but only on condition of numerous rallying points and refuges. Had the Christian knights worked permanently in the open, rapid Moslem concentrations against them would have destroyed them piecemeal.

Therefore did the fortifications of Palestine arise and become the models of all defense throughout the Middle Ages. From the little square towers, mere blockhouses, to the splendid castles which remain today the marvel of the Levant, the French military architecture of Syria, the product of the Crusades, is the scheme and chief type of all that was done wherever Christendom extended; and particularly in the heart of military Christendom, northern France and England.

The Syriac castle in the form which the French gave to it was all this. Was it also the origin of castle structure in the West? The answer to that question is doubtful. It will never perhaps be fully and satisfactorily given. The same doubt hangs round a number of other things peculiar to the rising strength of the Middle Ages—for instance, ogival architecture, the pointed arch, which some think they can prove to have been used in the Crusading Levant before Suger's Tower arose at St. Denis.

The commonest theory, less than a lifetime ago, was that the Crusaders developed the feudal stone castle. We know that most defensive works, in the time of the Norman Conquest and earlier, were no more than wooden palisades. There was stonework, of course, and plenty of it; for the thing was Roman in origin and nothing Roman is ever lost. But by the end of the Dark Ages, during the tenth and most of the eleventh centuries,

both the slight remaining evidences of image in tapestry, illumi-
nation, and carving, and the slight remaining evidences of a new,
very detailed contemporary description of fighting, show that the
great mass of strongholds were of the following type: a great
mound, made as steep as possible in order that assault should
be difficult, was crowned with a wooden palisade, and further
protected by the ditch whence the material had come to heap
up the mound. This was the sort of "castle" which probably
William of Falaise and Harold, the son of Godwin, stormed
together at Dinan. This was the sort of "castle" that William
himself raised for his troops when he scattered his first garrisons
over south and middle England.

Then come the Crusades. The preaching of the First Crusade
was half a lifetime after the battle of Hastings; the Crusades
were contemporary with the building of stone castles everywhere, and they developed everywhere upon the same lines.
Those in Syria, though sometimes on a grander scale than those
in contemporary France, are of the same sort as those in contemporary France. It is a natural conclusion that the novelty of the
Crusading march and its experiences created the typical castle
of the Middle Ages.

But as against this, there is the evidence which has been so
strongly emphasized in recent years, and particularly by the late
T. E. Lawrence, who worked very thoroughly on the subject.
The point is that the typical medieval castle with the remains
of which we are familiar all over western Europe, arose simultaneously in France and Syria. It was one of those French things
which stamped themselves on the Middle Ages, as did the
Gothic architecture; and its importance in making possible the
difficult holding of the seacoast belt during that increasingly
strained century is what we specially have to note.

This military feature, the castle, was omnipresent in the
Crusading State. It had to be so, for any considerable gap
between two neighboring fortifications would have been a gate
through which Moslem forces could have poured. There being
no frontier, and the failure to seize Damascus having left the
eastern road permanently open for the coming and going of

Mohammedan forces, the intensive fortification of Palestine and the Lebanon coast was unavoidable. At the very beginning of the effort this military accompaniment to it arises.

Torun was built in the very first years of the occupation; it was the first example of what the new work would do—and a striking one. It commanded the most direct road from the coast to Damascus over the mountains, and its presence at once prevented a whole column of refugees from rejoining independent Mohammedan forces beyond Lebanon.

Another early example was the building of Montreal right down in the Araba valley which the road to the Red Sea follows from Moab southward. That step was taken in 1115. Castle building continued uninterruptedly until the middle of the century, and one may put at about the date of the Second Crusade the moment when it had reached its final proportions.

Had the system not been completed thus early, the last difficult chapter of the Crusade, the staving off of Saladin's concentration, would not have been written. The Holy Land and Galilee and all the country under Hermon, the Phoenician coast, everything as far as Latakia, and certainly doubtful points in the central valley, were a net of tracks for armed mounted men, and the net was pinned and stretched upon the castles, each one of them being supported by at least two neighbors within a day's ride.

The system saved Christian Syria as long as it could be saved: when at last Saladin had achieved his great concentration against the Crusaders, the castles were for the first time denuded, and where not denuded, left insufficiently garrisoned. The army that was destroyed at Hattin had been gathered at the expense of the castle garrisons, and after Saladin's victory these had not the men left to defend themselves. They fell rapidly one after the other and with them fell the State.

It was inevitable. The strain of holding this imperilled ribbon of land with intermittent recruitment from the distant West, with no sufficient permanent body on the spot, could not be indefinitely sustained. It was bound to break down at last, and it did. But the temporary miracle of its survival was achieved by the Italian fleets, by the castles, and—much the greatest—*Monarchy*.

What monarchy could do in maintaining the Christian name under siege we shall see in the example of its first three kings, the two Baldwins and Foulque of Anjou. These in succession held the position, secured the Holy Places, for the active lifetime of a man. Not till the last of them was old did the breakdown begin.

8

THE THREE KINGS

The situation of the Crusade after the capture of Jerusalem was fantastic. There was no occupation of territory; there were no lines of communication; if you had set down upon a map those parts of Syria which were effectively controlled by armed Western Christians you would have had the county of Edessa in the north, the county of Antioch (which is no more than the somewhat empty territory surrounding the great town), and then, hundreds of miles away to the south, the town of Jerusalem itself, with the neighboring town of Bethlehem; with Joppa and Ramleh on the road from Joppa to Jerusalem. The rest was just anything; principally Moslem in the scattered farms, a mixture of Moslem and Christian in the towns, and these governed either by independent Moslem chiefs or chiefs appointed (in the south at least) by the Fatimite Caliphs of Cairo. And even that word "appointed" is misleading. On the seacoast you had local governors. Inland any local man powerful enough to be regarded as the head person of the town or big village (who might or might not give allegiance to Cairo) was the virtual sovereign of it.

Obviously that situation could not last. Jerusalem could not be held as an exception in the middle of a chaotic and half-Moslem population. If the Crusading effort were to survive, there must be a military occupation. But with what could it be accomplished? The numbers were already reduced in the south to a few thousand; they would be reduced still further by at least two thirds of their total when the knights and some of their greatest lords sailed back again for Europe.

There was not only the lack of numbers, there was also the

lack of cohesion inevitable in a feudal society. What saved the situation and led to the gradual occupation, of the maritime strip at least, by the French, the Western Christians, was a combination of two things: first, the manifest personal superiority of the Western fighting men over the Oriental; and second, the continued anarchy of the Moslem world—to which may be added a third element, the impotence of the heretical Moslem government in Cairo—the Fatimites. They had indeed garrisoned but lost Jerusalem itself, and they were to prove themselves incapable of withstanding the Christians in the field. The Egyptian blood was not warlike. The local strain there tended, as it always does, to absorb the new blood of its conquerors. The fighting Arab who had established himself in the valley of the Nile and had gradually changed the religion of its population was no longer the material from which the armies coming out of Egypt were recruited.

The institution of Monarchy was difficult to build up in Palestine. The Crusaders had come as feudal chiefs, great and small. In their native lands they admitted a certain tie, not very strong, between themselves and the King of France; or (in the case of the southern Italians and their Norman chiefs) the Norman King of Sicily. But they had no machinery in their new land, whereby to create a monarchy, nor any tradition for the setting up of that central, necessary thing.

At first even the name of king was lacking; more than a month was spent conferring in Jerusalem as to what should be done for the organization of a local government, and at last Godfrey of Bouillon accepted the post of head, but he did not bear the name of king. The traditional explanation is that he was too humble to wear a crown where Our Lord had worn a Crown of Thorns, and the phrase is ascribed to himself. But we must also remember that every one of his rivals was an equal, and would not easily be turned into a subject, and that the most insistent was the Patriarch with his claim that the Crusade was essentially a pilgrimage and that therefore the Church should command it.

Godfrey lived only just over a year after the capture of Jerusalem; he was to die on July 18, 1100. In this brief space the occupation of territory had begun, but the accidents which accompanied that effort sufficiently explain why it was so slow and imperfect. Indeed, as one reads of the very gradual expansion of Christendom and its power over the Levantine coast in that less than a century during which the French remained in effective power, the marvel is that they managed to establish themselves at all, even for those 88 years between the capture of the Holy City and the disaster of Hattin.

Almost immediately after Godfrey of Bouillon had taken up his task, an example of all these factors combined—the Moslem divisions, the superiority of the Western fighting man, the weakness of the government of Cairo—was afforded. The ruler of Cairo sent an expedition to Ascalon with the object of ousting the invaders; from Ascalon as a base he proposed, with forces far more numerous than Godfrey could muster, to turn the Christians out of Joppa, so cut the Jerusalem road to the sea, and then to recover Jerusalem itself. Godfrey marched at once upon Ascalon, but Raymond of Toulouse, who was encamped towards the Jordan, refused at first to follow his rival, and so did Robert of Normandy.

Ultimately the quarrel was settled, but the settlement bore little fruit; Godfrey's small army did indeed win a crushing victory over the far more numerous Egyptians; he and Tancred and Raymond of Toulouse and Robert of Normandy rode down the Cairene army. It was all over in a few minutes. Yet the town of Ascalon itself was neither attacked nor taken. It was to remain in Moslem hands for a whole lifetime—a land sea gate open to Moslem invasion for over fifty years. Ascalon ought, of course, to have been taken and occupied immediately after the rout which Mohammedanism had suffered outside its walls; but because Godfrey claimed it as a fief of Jerusalem neither Raymond nor Robert would help him to occupy the town. Then those two leaders went off northward to return to Europe, seeking their own countries and lordships at home; they departed by sea, taking with them the bulk of the fighting power at the disposal of the Christian cause. Godfrey was left with a few hundred knights and an insufficient body of infantry to continue the work.

Tancred stood by him and remained in Palestine. With only eighty of the mounted gentry and a correspondingly small force of men on foot, he went northward and seized Galilee, took Tiberias, which was to be his capital, and the whole countryside submitted to him. He was even strong enough to lead a raiding party away up under Hermon to the gates of Damascus; then, since Galilee needed a port, he joined Godfrey de Bouillon in the taking of Haifa. All this was quick enough work; Ascalon had been fought on August 12, Haifa was in Tancred's hands eight days later; but Tyre and Sidon and Acre and Beyrouth were still held by Fatimite garrisons, Tripoli by an independent Emir. There were, therefore, in these first months of the slowly spreading occupation only two ports in the Christian hands—Haifa and Joppa. To hold these ports and acquire more entries by sea was essential to the endurance of the Crusading State—if State so loosely knit a thing could be called.

The Crusaders had not approached by sea, but the sea was necessary for their reinforcement and continued support by the west of Europe, and the ports attracted what was of the first moment to the lords established in Syria, the trading fleets of Pisa and Genoa and Venice.

It was the fleet of Venice which had helped, for instance, to take Haifa. The town was held almost entirely by Jews, who defended it with intense courage. But no one came to their aid. Each town was left to defend itself, for, during the whole of the first years after the great invasion, except during the ephemeral gathering of the host under Kerbogha, the world of the Levant was a mere dust of personal rivals. The Emir of Tripoli for instance felt so strongly his rivalry against the Emir of Damascus that he soon became the active ally of Jerusalem.

Apart from this disintegration of Moslem power, which, coupled with the great numbers of Westerners in the first attack, had made the precarious success of the First Crusade possible, there was the main cleavage between the two religious divisions of the Mohammedan world, with what one may call the Orthodox centered in Baghdad, and the Dissidents, the Fatimites, centered in Cairo. More than once during the advance the better-

advised among the Crusaders had considered an alliance with
Cairo: the capture of Jerusalem and, much more, the massacre
which followed, had made that difficult. Cairo, that is the Moslem power to the south and west of the Crusaders, remained
spiritually hostile to, and therefore socially separate from, the
Orthodox Moslems to the north and east. It is perhaps somewhat
misleading to use the terms "Orthodox" and "Heretical" of this
prime (and still enduring) division in the Moslem world. The
quarrel was rather as to dynastic claims—as to who should be
the spiritual and therefore military head of Islam. But though
neither as bitter nor of the same texture as the later Christian
quarrel of the sixteenth century, the quarrel between Cairo and
Baghdad helped to paralyze still further the Moslem forces
already so gravely weakened by the lack of political unity.

At Godfrey's death, in that July of 1100, there was a moment
when it looked as though the mastery of Jerusalem would pass
to its ecclesiastical authority, the patriarch who represented the
pope. Such a conclusion would have been fatal to the Crusade,
which could only survive by the office at least, and if possible
the power, of monarchy. A theocracy could never have held the
land. Under such a government the feudal turmoil would have
grown worse than ever. Nonetheless there were some months
during which a theocracy seemed possible, for it was not until
the autumn that a new chief was chosen. The barons of the south,
the men responsible now for Palestine, including Galilee and the
two ports now held on the seacoast, offered the Crown of Jerusalem to Godfrey's brother, Baldwin of Edessa in the north.

It was this choice which bred all the results, such as they were,
of the next half lifetime in the consolidation of Christian power
upon that coast, for Baldwin was suitable to his office.

BALDWIN I

Baldwin of Edessa handed over his town and principality to
his cousin, a man of the Ardennes like himself, the son of the
lord of Rethel, beyond Rheims (called "Baldwin of the Borough"), and then rode down southward with a very small force

to take up authority at Jerusalem as the main leaders had invited him to do.

So hostile was the patriarch to the lay power that he would have had Baldwin's road barred at Antioch, but happily the intrigue failed. A greater danger was the mobilizing of a considerable army by the Emir of Damascus. He blocked the road near Beyrouth where the jutting forth of a bold headland leaves but a narrow passage. Baldwin fought an action which cleared the way. How he was able to succeed against such greatly superior numbers we can now hardly discover; the account is confused and no sufficient reason can be found for his success. It was probably only one more example of the superiority of the Western knights when they could charge home against any number of Orientals.

At any rate this host from Damascus melted away as was the habit of a Moslem force after defeat; and the Moslems of the seacoast actively helped the Christians against their rivals of the interior.

Baldwin of Edessa then went on to Jerusalem in safety with his small force, was received with enthusiasm by the native Christian population (the Moslems of Jerusalem had been driven out). He was crowned King in the Church of the Nativity in Bethlehem on Christmas Day, 1100, and began that great work of effective monarchy which was to save—for as long as it could be saved—the great experiment.

Here there will occur to any modern reader a decisive question; when such great hosts had swarmed eastward to recover the Holy Sepulchre, since the Infidels of the Orient as a whole were clearly so much more numerous than even the Christians of the Main Crusade, why was not every effort made to keep up the strength of the Crusading garrisons and mobile forces to something not wholly inadequate to their task? The Crusading State, reduced to a strip of coast held with the utmost difficulty, was starved for men. It felt the superiority of its fighting *personnel:* but equally—as have so many isolated bodies in all ages who feel personal superiority in fighting power—it dreaded its insufficient and dwindling effectives.

Why was not something done to reinforce immediately, and still further to reinforce the Westerners holding on with such difficulty to their conquest? Why did not Europe maintain a continuous recruitment of her sons in the Orient who held her outpost against such odds?

The answer lies in two things. First, feudal society had no machinery for carrying on one continuously united effort: second, the communications with Syria from the West were too long and too difficult for the resources of the time. The truth of this can clearly be seen in the failure of the one great expedition which did envisage something of the kind. The necessity was apparent, the attempt was made, but the effort came to nothing. It was dissipated altogether, eaten up by the double obstacle: impossibility of coordination in disjointed feudal forces and the physical difficulties of transport.

Just after the difficult but final achievement of the Crusade a second wave, not on the same vast scale but still very large— half the first, perhaps—flowed out from Western Europe.

It was as though the Latin Christian society of the late eleventh century were inexhaustible, but indeed the whole story of the Crusades is the story of successive expeditions, sometimes considerable, which, continually thrusting at the goal of securing a Christian State in the Levant that should cut the Mohammedan world in two, failed perpetually to reach this result.

This second effort, following so closely on the heels of the first, ending in complete failure, showed at once how exceptionally fortunate the first main effort had been and what the difficulties were of keeping communications over 1500 miles of ruined land: difficulties which, in the long run, made the maintenance of the Holy City impossible.

This new thrust began with a body of fifteen thousand Italians from Milan marching east and reaching Constantinople in March, 1101. Immediately after that came a smaller body of southern French under the Duke of Aquitaine, and a much larger body of French and Germans who seemed surely sufficient to do once more what the former attack under Godfrey and the rest had done. All these successive bodies were destroyed.

The largest group which massed together first for the eastern advance across Asia Minor was annihilated. It was checked at the river Halys. It thence blundered back northwards towards the Black Sea. A Lombard contingent therein was stricken with panic at the first main Turkish charge; in the confusion of the night there was a general massacre and only a few of the mounted leaders escaped. These reached the shores of the Black Sea at Sinope, took ship there, and came back to Constantinople. The principal man among those who thus reached the coast after the abandonment of the army was Raymond, the Count of Toulouse, the same who played so great a part in the First Crusade, and who had now returned to get the support of the Byzantine court against his rivals in Syria.

He had become, since thus leaving the Holy Land for Constantinople, both the chief name among those who proposed to make a new effort and the ally of the emperor against the growing feeling of the Crusades that they must be independent of all imperial claims. He had been disappointed in the partitioning of power and of territory. Godfrey had been made head in Jerusalem, the Normans held Antioch, Godfrey's brother, Baldwin, held Edessa; he, Raymond of Toulouse, much the richest and on the whole the greatest of the feudal princes who had started out from France five years before, had no capital city and no feudal government in Syria to show as the fruit of his labors.

When he thus came back from Sinope, flying from an army destroyed, his prestige, since he had separated himself also from his fellows in the Holy Land, sank further. But his loss was of some advantage to him, for in the long run, when he did get back to Syria it was to find himself at last master of Tripoli, and he became the first chief of that new middle state, built up of the town and villages of the seacoast between the boundaries of Jerusalem on the south and of Antioch on the north. He became the lord of the Lebanon district and could call himself Count of Tripoli, though he did not live to hold that main port which gives its name to this coastland.

The feudal lord of Nevers followed on after the first great body had been routed on the Halys. He intended to catch up with the Italians and the rest, missed them, turned south and was destroyed in the tangle of the Taurus mountains. The third body, German and French mixed, attempting the original way across Asia Minor, was massacred as had been the first. Their destruction fell on them at Heraclea in August, and with them the effort at a great following Crusade to complete the work of the first came wholly to an end. The Duke of Bavaria escaped from the slaughter, so did William of Aquitaine, but of all those hosts very few returned alive.

It is possible that, if the stroke of 1101 had carried through, if there had been no breakdown on the Halys, the Crusading effort in Syria might have been rendered permanent. If the second column, that of Nevers, had joined an army still intact they would never have turned down single-handed southward to be destroyed in the Taurus. Then the third body of French and Germans, having so many of the first names of Europe among them (the Marquis of Austria, the Archbishop of Salzburg, the bishops of Paris and of Laon and of Soissons and Bavaria and Burgundy and Blois), would have come in with the rest, and all combined would have advanced on Syria as their immediate predecessors had done. There would have been heavy leakage on the way, of course; but even had this been on the scale of the First Crusade more than one hundred thousand armed men would have reached Syria to strengthen the depleted Christian garrisons.

Most important of all, Damascus, which had remained in Mohammedan hands, might have been seized. Had it been seized, as we have repeated, the whole "bridge" uniting the two halves of the Mohammedan power would have been cut. The military success and the political success would have been complete. As it was, this complete destruction in Asia Minor of all the bodies which attempted the reinforcement left the position in Syria undecided.

Yet in their insufficient numbers the Crusades did maintain themselves—in spite of the failure of the relief they had expected and in spite of jealousy and conflicts among themselves and in spite of misfortunes befalling individual leaders. Bohemond, for

instance, was captured in a raid to the north. He was taken by
the Turks and not ransomed for two years, and when he was
free he set out to the west to raise more men. But Antioch stood.
Bohemond's nephew, Tancred, had taken his place and maintained himself, not only against the pressure of the Mohammedans to the east, but against the rivalry of Christian Edessa
to the north. There was even a moment when Tancred was seen
in alliance with the Mohammedan ruler of Aleppo, raised against
the Christian ruler of Edessa and *his* Mohammedan ally.

We shall see how Tripoli was organized by Raymond of
Toulouse. When he died, half a dozen years after the capture
of Jerusalem, his son, Bertrand, and his nephew, William of
Cerdaigne, came up to take up an extending inheritance. William
came first, and Bertrand, claiming a legal right, could not oust
him. The new ill-founded strip of the county of Tripoli was broken up. It did not come together until William was dead; and
for his death some blame Bertrand.

So, as the first years passed, the power of Christendom strug-
gled to carry a military burden which seems to us too great to
be borne. The position was very perilous, but it endured, and
what had been at first a military expedition soon turned into
something like a colonial one. The invaders mixed with the
Christian population of the land; they grew familiar with, and
took advantage of, the Mohammedan politics, especially the continual rivalry between the Emirs and the lesser Moslem lordships
of separate castles and walled cities. That welding of the
Westerners into an Eastern society was to prove in one lifetime
a weakness, but it enabled the beginnings of the Crusading State
to strike root.

Through the failure of the attempted reinforcement *en masse*
the very few small and isolated bodies of armed Frenchmen,
south of Antioch, left "in the air," without proper communications, without permanent resources, without reserves, had to
accomplish the impossible under their new king. They had to
consolidate and found a State. They did so through an inborn
military sense of strategics, and through a large measure of good
luck, without which nothing difficult is ever done. Their sense

of strategics led them to make the conquest of the seacoast and its ports their first task and to divide in right proportions their very insufficient effectives between the business of garrisoning the strong points—especially Jerusalem, the main base—and the business of forming armies for attack and siege.

Their good luck furnished them with three leaders one after the other, Baldwin I, his successor and cousin, Baldwin II, and Baldwin II's son-in-law, Foulque of Anjou, who were the three first kings of Jerusalem. That good luck also gave to each of them a fairly long tenure of office between his crowning and his death: and length of reign is a factor in the strength of monarchies. Between them they totalled 43 years of consecutive and organized rule. Such a span is the active lifetime of a man. Only the youngest of the knights who rode by the side of Baldwin I on his accession could on the death of Foulque still march and fight, for by that time a lad who had been 18 when the first king was crowned would have come to be over sixty.

The three reigns were well spaced, too, and (what was important) the first, during which the foundations had to be laid, was the longest. Baldwin I governed for over 18 years, Baldwin II and Foulque of Anjou for over a dozen each.

It was good luck also that the merchant and pilgrim fleets of the West were present in numbers during the first years when it was life and death to seize the seaports. The French knights working from inland were never in numbers sufficient for that task. It was made possible by the Italian sailors. But the best of their luck lay in the character of these three men each exactly suited to his share of the development: Baldwin I to the difficult planting of the Crusading State, Baldwin II to its guarding and strengthening, Foulque to the maintenance of it when it was already beginning to weaken from within and to feel the approach from without of the Menace which at last destroyed it. Indeed Foulque, the third king—and the best—created by the excellence of his rule a sort of façade which kept up the illusion of full strength after full strength had begun to pass away.

Baldwin of Edessa, first King of Jerusalem, was a man tall and bearded—while around him men followed the common cus-

tom of the northern French in being clean-shaven and were
mostly of that short square build which marked the northern
French knighthood. He, like his brother, Godfrey of Bouillon,
before him, and his brother, Eustace of Boulogne, who might
have followed him, were all sons of that frontier ruling house
in Gaul, the House of Flanders, governing the lowlands of the
Meuse and Scheldt and the coast of the Straits of Dover. He
was a great horseman, self-willed, but not without finesse, impa-
tient of clerics and rapid in decision and action: also promiscu-
ous with women. He was vigorous in perpetual exercise of
authority over inferiors, and in·organizing the resistance to
Islam. The harvest of fortification which went on in his time—
Toron, commanding the road to Tyre, the castle northeast of the
sea of Galilee (the site of which is disputed), the great and noble
experiment of Montreal which guaranteed the connection with
the Red Sea—though none save the last were his own work, yet
fell in his reign, and it was under him that the fixing of stone-
defended, heavily walled garrisons as the foundation of the
Christian power began.

   He also had a high political sense; perhaps he even exceeded
on this side, but at any rate he worked it thoroughly. Since there
had been no capture of Damascus—as there ought to have
been—on the original march to Jerusalem, he did at last work
an alliance with Damascus against the main Turkish power to
the north; and this tradition of a Damascene alliance, often interrupted but always renewed, divided the enemy forces and kept
the balance for a lifetime between the Crusaders and the forces
of Islam pressing against them from the east. It survived the
original diplomatic conception of Baldwin by more than twenty
years.

   The same political preoccupation guided him in his marriages;
in Edessa he had made a political alliance with the daughter
of an Armenian chief, the better to control his Armenian subjects. Now later, being king in the south, he repudiated her and
married the widow of Roger I, King of Sicily, the mother of
the young King Roger II. It is true that, the marriage being
denounced as bigamous by the Church, he later undid it; it is

true that this political stroke did him no good, but rather earned him the enmity of the Sicilian power, the nearest Western Christian power to Palestine and the one with most maritime resources; but it is an example of his industry in political combinations. His first wife, the Armenian Arda, he would never get back—she had gone off to Constantinople after her repudiation and was giving every sort of scandal by her life—while his second wife, Adelaide, was too old for him and his divorce from her did him nothing but harm. But his two marriages, though the purpose of each was frustrated, prove his way of sacrificing everything to political combination.

It was this same political character in him (which, though he was a remarkable soldier, was still stronger than his strategic sense) that made him consider the attack on Egypt—an idea premature for his time but destined to bear fruit. It was the same political character in him which made him take on something of the Syrian manner; clothing himself in a fine white burmous embroidered with gold, sitting cross-legged on the floor for his meals and for audiences. The natives called him the "Sultan of the Franks": and in this Tancred imitated him, wearing a turban to promote good will, but putting a cross on it to affirm his creed.

The main affair of these twenty years was, I have said, the capture of the seacoast, on a strip very long, narrow, and ill-provided with communications, crushed, north of Acre, between the sea and high mountains. The conquest of this flat coast in so short a time would seem, if we look at the map and think of the place as Mohammedan territory, and of the Crusaders (after the repatriation of the main body) as a handful of aliens, inexplicable. When we read of such things being done we find they have been done as a rule only through some overwhelming superiority in technical power and armament over a native population. Such superiority the Crusaders did not have over the Moslems. They fought with the same weapons, the same lack of maps, and so on. But the ports were vulnerable because they were isolated; though they were thickly populated, the territory in between them was sparsely populated. One port never helped the other, in the whole story, save now and then, rarely, by sea.

The geographical conformation of the coast accounts for this; until you get south of Carmel the life of the coast is not continuous. Tyre, Sidon, Beyrouth, Latakia, Tripoli, Byblos, Acre and Haifa, stand in fertile but restricted plains with a mountain mass immediately behind them and spurs of the mountains cutting off each from its neighbor. They were also morally divided. Islam all along this coast was overshadowed by the Egyptian power, which was not popular with the local Moslems; it was cut off by desert and mountain from the Turkish power inland; it fell naturally into small local commands where the head of each desired to make himself independent, even at the expense of occasional alliance with the Crusaders.

Nor was it only that the local governors of the ports desired to be independent; it was also that such of their subjects as were Moslem desired the same thing. They were perhaps at the moment less conscious of a universal Moslem culture on this particular belt of seacoast than they had been for centuries past or were to be again for centuries later; the Crusaders found Islam, in this particular region, at a low ebb in its cultural patriotism.

Finally there was a large Christian population. We have no means from the records of the time for estimating exactly how large it was, but the proportion was very large. We have seen how in Antioch it was much the greater part of the town. It was to be found scattered all over the countrysides; it was represented in every town and port and it was presumably much larger than it is today; for though the Crusaders encouraged it and protected it, the Moslem reaction following and continuing in power for seven hundred years certainly reduced the Christian numbers severely. These Christians were not, of course, of the Latin rite, they were Orientals; but it is to be remembered that the gulf between the Oriental Christian and the Christian of the Western Latin liturgy was not as wide and deep in those days as it is now. What confirmed the schism and bred a mortal enmity was the forcible Latin conquest of Constantinople, just after the main Crusading experiment had broken down, rather more than a century after the capture of Jerusalem. During the twelfth century, when the Crusading effort still looked for success, the various rituals and liturgies could exist side by side in a common cause against the Moslem. Even today territories in which the Christian proportion is large, such as the Lebanon coast, have much more in common with Western civilization than has the almost entirely Moslem hinterland.

It is well to set down certain pivotal dates of these remarkable twenty years. Jerusalem, as we have seen, was stormed in the high summer of 1099; within four years the near coast, Haifa, Jaffa, Arsouf and Caesarea were solidly held and garrisoned. Tortosa went in 1102, Acre and Byblos in 1104. Tripoli we shall find seized by 1109; Beyrouth was stormed in 1110. Therefore, though there remained exceptions, islands as it were of Moslem power, commanding sea communications, the bulk of the coast was in Crusading hands within a dozen years of the first plan to consolidate the whole seacoast under the rule of the Crusaders.

Only Tyre, the most important point in those days of all the middle coast, did not fall in that first rapid movement but was to hold out for some years more.

While Baldwin I was laying the foundations of that royal power which was to be the saving of the Crusade so long as it could be saved; while he was laboriously establishing his communications by sea through the ports nearest to Jerusalem, another province was being slowly pieced together to the north of the royal domain proper. This province was the province of Tripoli, and it became the special fief of Raymond of Toulouse.

It is curious to note how the most politically important of the Crusaders had had the worst fortunes of them all. He had been elbowed out of Antioch, he had lost his chance of a domain beyond the Orontes when the impatience and suspicion of the remaining pilgrims had forced him to abandon that northern territory and take up the march to Jerusalem. Then he had suffered that disaster just described, "The Reinforcement," all broken in the wastes of Asia Minor, himself barely escaping with his life.

He, the man who had always stood out against subservience

to Byzantium, now had to seek Byzantine aid if he were to recover any footing at all on the Phoenician coast. It was as a vassal of Byzantium that he undertook the reduction of Tripoli. When the Crusaders had passed down that coast on their way to Jerusalem, Raymond had already coveted an establishment there, he had tried to seize Arqua and failed, he had got hold for a moment of Tortosa, he might have got Tripoli then had not the Mohammedan Emir of it saved himself by an alliance.

What had really prevented Raymond from establishing himself at Tripoli and all along that coast was the determination of the original Crusading army to march on Jerusalem. Now, two years later, he was free to return to his attempt. He found that Tortosa had done; while he was suffering his disaster in Asia Minor, the destruction of "The Reinforcement," an Arab family had seized it. It had to be retaken and it fell to the Christians again, and to Raymond, some time in the early part of 1102. The success was as usual due to the help of an Italian fleet, the Genoese.

With Tortosa as a base he determined to seize the much more important Tripoli to the south. The Emir of Tripoli, though he desired independence above all things and, like almost every Moslem notable at the time, refused a superior of his own faith and promoted the chaos into which Syrian Islam had fallen, appealed to the Moslem masters of Homs on the Orontes inland and to the master of Damascus. There was a battle which saved Tripoli for a moment, but in that battle one could see the perpetually recurring feature of a handful of Western French knights withstanding great bodies of the mounted Orientals.

Raymond had only a hundred knights watching Tripoli, only fifty surrounding his own standard, another fifty to stand in line against the whole force of the Mohammedans from Homs, a hundred to stand in line against the much larger force from Damascus. He had, of course, his much larger complement of foot soldiers as well, for without them the knights could not do their work; but it is remarkable that in this shock were only these three hundred fully armed mounted gentlemen of Languedoc and Provence to meet the onslaught. Still more remarkable was it that even by the Mohammedan account these southern

French knights and infantry between them accounted for seven thousand of the Orientals.

He had won his battle, but he could not take the town, though the bulk of the population was still Christian and came in from the farms to help him. He fell back on Tortosa. Thence he tried to seize the Bequaa inland valley beyond Lebanon and Homs beyond the mountains. He had too few men; he returned and tried his hand again at Tripoli in the summer of 1103, was repelled, seized Byblos the next year and once more returned to force Tripoli, the central port of them all and the capital of the Lebanon plains. He built his castle on the hill commanding the peninsula on which Tripoli harbor lies, and began a steady blockade. He did not live to see his own triumph, he died early in 1105, but a nephew of his, William of the Cerdaigne, pending the arrival from Europe of the son and true heir of Raymond, carried on the work in the hope of seizing all that would have been Raymond's new fief. He took Arqua[5] at last, but the harbor town of Tripoli still stood out. Tripoli was still besieged when the son and heir of Raymond arrived, Bertrand by name. Bertrand claimed the succession by right of blood, William of Cerdaigne by right of prior arrival and conquest, and then there happened a thing important to the history of Christendom on the Levant—the two rivals submitted to the arbitration of the King of Jerusalem.

Baldwin held a Royal Session in the castle Raymond had built whence the blockade of Tripoli was being conducted, and to this session came all the Christian chiefs of Syria: Baldwin of the Borough, the master of Edessa, Tancred from Antioch, and the rest. It was a most imposing recognition of the new royal authority which was to strengthen the new Christian State all down the Levantine coast.

Baldwin's award was a compromise; he gave Tripoli (when it should be taken) and the southern part of the coast to Raymond's heir, Arqua and the northern part to William of

---

5. The name came from the arches of the Roman aqueduct, like the many "Arcs" and "Arques" of western Europe, called after the same fashion.

Cerdaigne. It was from this award that the house of Toulouse ultimately became counts of Tripoli and masters of all that district. But the historical value of the thing lay in this: that for the first time a kind of unity had been forged between the separate adventurers from the West.

While their forces were all thus assembled, advantage was taken of the exceptional numbers, a general assault delivered and Tripoli fell. It was July 12, 1109, ten years almost to a day since the storming of Jerusalem.

Soon after, William of Cerdaigne was killed. A chance arrow pierced him. Men accused his rival, Bertrand of Toulouse, but nothing was proved: the whole county of Tripoli was now in one hand, from Tortosa in the north to the River of the Dog by Beyrouth; and though isolated islands of Mohammedan command still remained (Tyre and Ascalon, the chief), one may henceforward call the whole Levantine coast a part of Christian government and the main lines of the new Christian state established—until the breakdown began, nearly 40 years later.

There you may now see the kingdom of Jerusalem in its four divisions; Edessa the bastion of the north; the principality of Antioch next south; then the county of Tripoli lying on the narrow coastal belt between the mountains and the sea; last, on the extreme south, and marching with Egypt, the royal province of the kingdom of Jerusalem. Fixed frontiers to the east the Crusading State had none; it held what it could, attempting, and failing, to pierce beyond the Orontes; leaving Damascus independent; warring for Moab; never properly controlling that eastern road along the edge of the desert which, could the Christians have seized it, would have made them secure.

There along the seacoast and from one to two days' ride inland from it the Christian lords were established with tenants, Moslem and Eastern Christian, providing them with tax revenue and rent; Antioch, the richest, Edessa, the widest in extent, Tripoli, the most fertile, though very restricted, coastal ribbon of soil; Jerusalem, far on the extremes, quite ill-suited for a central command, but politically, and still more through devotion, the nucleus of the whole affair.

There were the seaport towns filled with the counting-houses and the guards of the Italian maritime cities. The Crusading land as it was to remain for a lifetime was formed: formed but not bounded, save by the sea. The eastern landward side lay open. Thence Islam could raid; along its main eastern road from Aleppo, up the Orontes and through Damascus southward Islam could rally, and when once Islam should be united and should rally, the Crusading State must fall—for it had not cut that road: lacking Damascus.

BALDWIN II

When Baldwin I died there was some hesitation among the Christian notables at Jerusalem upon the succession. A general opinion was that a third brother of the great House of Flanders, Eustace of Boulogne, should be summoned.

But the journey was long and the military necessity of the State pressing. They wisely chose the late King's cousin, to whom he had handed over Edessa. This cousin was also called Baldwin—Baldwin "of the Borough" *("Du Bourg")* came from the same Ardennes country and continued the tradition of the reign before. His candidature was supported by Jocelyn of Courtenay, and as the two men were known enemies, that support carried the day. For men agreed that if Jocelyn, in spite of the ill treatment he had received at the hands of this second Baldwin, his suzerain at Edessa, when both were up in the north together, gave his vote for that superior, it could only be because the good of the State seemed paramount.

But Jocelyn had another motive. With his old suzerain Baldwin of the Borough safely away down south in Jerusalem as king, he, Jocelyn, might have Edessa. Jocelyn became, indeed, lord of that place, and from this accession of wealth and power, though Edessa did not long stay with them, springs the great part played by the Courtenays thenceforward in the story of western Europe, and even in England.

The new king was tall and bearded like his predecessor, and, like his predecessor, an excellent horseman and an eager soldier.

But in character he differed widely, and that with a difference very suitable to the next phase of this kingship. For the eighteen odd years of Baldwin I's reign went well with a neutral temper and even with a certain measure of antagonism to the clergy, lest the State, in its difficult beginnings, should fall under clerical rule, unsuited to its military peril. But the next twelve years needed rather a temperate wisdom and a superior whom men would universally support through attraction: for now that the foundations were laid and the posts held, the danger was one of feudal incoherence and local war. Baldwin II received universal support and his temperament raised no enmities. It is remarkable that the Mohammedan rulers felt the attraction and revered his memory after his death. His virtuous life and his piety recommended him to both camps.

Yet Baldwin of the Borough, now Baldwin, the King, had by his virtues done one harm to the State. He had married, and was true to, an Armenian wife. He was devoted to his children by her, three daughters. The elder, Melisande, was to bring the crown of Jerusalem to her future husband, but with that dowry, an Oriental character of her own with her fortunes attached to it: her younger sister, married to Antioch, later nearly brought about as dowager in her widowhood the ruin of that principality.

Three things marked the twelve years of this reign: the saving of Antioch, the capture of Tyre, and an attempt on Damascus, which failed.

Antioch, Baldwin saved after the capital Christian defeat in the north which came just at the transition from the first reign to the second. It was the first main act of the new king.

The young prince of Antioch had marched out towards Aleppo and camped in that plain on the Antioch side of the pass between the two towns. There he was surprised by the Mohammedan army and cut to pieces. The Christian force was annihilated, and if the victors had followed up, Antioch itself would have fallen, and with it all the north: Edessa cut off and only Tripoli holding to Jerusalem. Baldwin marched at once and restored the balance. There were lost towns in the marches of Aleppo which could not be recovered, but Antioch was saved.

As for Tyre, although at the moment of the siege Baldwin II was a prisoner in the hands of the enemy, it was the strength of the monarchy that triumphed and seized the last great port still in Moslem hands on the Phoenician coast: the last exception which—north of Ascalon—seriously interrupted the now continuous Crusading hold on the seaboard.

On February 15, 1124, Tyre began to suffer siege, the Christian army held it on the land side where a narrow neck of sand had drifted up over the ruins of Alexander's mole. From the sea the ships of the Venetians maintained a strict blockade. After a seesaw of adventures and attempted relief, that most ancient, most famous of the Oriental ports offered to surrender. It surrendered honorably under full capitulations with a regular treaty signed, and on July 7 the Royal Standard of Jerusalem was raised above the main gate. Baldwin II was still a captive, but his Constable represented the magic power of Monarchy and it has been well said that "the spirit of the King of Jerusalem was there."

Subject to that banner, the lord of Tripoli set up his upon one tower, and the Doge of Venice's flag floated above another. Here as everywhere the Mediterranean maritime cities—in this case, Venice—took firm root; Venice had separate jurisdiction in the town over her own subjects and even a dispute between a Venetian and any other must be tried in the Venetian courts, save in the case where the defendant were a direct subject of Jerusalem. Venice had nearly all the maritime trade, a whole quarter of the city to herself alone.

In a sense Venice and the rest were to outlast all that soldiery of which they had only been occasional allies, for when the last garrison had disappeared from Antioch itself and the last Western Mass had been said in the chapel of the last independent lord, the commerce of Venice and the rest filled that sea, and her profits from freight and banking continued to draw a tribute from the Levant long after the last Christian knight had disappeared from it.

Nevertheless, a new factor had appeared, and gave to an attack on Damascus a chance of success. This new factor was violent religious division between the two factions of its Mohammedan population.

There had come in from the East a sort of heretical preaching which had gained importance; and the strength of it, already appreciable in Mesopotamia, concentrated upon Damascus. The orthodox Moslem population of the great city was full of anger against the novelty; but that novelty was officially protected. There were all the elements present for civil war and a consequent impotence in defense should the Christians decide to march north from the kingdom of Jerusalem and seize Damascus. Baldwin II, knowing that in spite of the opportunity his weakness lay in lack of numbers, summoned every force available, but especially tried to gather a really strong army, yet another reinforcement and supplementary Crusade, from Europe. He sent Hugh, the Master of the Templars, to France with that object. A certain amount of recruitment was obtained, but not enough, because the chief feudal families of France with their large personal levies hung back. They could not judge, as the men on the spot could judge, the new and considerable opportunity. Even as it was, however, the force mustered by Baldwin II might have sufficed but for an accident of weather.

The dissident heretics had betrayed the castle of Banias, northeast of the sea of Galilee, under the lower slopes of Hermon, to the Christians. That was an added strength, and the expedition went forward fairly confident of victory. But in any attempt against Damascus, especially from the arid south, there was always this handicap—that the thing had to be done quickly if it were to be done at all.

The stores of provisions were within the walls of the town; the great belt of orchards and gardens outside the city could not of themselves maintain an army. A force attempting Damascus must therefore bring a heavy train with it, and even so its provisioning would last for but a few days. It was probably this feature which has saved Damascus so often during the many attacks on it in its 4,000 years of history, from Assyrian days onwards. The town was of so great a circuit and population that to attempt it meant an especially large body, and yet to feed that especially large body on the edge of the desert for anything but a short time was impossible.

Baldwin appeared before the town on the south and east side in the month of November. During the critical action between the besiegers and the Moslem sortie from the walls, there burst one of those storms which are only seen and heard on the edges of the desert.

There is irony indeed in this salvation of Damascus—of all places!—through blinding torrents of rain. For rain fell in that winter day of such tropical violence and in such long continued downpour that those who were present said it was "like fighting in the night." Cohesion was lost; the Moslem attack got well in among its foes. Baldwin's army fell into such confusion that it almost ceased to be an organized body. There was not, properly speaking, a rout; but there was a disarray which forbade any rally. And by the time the episode was over there was not enough munitionment left to attempt any renewal on the Christian side. The army of the Crusade retreated over the runnels, nearly always bare and dry, now still foaming with the waterspout of the great two days' storm, and the best chance of clinching down the Christian power upon that key city which determined, and still determines, the fate of Syria was lost.

The death of Baldwin II, in 1131, fell at a moment when the first serious menace of a united Moslem Syria was rising against the Crusaders of Palestine, Edessa, Antioch, and the West. Unity, temporary but formidable, would raise larger armies than the Christians could withstand, and unity would come when a leader, conquering and grasping all Levantine and Mesopotamian Islam in one hand, should arise. Such a character had already appeared in one *Zengi*.

His captainship had made him. The chief men of Irak sought the Sultan in Persia and told him, in the last moments of Baldwin I's conquests, that Islam had lost Syria. All was gone unless a captain could be found. They begged for the appointment of Zengi, who came thus as official master to Aleppo in the last months of Baldwin I's reign. Shortly after the loss of Tyre, in 1126, he was master of Irak as well. Within a score of years he was to strike the blow which first shook all the structure of the Crusading State.

But the advance of Zengi was for the future. When Baldwin II died, the State seemed well established, the succession secure, for there lay ready to hand one of the chief feudal masters of western Europe who had stood in Syria already for ten years as the husband of the king's elder daughter and heiress, Melisande. It was Foulque of Anjou, who was to be the last and perhaps the greatest of the three kings.

FOULQUE OF ANJOU

The third and last of the men who founded kingship in the Crusading State was the most remarkable of the band.

It is possible that if, at that moment, 1131, when the original Crusaders were grown old or were dead and when there was already arising that dangerous new population of mixed blood, neither French nor Syrian, a less competent man had taken the throne, the decline of the realm would have appeared. As it was, he staved off that decline for a dozen years, and the Holy Land seemed at his death, in 1143, to have reached a strength not yet attained. Especially did he seem to have made it stable and destined to a life indefinitely prolonged. He crowned the work, and none watching his success could have expected what was to follow.

He suffered one heavy defeat when he surrendered at Montferrand beyond Lebanon in the very middle of his reign. He witnessed the passing, without fruit, of that capital hour in which, by an understanding with Byzantium, the eastern road might have been seized and the gates of invasion from the Mohammedans shut for good in their faces. The opportunity was lost. It may be argued that Foulque was in part responsible for the failure. But he lived to see his kingdom everywhere consolidated and its future apparently secure.

Foulque V, Count of Anjou, had all the qualities required in a medieval leader continually occupied with the task of maintaining an armed society against the threat of destruction.

He had, to begin with, what is always important, though it was not here a factor of the first importance, prestige, both within and without. That is, he felt himself from within, by his own family tradition, to be a man of high consequence, and he was regarded from without by all as one specially called upon to rule. None of the leaders of the Crusade had taken their places there as monarchs; that is, as men accustomed to direct command over a very great number of their fellows. Two of the original leaders had indeed been of this position politically: the Duke of Normandy and the Count of Toulouse; but one had not wished nor was the other able to exercise great personal power in Syria. Normandy was but a pilgrim fighting for the sake of the religion and glory and bound to get home again when the adventure was over. The misfortunes of Toulouse we have seen. Even at the end of them he was no more than a vassal of Byzantium, and with his death the lordship of Tripoli passed through a phase of conflict.

Bohemond had been born the cadet of a newly great house, not the head of it; Tancred, a nephew or cousin of the same; Godfrey and Baldwin I and Baldwin II all of the same standing, younger branches of a main ruling house, that of Flanders. But the Count of Anjou, Foulque V, who now took over the government and was to give it such stiffening against the growing menace of a united Islam, was a man of monarchical training: he had lived his life in Europe as the successful and tried ruler of a wide, highly centralized province wherein he had, like all his immediate ancestors, acted the part of a local king.

In the breakup of the transformed Roman Empire during the ninth century the House of Anjou had come to be what it was, after the fashion of all the great provincial ruling houses.

During the profound internal changes of Christian society which followed the death of Charlemagne, when what had been offices of government turned into hereditary properties, a certain Ingelger, a man of peasant and probably servile birth, had distinguished himself in the imperial service by his energy. Robert the Strong, the ancestor of the House of France, to whom the Emperor of his day had allotted the government of the western Gallic districts against the Norman pirates, left a son to administer the rich county of Anjou, and this son had shared his power with one whom he had appointed to act as delegate, and whom he called the "Viscount" of Anjou, that is, the Lieutenant of Count of Anjou.[6] The man with whom this acting count or governor of the time chose thus to share his power was the son of Ingelger, famous and even legendary for his prowess of the generation before, and the name of this son of Ingelger was Foulque.

There were, of course, no family names remaining save here and there the dim tradition of a few which had come down from the old senatorial tradition of the Roman Empire. This Foulque was known only by a nickname common enough, due to his complexion or his hair, "Foulque, the Red." Within a century of the death of Charlemagne this man Foulque, the Red, grandson of a serf, was accepted fully as Count of Anjou, that is (now that the imperial power was dying out) as the local monarch of Angers, town and stronghold and all its district. He is recorded as the first independent Count of Anjou and is remembered as Foulque I.

Through the next century and a half, five generations followed, growing in power and now accepted without question as the natural hereditary lords of the Angevin division. The great-grandson of the grandson of Foulque, the Red, was one Geoffrey, known as "the Hammer." He had no son, and with him the first dynasty of Anjou ended.

But his sister Ermingard had married one of that most ancient family, the Ferreoli, the same senatorial Roman family of the Gallic Narbonnese from which Charlemagne also had descended. The son of that Ferreolus and of Ermingard was called Foulque in his turn, after his uncle. He was known as Foulque IV, or *"le Rechin."* He was contemporary with the Conquest of England by William of Falaise, "William the Conqueror," his neighbor feudal monarch close at hand to the east, the lord of Normandy. With this Foulque IV *"le Rechin"* begins the second

---

6. We must remember, of course, that these names "Count" and "Viscount" stood in the twelfth century for office and real power. They were not titles. They meant rather "Hereditary Governor" of the district.

line of the counts of Anjou, maintaining, although they are descended through a woman, the old traditional names of Foulque and Geoffrey.

This Foulque IV, contemporary with the Norman Conquest, died in 1109, ten years after the storming of Jerusalem. He was succeeded by his son, a rare good fighter, and, what was of advantage in a ruler of those days, quite young. This lad, Foulque V, was only 18 when he came into his inheritance, and for eleven years, until he was close on 30, he continued to extend the boundaries of Anjou and consolidate them.

He was the very man for the task. Short, broad-shouldered, quick, red-headed like all his tribe, enormously energetic without violence, a strong fighter, and an excellent organizer, he had in high degree the qualities which made a feudal leader. But he also had continuously applied political talent. He it was who made of Anjou the best centralized of all the northern French states: more secure against internal rebellion than was even Normandy.

He had also the advantage of close cousinship with the House that was, in name at least, the head of all such as he, the Royal House at Paris. For his mother had married the King of France. In the midst of this triumphant youth of his he took the Cross and went off on the great adventure, leaving behind him a child, Geoffrey, who should have been his heir and whose counsellors should rule Anjou while he himself was warring in the Holy Land.

We have seen how Foulque in Syria married for second wife, Melisande, the daughter of Baldwin II, and now he was chosen with enthusiasm for the next king after Baldwin II in 1131—a man of 40 and of already ten years' experience in the Syrian wars.

When he was thus raised to the throne of Jerusalem, Foulque V abandoned his rights over Anjou to his son Geoffrey, of whose name history is full; for that young Geoffrey of Anjou, so succeeding to power in his father's lifetime, was the same who wore for a badge in his cap and helmet a plant of broom from the western heaths, a bunch of *planta genesta,* whence he got called

"Plantagenet." His son, Henry, inherited England from Maude, his mother, grand-daughter of the Conqueror. He is that Henry II who founded half our institutions, and from him descend all the kings of medieval England in direct line, the High Plantagenets, until the last fighter of them went down on Bosworth Field and the usurping Tudors came in, changing all.

The monarchy of Jerusalem had special opportunities for consolidating itself during the reign of Foulque because that reign included a regency over Antioch (the young heiress of which was his niece, born of Melisande's sister), and the opportunity of Christian suzerainty or at any rate protective power over petty Mohammedan border states. The monarchic idea grew all the stronger also because Foulque, unlike any of the chief resident leaders of the Crusades, had been at once the head of the State in Europe and head of a State in the Orient. The Count of Anjou and Maine, before he was King of Jerusalem, Foulque of Anjou brought the whole moral strength of a western European principate; he came with the prestige of it behind him, and the effects of it upon his character in his own person.

The reign of Foulque, from 1131 to 1143, illustrates also most vividly that factor of blood and climate which plays so large a part in the rise and fall of the Crusading effort. The climate ultimately affected (as we know) the Westerner; inter-marriage with natives of that climate affected their lineage. Foulque brings in fully the Western blood, he comes fresh from western Europe in all the vigor of his age; but immediately after his time that climate and the mixture of blood begin to affect the strength of that small Christian armed force which stood in a chain of garrisons cutting off Islam from the sea.

This effect of Eastern blood upon the Crusading families was the more strongly illustrated in Foulque from his devotion to the half-Oriental Melisande. That princess, and her sister, the Regent of Antioch, were born of an Armenian mother, the Oriental woman whom Baldwin of the Borough had married when he would possess himself of Edessa. She was younger than the Angevin by many years and the difference in age nourished his affection. He bore with her passionate temper and, perhaps, her unchastity. She had certainly a high favorite, a friend from childhood, who was perhaps her lover. Her contemporaries believed the worst things of her. They may have judged her harshly as being foreign to their blood, but her reputation was low. Yet old Foulque bore with her until, on the approach of middle age, she sobered and turned to religion. She was closely bound in his heart to the end of his life. Had he less loved her, he might have provided wiser counsels for her regency which followed on his death.

That death, it is worth remembering, was an accident connected with her whims and his attention to them. The Court was at Acre. The Queen planned an unexpected picnic in the fields and they all rode out. As they rode, a hare started from her form; the King spurred, his mount stumbled, threw him—a man well over fifty—and rolled on him so that the heavy saddle crushed out the rider's brains—and Melisande, seized by a frenzy of grief, or remorse, sat by him on the ground quite tearless but torn with shrieks and kissing the blood on the wounds: a woman from the hills.

I have said that Foulque, the King, in the midst of his good fortune and high victories had suffered two grievous moments. The first was when Zengi had caught him unawares, him and a small army in the little stronghold of Montferrand, beyond Lebanon, and compelled him to surrender.

That was in 1137: six years after his accession and six before he was to die so suddenly. He was released, and he owed his freedom to the fear in which Zengi stood of a great advance which approached and nearly changed the history of the world from that day to this.

The Emperor John Comnenus, son of that Emperor Alexius who had assisted at the passage of the great original Crusading host, had been on the throne of Constantinople since 1118. His reign exactly coincided with the two reigns of Foulque and his father-in-law: 1118-1143; a long time for one man to hold power in Byzantium, and he held that power to great purpose: a man of strong will and strong intelligence combined. He saw further than did the Crusaders, he had a wider view of the whole con-

flict between Christendom and Islam and a much deeper memory of the distant past and the Mohammedan conquest which
had imperilled all our civilization. He came with a strong army
eastward to make sure of Asia Minor. He claimed Antioch on
the old lines and almost took it by force. Then, in this same
year 1137, he proposed a policy of genius.

Let the lords of Antioch take *Aleppo* and surrender Antioch
to the Byzantine crown. He would help them to seize that frontier town of Aleppo, the head and gate of the only road by which
Islam could come in from the east and attack the Christian State.
The vital line—Shaizar—Hama—Homs—Damascus—would be
seized and give the kingdom a strong desert frontier. He had
brought a fine siege train, something much more powerful than
any the Crusaders had seen. He got them to come with him
and began to storm the cities in the Orontes. It looked, at one
moment, as though the large strategic scheme had succeeded.

But the Crusading lords were half-hearted and doubtful. They
were jealous of Byzantium's presence in Syria, they feared for
their independence. They considered their known possessions
and dreaded any exchange and new adventure in which they
might lose all.

On the night of May 11 to 12, 1138, the siege of Shaizar
was raised and the moment for success had passed.

John Comnenus still dreamed of alliance and of a common
Christian pact. He was preparing a pilgrimage to the Holy Sepulchre which might have raised a threat of suzerainty, when he
died and his plan of a revived united Christendom of the East
rolling back Islam died with him.

Would it have succeeded? In its failure the strength of Islam
under Zengi gathered. Foulque met that gathering strength with
a strength of his own; it did not destroy him as it destroyed his
successors, but it pressed him hard.

The Crusaders in their original advance had found before them
a Mohammedan Syrian world divided into fragments. Their triumph was in part (but only in part) due to this internal crumbling
of Islam throughout the territory they invaded. There were bound
to come sooner or later leaders on the Moslem side who would

bind the Moslems in Syria together. It was not in the nature of the Orient to produce strict permanent monarchy upon the French and European model. Islam must needs be always breaking up, but there was certain to come some temporary leader who would gather strength for a time into his own hands. We have seen an effect of it in the case of Kerbogha; but we have also seen how Kerbogha was destroyed in front of Antioch, mainly because his supporters were not subordinates, but local rulers of Damascus and Aleppo, jealous the one of the other, and jealous of their temporary commander. What Kerbogha had failed to do, Zengi came much nearer to doing. He did not unite all the Moslem East as later Saladin was to do—the man who would first do that would indeed be a menace to Christendom—but he did unite all the northwest of Mohammedan Syria and Mesopotamia. He came at last to hold Mosul, Aleppo, and all the middle Orontes. He as yet held neither Christian Edessa on the north nor Moslem Damascus on the south, and during the whole reign of Foulque, both remained outside his power, partly from his respect for the King of Jerusalem's strength. But Zengi was of sufficient power to balance the power of the King of Jerusalem.

The reign of Foulque was also typical of the whole Crusading story in this, that under it was set forth the most doubtful question of the whole affair—the paradox of Damascus.

For the Christian princes of Syria and especially for the King of Jerusalem, who was their head, it was an apparently obvious policy to be friends with the Mohammedan government of Damascus. The government had always been jealous of its independence; it had always been ready to betray its fellow Moslems of the north and east in order to maintain that independence; it had come to be, of all the cities mainly Mohammedan in population, the most sympathetic to the Western invaders, and they to it. With the French Christian princes of Syria acting almost as protectors of Damascus, their Moslem enemies were not only morally divided but geographically cut in two. All this was clear to any intelligent man of the day, and especially clear to Foulque of Anjou. He made the protection of Damascus and his own friendship with it the very center of his policy.

Well and good. But there was an alternative consideration. From the moment when an attack on Islam was launched by the West, right on throughout the centuries, Damascus was the key point. It is so still—in spite of steam and petrol, rail and airplane.

It was all very well for the invaders to keep Damascus as an ally; but so long as it remained Moslem, it was bound sooner or later to become a main Moslem capital. Only with Damascus taken and all held by Christian armies, only with Damascus as thoroughly grasped by the Crusading power as was Antioch or Jerusalem, could the feudal French kingdom in the Levant, the Christian outpost, the bulwark against Mohammedan invasion of Europe, be certainly secure. We saw how the Crusaders failed to appreciate in their first advance the meaning and value of Damascus; saw how Baldwin II attempted a conquest and fell back; we shall see how later they attempted to seize the city and failed. We shall see how that failure involved the ultimate breakdown of the whole Crusading scheme.

Modern historians, seeing the arguments for and against the conquest of Damascus by the Christian power, and the firm and permanent tenure of it by them, as against the policy of alliance and protection, have mainly decided for the latter. Modern scholarship upon the Continent of Europe, and especially in France, inclines to the belief that Foulque proved himself the statesman of the Crusades, because he determined to turn Damascus from an enemy into a friend and abstain from the temptation to attack it. Foulque was certainly the great statesman of the Crusades, but the alternative to his policy—a further effort against Damascus—would ultimately be urgent—and the event proved it.

After Foulque's death, a powerful contingent of men from the West, of newcomers, arrived to secure the Holy Land. They struck the blow for Damascus, and they failed.

Perhaps the true answer to the question put by Damascus is that the strength of the Christians in the East was never great enough to permit them the permanent capture of the city.

Foulque's policy of alliance and quasi-protectorate was only a second best, and he may have known it; but it was a second best imposed by the very nature of the Crusading position, by the difficulty of reinforcement from the West, by the numerical weakness of the Crusading units left free to march after the garrisons of the kingdom of Jerusalem had been furnished.

While we still speak of this interlude between the first triumphal advance of 1097-99 and the fall of Edessa in 1144, we must understand how successful and how necessary was another feature of the time. This was what some called the "colonial" effort of the French.

The term is not very accurate, for the idea of a colony connotes the transplanting of men from one place to another and the vigorous growth in the new soil of the thing so transplanted. Now, the Crusaders did bring all this Western blood onto the coastal plain of Syria, they did plant our religion, our customs, our social organization. But the new thing flourished as a thing transplanted, it flourished as a mixture. There was intermarriage and there was a corresponding change of blood; there was the adoption of Oriental social habits by the descendants of the first Crusaders. It had always been so with every effort made by Europe to impose itself upon the confines of Asia and set up a barrier there. Men living in Syria had to live under Syrian conditions, or very soon they would not have lived at all. The kingdom of Jerusalem and its dependencies could not remain wholly like ourselves. They took on an Oriental color and upon the whole this weakened them in their task, that of resisting the Orient. In the capital point of religion they more than held their own, but all that social structure which goes with the climate of the West, invigorated by the northern winter and nourished by the well-watered lands of Gaul and Britain and the Rhine, was altered. It was altered to advantage insofar as it enabled the transplanted to survive—but it was altered to disadvantage insofar as it lessened the pristine energy and tenacity of the transplanted.

9

HIGH TIDE AND SLACK WATER

There are many places in the seas and rivers of the world where to the onlooker the tide still flows (though slackening) to its height, while, below the surface, the stream has already turned and the ebb has begun.

So it is with most states in human history. They are reaching, or have just reached their highest. The vital spirit of their growth is still apparently at work though not in its pristine force, the momentum of their triumphant past still seems to move them, their memories are still proud and too secure; but beneath these still obvious things which all observers take for granted, the change has begun, the decline is prepared, and the first warnings of doom are at hand. So it was with the Crusading State on that November day when Foulque of Anjou, the source of the Plantagenets, fell from his horse upon the plains of Acre and died.

At the close of 1143 the kingdom of Jerusalem had reached its climax in outward show of strength and in extent of territory, but that which was to destroy it, the reunion of Islam in a Holy War, had already risen in the passionate mind of that great soldier, now mature and about to spring, after a tenacious gathering of power through a long seventeen years. The shadow of Zengi was upon them. Certain elements of strength peculiar to the French would permit a prolonged though doomed resistance for half a lifetime and more; also some reinforcement from Europe, but never sufficient; the mercantile Italian wealth of the seaports helped; a remaining zeal kept alive by recurrent pilgrimage helped also; and, most important of all, the growing power of the military orders with the Templars for main guard were an armor for the Crusading State to the end. But the adverse pressure must prove too strong when once it could be drawn in together from the wide spaces and swarming numbers of Islam to the landward side. This now gathering power could meet upon, and use for its action, that all-important eastern road which ran uninterruptedly in Moslem lands from Aleppo through Hama and Homs to Damascus, from Damascus on south through Moab to the south, the Holy City of Mecca and the unextinguished fires of Arabia.

Meanwhile let us estimate, as it stood in this summit of its fortunes, the incomplete Christian conquest.

The kingdom of Jerusalem, now, in this close of 1143, organized as a feudal State, was in its greatest extent from four to five hundred miles long. One cannot give the exact dimensions because although it had a sort of rough fluctuating boundary on the north it had no definite frontier on the south where it merged into desert land. Moreover, it is not, in that direction, to be fixed at any limit. From the hills which look on Antioch to the south of the Dead Sea is some four hundred miles, but the Araba Valley, stretching on nearly another hundred miles to the Red Sea, was imperfectly held by Crusading works and open occasionally to a Christian advance to the Gulf of Akaba.

On the west the frontier of Christian power was marked enough, for it was the seacoast, save in the extreme northern part where one may fairly say that the heights of the Taurus had been for a moment and might be again, the boundary on the one side (for Cilicia, though changing hands, remained Christian) and the vague eastern marches of the Edessa far beyond the upper Euphrates on the other.

On the eastern side towards the desert no frontier could ever be determined; it was but one perpetual battlefield forever in dispute, the very arena of the Crusading war. Hence the pushing back of the Christians into the sea was the whole business of the men of the desert, the Mohammedans. The maintenance of their hold upon the seacoast and the immediate inland parts thereof, including Palestine, was the whole business of the Christians.

During the first years after the initial successes of the Crusade one can give the kingdom of Jerusalem something of a shape upon the map. It included the plain of Cilicia, with Tarsus for its most western town. That plain was soon lost to the Normans and was later garrisoned, now by Armenians, and now by Byzantines. But the territory of Edessa remains part of the Crusading States. It stood on either side of the upper Euphrates, and ran west from the borders of Cilicia right away to the upper waters of the Tigris; for Edessa menaced entry into Mesopotamia itself.

It must be understood of this northern extreme of the Crusading State, as of all the rest, that there was never full occupation in the modern sense either Moslem or Christian. Today when we talk of, say, French territory and German territory on either side of the Rhine, we mean land fully policed and patrolled, with boundaries plainly defined and watched and, internally, all the organization of a strictly governed society. But in twelfth-century Syria it was not so. A strong town—always walled—and its citadel, or an isolated castle, had a radius of action over a certain district, such action being less and less certain as the distance from the city or stronghold increased; but the intervening spaces were vague. The more numerous the fortified points and the closer together, the more thoroughly was a district held by the Mohammedan or Frankish masters of these posts. Thus Palestine from the southern chain of castles to Acre and Hermon was a fairly close-built body. But even over the most of Palestine one might meet bodies of armed Moslem mounted men, and Moslem caravans came to and fro regularly. Perhaps the most united territory of all was the very narrow fertile strip between the long high crest of Lebanon and the seashore of the Mediterranean which it overhangs: the county of Tripoli. Many Moslems lived there, but all were under Christian lords.

The least consolidated part was the unfertile extreme south between the Dead Sea and Egypt. It was a wide stretch which during all the Crusading century, armies, Mohammedan and Christian, crossed and recrossed at will. It may also be fairly said that all the district linked up by the eastern road from Hama southward (Hama, Homs, Damascus, etc.) was unitedly Mohammedan. But the northern part of that road above the Orontes between Hama and Aleppo was open to continual Christian incursion. Aleppo itself was always firmly held by Islam, as was Antioch by the Crusaders.

As you go south from the vague junction of Antioch power and Edessa power, the Christian territory gets narrower and narrower. *All* inhabited territory gets narrower and narrower as you go southward from the Cilician plain and the mountain country of the upper Euphrates, because south of parallel 36 the desert begins to press in upon the habitable belt, watered by winter rains from the neighboring sea. That inhabitable belt itself gets narrower and narrower as one goes south, until, at the level of Damascus, it is barely fifty miles wide.

Thus the Crusading State at its strongest was a band of territory very narrow, though in the north, from west to east of the territory under the influence of Edessa, there was an extreme width of well over one hundred and fifty miles—one might stretch a point if one included the most eastern frontier castles and villages and call it two hundred miles. From Aleppo to the sea is not much over sixty miles and the eastern third of that was never held by the Christians.

As you get further south, following up the Orontes valley, you come to the point where the great Mohammedan stronghold of Shaizar is not much more than thirty-five miles from the sea. The Christian outposts made a rather better show immediately to the south where they reached the sources of the Orontes, and where the main permanent Mohammedan garrison of Homs is forty-five miles from the Mediterranean, but when you come to the great mountain mass of the Lebanon and Anti-Lebanon, hardly inhabited at all, the most easterly post is so close to the sea that there is not a day's march between it and the water. Virtually, the Tripoli frontier runs along the summit of the Lebanon, and the county of Tripoli at its narrowest was, after the loss of Montferrat, hardly twenty-five miles broad. There were Christian posts held on the eastern slope of the great mountain range, but they were isolated. There was never any full and permanent Christian domination over the great trench of the Bequaa.

From the county of Tripoli southward the district which may be fairly called Crusading territory, in a permanent sense, begins to spread eastward again. It covers all the plain of Tiberias, the southern and western slopes of Mount Hermon, and then southward it precariously follows the Jordan, with intermittent attempts to hold a belt to the east of that profound valley. But east of Jordan and the Dead Sea there was only one point that was really held in strength through the whole century, and it was the famous castle of "Kerak-in-Moab," which was Christian until the final disasters, Hattin and its consequences. From Kerak to the sea is in a straight line not more than seventy miles. Thence southward there was not even a vague frontier. There were Christian strongholds all the way down the Araba valley to the last one on the Red Sea by Akaba, including the important one of Montreal, "the royal hill"; but in Palestine itself all effort to hold a regularly fortified limit in the south ceased beyond a line running west from the southern end of the Dead Sea to the Mediterranean.

The southernmost fortified post along the seacoast was that of Darum, just south of Gaza. Behind it and the Dead Sea at long intervals were two minor posts, south of Hebron. It was not a frontier to hold, because everything was there fading away into the desert.

The general shape of the kingdom of Jerusalem, more or less effectively occupied, may be compared to a battle-axe, of which the handle has been pared away in the middle but left heavier and thicker at the ends: a battle-axe, the head of which (the Edessa district) has the broad part turned eastward.

In spite of its impossible shape, this Christian colony or unit planted right on the critical junction of Asia, Africa, and Europe, and thereby threatening the central vital link of the Mohammedan world, preserved political unity for many years. Even after it had lost its northern bastion with the fall of Edessa it remained, until the catastrophe of Hattin, one thing.

It owed such permanence to two causes: First, that dependence on fortification already described; second, what it is very difficult for the modern mind to grasp, its feudal organization.

In feudal times, the local unit down to the smallest manor was far more independent of superior authority than the members of a modern state think consistent with any kind of order or government. The private local jurisdiction even of the village lord and the existence of a multitude of such lords side by side looks to us like a sort of anarchy. Any two neighbors might indulge a private quarrel in arms, and great overlords might wage independent wars one against the other.

Yet there was a cement. It was the sense of feudal honor and unity binding vassal to suzerain and overlords to the crown which stood above them all. That moral bond of loyalty was very strong. It did not prevent internal dissensions of jealousy and treasonable ambition, but it did prevent the breakup of the political body as organized.

The feudal kingdom of Jerusalem, which seems to us so fantastically loose, four hundred miles of scattered strongholds in a chain, had, on the spiritual side, this element of unity. It, therefore, must be taken seriously as a State, and its careful organization on paper, its careful *theoretical* organization, must not be ridiculed as a mere make-believe. The kingdom had real existence through its king's real authority in the hearts of its component governments, great and small.

In order to understand the feudal arrangements and hierarchy of the kingdom of Jerusalem, we must begin at the south. From south to north you have four main divisions. First comes the kingdom of Jerusalem proper, the king's special department, Palestine. It claimed the coast to just north of Beyrouth.

Next, to the north of it, comes the county of Tripoli beginning just north of Beyrouth and following the coast to the great castle of Markab which dominates the shore from a high spur of land.

Next, to the north of this, comes the principality of Antioch reaching to the entrance of the Gulf of Alexandretta.

Next, to the northeast of the principality of Antioch, comes the County of Edessa.

The kingdom of Jerusalem proper, that is, the territory immediately dependent upon the king himself in the capital, stretching from the Egyptian desert on the south to just beyond

Beyrouth on the north, counted sixteen high lordships holding directly of the king, four major ones, the chiefs of which could properly be called barons, and twelve minor ones. The minor ones (such as Beyrouth itself, Hebron, Haifa, and the rest) centered round individual fortified posts, especially the towns of the seacoast. Of the four important baronies, one had for its center the port of the capital, Jerusalem, the most important town of the near seacoast: for the port, or rather roadstead, of Jaffa had always formed the gate of entry to Jerusalem from the Mediterranean.

The great castle of Kerak in Moab, beyond the Dead Sea, on which depended the fortresses southward towards the Red Sea, was a second barony of even higher importance than Jaffa in a way, because it was the obstacle to communication between the eastern parts of the Mohammedan world (Mesopotamia and Syria and Arabia) with Egypt and thence to the western parts, to Tunis and so to Morocco and Spain. This position it was which, as we shall see, gave Kerak of Moab its vital importance up to the very end of the Crusading century.

The third great barony was that of Sidon south of Beyrouth on the seacoast. Lastly, there was the natural geographical and social unit of Galilee, including the Lake of Tiberias, which made the fourth barony.

Thus was the head division of the kingdom of Jerusalem, sometimes called in a special sense, "the kingdom," arranged; and it is important to note that the great castle in Moab, upon which strategically all depended, was in theory at least directly vassal to the king at Jerusalem. This was exceptional. The castle in Tiberias, for instance, was held of the king only as part of Galilee. But Kerak in Moab was held of the king as a thing by itself, not as part of a district. This difference of tenure is an essential point, for on it was to turn the final quarrel with Saladin.

Beyond the northern frontier of the kingdom of Jerusalem proper, beyond Beyrouth, that is, the feudal tie with the capital was weaker. That frontier seems to have lain on the torrent bed, nearly dry in summer but fed till very late by the snows of Lebanon, which all through the ages for four thousand years has been the dividing point along the Syrian coast and has been called, since the Arabian conquest, the River of the Dog *(Nahr el Kelb)*.

The county of Tripoli was of comparatively small extent, and went northward, as has been said, to the great and often disputed castle of Markab, if as far. At any rate Markab was the northern fortress which, whether holding of Antioch or of Tripoli, was the marking point of the passage from one to the other.

North of this has been noted the principality of Antioch, which had been made into a nearly independent state from the day when the Normans of South Italy had established themselves at Antioch itself and claimed lordship over all the Christians in the Cilician plain.

The word *principality* expressed that special position which Antioch held. It had begun by being attached by oath to the Emperor of Byzantium, and though the oath counted for little, and the tie was soon severed, the event was symbolical of the practical independence which Antioch hoped to establish for itself. The contrast between the county of Tripoli and the principality of Antioch in the matter of size is striking. The whole coastline of the former from the River of the Dog to Markab is not more than seventy miles, and in depth the county nowhere held more than thirty. Of all the feudal divisions of the kingdom of Jerusalem this also was the most oddly intermixed with Mohammedan effort. Up in the mountains above Tortosa the Mohammedan strongholds would form more or less permanent "islands." Beyond these hills, near as they are to the seacoast, the Crusaders never penetrated thoroughly or permanently. Further, this county of Tripoli was divided into a number of separate little fertile plains, of which the largest is that just north of its capital, but of which none can support any great population. Yet the county of Tripoli was a critical district, comparable in importance to Kerak of Moab. It was essential to the Crusading effort because it held the "waist" of the occupation. And there ran through the county of Tripoli the main road from the Mohammedan interior to the coast, the road which most easily unites the upper Orontes valley with the Mediterranean. This road was commanded to the end of the Crusading century by the strength of the gigantic castle which lies beside it, "Kerak of the Knights"—so called to distinguish it from the Kerak of Moab, more than two hundred miles away.

The great principality of Antioch to the north was held easily as to Antioch, its very important capital, but the wealthy Cilician plain—the country of Tarsus—it held for only a short time and precariously. Armenian chiefs and kings entered it. The Emperor of Byzantium claimed it, as, indeed, he had a right to do. He got hold of the most of it within forty years of the first occupation. The princes of Antioch recovered it intermittently, and only gave it up finally to the Armenians after the catastrophe to the kingdom of Jerusalem and the victories of Saladin.

Last, to the north, the county of Edessa, covering a large area of territory but mountainous and sparsely populated, lay still more separate from the central power at Jerusalem. There were fairly good crops on the southern limit of this state where the torrents from the mountains come down towards the sandy plains which ultimately turn into desert. There were considerable towns here and there in the mountain country itself, with Edessa the chief of them. Far off as it was, the Crown of Jerusalem was able to assert itself there and exercise suzerainty. It was the first of the Crusading divisions to fall to the Mohammedans. But in this year 1143, the moment of the kingdom's greatest expansion, it still seemed secure.

This kingdom of Jerusalem, this new Crusading State, this difficult experiment in thrusting back the Orient and re-establishing our culture as Alexander had established it for so long in Asia, had one strategic weakness—which was mortal. Its success depended on holding the "Bridge," the "Neck," the "Link" whereby the two halves of our enemy, the Mohammedan world, hung together. It is a point already emphasized, but I will repeat it here. *The Kingdom of Jerusalem did not hold the whole width of that "Neck," that "Link," that "Bridge."*

Summarizing what has hitherto been said on this point, the following facts may be recalled and our conclusions drawn from them before proceeding further.

Had the Crusaders permanently occupied the *whole* maritime belt of Syria between the Mediterranean and the Desert, they would have cut Islam in two. That is the central strategic truth of the Crusades—but they never occupied the *whole*. They held the western side of it; they failed to hold the eastern side, and along that eastern side of the "Bridge" which the Christians never mastered, the Moslems could communicate at will, pass from their eastern to their western half and bring armies down behind the western invaders of the seacoast.

The failure to hold the *whole width* of the Syrian maritime belt is the explanation of our breakdown: of our failure to restore to the traditions of Greece and Rome all that half of the Mediterranean world which Islam has ruined.

Of the two ways possible to armies desiring to pass from the north of the corridor to the south: one is by the coast, the other along the fertile belt which fringes the desert. The first the Crusaders held. The second they failed to hold. They might have held it when they first came into Syria in their original great numbers. We have seen how they delayed and why, and how, after that fatal halt and wastage of 1098-99, their reduced forces made directly for Jerusalem.

That initial error could never be repaired, because the Crusaders never afterwards had enough men. Reinforcement came only spasmodically and was often destroyed on the way. Europe was not moved to further large and serious combined expeditions save under the stimulus of really bad news from the Holy Land. A conspicuous defeat, the loss of a capital city, would rouse Christian feudal society to some great effort—only when it was too late.

But though they failed to hold the eastern road, might they not have cut it and so destroyed its usefulness as an avenue of approach for hostile armies? Yes, they could have cut it at Damascus, and to have cut it there would have been permanently effective: for just at the point of Damascus the desert approaches the inhabitable belt, so that, with Damascus held against them, Moslem armies could not have marched round it on their way south. But they never had quite enough men to capture

Damascus and to garrison that great town. Every effort of theirs to master Damascus, and so cut the eastern road and therefore close the "Bridge" between the two halves of Islam, broke down.

The Crusading state was, therefore, ever on the defensive against menace from the eastern half of the Syrian corridor whereof it held only the western half. It maintained that defensive heroically enough in face of increasing difficulties right up to the death of Foulque at the end of 1143, the halfway point between the triumphant on-rush of the first great Crusade and the final disaster of ninety years later.

The Crusading state was able to support the strain thus long through three supports: through the wealth of its seaport cities, through the recurrent revival of enthusiasm by new arrivals, and most of all through the great Military Orders, half monks, half soldiers: the Temple and the Hospital.

These were the supports of the imperilled Holy Land. They were insufficient to save the State, though sufficient to prop it up even after its decline was manifest.

Now the decline, which we shall see advancing so rapidly after the critical turn of the years 1143-44, the death of Foulque, the blazing triumph of Zengi, and his uniting of Syrian Mohammedans against the Cross, was one *positively* due to the newly arisen monarchic singleness of aim and command in the Mohammedan world; but *negatively* it proceeded from certain disabilities on the Christian side: the new interests of Europe which led to neglect of the Crusading cause, and the weakness of mixed blood, of half-breeds, neither Western nor Eastern, coming to characterize the Crusading land. This last was perhaps the chief element of the three. Had it been possible to maintain in Syria the old excellence of the Western knight and his chiefs, the breed of men that governed from the Grampians to central France, the chivalry which used the same northern French tongue and lived by the same social code in York, in London, in Rouen, in Paris, in Rheims, in Poitiers, in Normandy, in Anjou, in the Ardennes; had it been possible to maintain that class in Syria not only unmixed in blood but sufficient in numbers, recruited from Western Christendom, it might have won its war. But it was not possible so to maintain it.

One common cause of decline was absent. There was no new development in armament or maneuver adverse to the Crusading power. No new weapon or new arrangements in the field appeared on the enemy's side to embarrass the Christian Crusader.

It is remarkable that in the decline of the French Syrian State, though it lasted longer than one full active lifetime, little was accomplished by a change in material or in tactics.

Even after the end of the affair during the abortive effort at recovering the Holy Places when they had been lost (called "The Third Crusade"), it was still the same story of Christian heavy-mailed cavalry charging into the heart of the opposing line and Moslem lighter cavalry swooping round the wings, darting forward in a swarm, retiring and darting forward again.

Siege work had developed, but hardly changed in character. The fortified works had reached a magnitude unknown to the previous century, but assault upon them by rolling towers, catapults, scaling ladders, Greek fire remained after the fall of Jerusalem what it had been at the taking of Nicaea ninety years earlier. There did not even appear (what one might have thought inevitable) a new and stricter discipline on either side: proper unit formations and their collection into large bodies under one hand. The first great Crusading march had been wholly feudal, with leaders moving at will and the mass of their inferiors incohesive; after a century of war the last bodies were of the same structure, save perhaps for a somewhat larger proportion of mercenary troops.

On the Moslem side there was similar lack of internal military change. Great hordes gathered and dispersed at the very end of the twelfth century as they had gathered and dispersed three generations before. Unity imposed by a Moslem leader like Saladin broke up at once upon his death as rapidly as the unity imposed upon his forces by a routed Moslem commander like Kerbogha dissolved on his defeat.

The lance and the heavy sword were still the Christian

weapons of the Third as of the First Crusade. So with the Turks
of the last battles as of the earliest. It was still the same short
stirrup, the same light curved sabre, small round target, and
small, very swift, Arab mount, rapidly wheeling. The social
structure of feudal western Europe had greatly changed in the
hundred years, the social structure of Syria and Mohammedanism
much less, but the military structure of either party inappreciably.

In one or two details a contemporary observer would indeed
have noted changes: the Christian knight gradually discarded the
long shield for the shorter triangular one. The vizor shielding
the face also had begun to appear at the end of the century;
but nothing of importance had changed, unless we call ornament
important—for it is true that, whereas heraldry was unknown
to the original Crusaders, some few of the great leaders were
displaying special marks upon their coats of arms before the fall
of Jerusalem. In the century after we had lost Jerusalem, when
the Crusades were losing their meaning and had already lost
their objective, heraldry began to appear, but during the first
active struggle it was unknown. The *Fleur de Lys* of the House
of France, the Three Leopards of Anjou, were, in the thirteenth
century, familiar and established emblems. In the twelfth they
were, at least until towards the end, no more than suggestions.

It was, then, no growth in the art of war that favored Islam
against Christendom—nothing corresponding to that mechanical
development which today still favors Europe against the Mohammedan world. Rather was it the political change in Europe dis-
tracting attention from the Holy Land and the deterioration of
our own blood in the Levant.

The mid-twelfth century was making all things new in the
Occident: the main buildings, the philosophy, and the structure
of society—all were recast. One most obvious external political
effect of this change was the maturing of the national idea and
its accompaniment, Kingship. It was the Crusades themselves
which had thus poured new vigor into Europe, and one may
even say that the early example of kingship at Jerusalem reacted
in favor of stronger kingship throughout the West. In other words
there would have been, anyhow, a certain growth of conscious

nationality. The idea of France as some sort of dim unity, symbolized by the Crown seated in Paris, was passing into active consciousness. Rivalry between a French feudal system, though only loosely and theoretically bound together under a French king, and the still looser German feudal system could not but be felt. That rivalry was to appear during the Second Crusade. In the last rally, called the Third Crusade, dynastic rivalries were to be still more pronounced. In general, because the civilization of Europe was being invigorated and transformed even as the stones of the great cathedrals were being renovated and changed, particular interests, stronger in action than the general interest of Christendom against the Mohammedan, could not but pierce the surface of that world and begin to act independently.

It has been said, not unjustly, that the French Crusading State in Syria broke down through the inability of the Western kings to combine permanently in its defense, but it is justice also to add that with Europe as it was now becoming, unity of action in the East would be less and less possible.

There was one particular new political development which was later to have more effect than all the rest: for it prevented the recovery of Palestine: this was the rise of Plantagenet power.

When Louis of France had divorced Eleanor of Aquitaine and she had married young Henry Plantagenet, to whom fell the crown of England and the districts of Anjou, Normandy, and Maine, she brought with her central and south-central France on its western side. There was thus gathered into one Plantagenet hand ultimate lordship over nearly half of Gaul, and though the man who held that lordship was nominally the feudal vassal of the King of France at Paris, he was also the independent King of England.

Henry, the Plantagenet, Henry II, as he is called in English history, had a greater revenue and far more manpower at his disposal than his suzerain, the Capetian king in Paris. Henceforward, therefore, from the second lifetime of the twelfth century there arose in Western Christendom the makings of a mortal feud. The King of France, the Capetian, had under him a vassal, the Plantagenet, more powerful than himself.

It would have been shocking for the morals of the time that the powerful vassal should openly supplant his less powerful overlord. But it was in the nature of things that the tendency to such a supplanting should be at work throughout the West for generations to come. The latent quarrel between the Plantagenet and the Capetian forbade succor to Jerusalem while Jerusalem was still held. When Jerusalem had been lost, that quarrel was to flame up on the very soil of Palestine when Richard Coeur de Lion, Henry II's son, stood there a manifest rival to Philip Augustus, the grandson of Louis VII. This, which may be called "the political schism" of the Occident, rendered imperfect the spasmodic efforts at restoring the Crusading State, and in the interval between such efforts left that State unsupported.

The rivalry of Plantagenet and Capetian was to have longer effect than this weakening of our hold upon Syria. It was to lead to a partial driving out of the Plantagenets from France a few years after the Third Crusade; it was to lead, when the whole Crusading effort was dead and done for, to the devastation of the Hundred Years' War. The conflict as to who should lead the great Anglo-French State of the future was not even settled when, after Joan of Arc, all the possessions of the English Crown in France fell back into the control of French kings. Indeed, the last flicker of that flame was not extinguished until the youth of Henry VIII of England (who dreamt of reviving it), the end of the Middle Ages, and the first tumults of the Reformation. But for our purpose in the story of Christian and French Syria, the Anglo-French dynastic struggle meant only this: that after the marriage of Henry Plantagenet with Eleanor of Aquitaine, the King of France would be more concerned with the rivalry of the House of Anjou, and the House of Anjou more concerned with the rivalry of the King of France, than either were concerned with the maintenance or recovery of the Holy Sepulchre.

But, at that central date, 1143, all this was yet to come. The rapid development of Western Society had not yet awakened active and conscious conflict between what were to become the separated national groups of Western Europe, but was already by that mid-twelfth century a grave impediment to the common action of Christendom against Islam. Another problem was the emergence of the new strong lay governments and the simultaneous organization and definition of the clerical power.

The kings and their officers were creating new and more powerful instruments of administration. The Church was also becoming more [strongly] centralized. The Papacy, challenged in a sense by the new bureaucracy and judiciary of the kings and the greater feudal rulers, was consolidating that expansion which had begun under Hildebrand a lifetime before: Hildebrand, who became that great Pope, St. Gregory VII, and had, before the time was ripe, already envisaged the Crusades and the launching of Europe against the encroachments of Asia. The Lay Power—the Empire, the central governments in England and in Sicily—had now an established quarrel with what they called the new pretensions of Rome—with what Rome called (more justly) the corrupt increase of laical power over the Church brought in during the dark time after the breakdown of central rule by one head over Christian men: "The darkness of the death of Charlemagne."

This new active debate deflected men's minds from the recruitment of the Christian forces in the East, and it did so just at the moment when the strengthening of the kings made their great vassals reluctant to leave home lest their local powers should be attacked by the kings during their absence.

But this returning of Western Europe to its own interests, a product of the new energies of the time, was not the chief peril of the Holy Land. It checked reinforcement, but it did not weaken the distant and soon-to-be-imperilled Crusading State from within. What did *that* was the ebbing of energy due to the gradual effect of climate, but, much more, to the intermarriage of Syrian and French. This mixture of blood proceeded rapidly in the period of Baldwin I. The new generation of mixed Oriental and European blood was growing to manhood under Baldwin II. Under Foulque, that now mature generation was occupying every place. The throne itself, after Foulque's death, was an example of it: his son, a boy king, half Armenian, half Angevin, was crowned over Jerusalem. To the man of the Atlantic and the Channel was coming in, as companion or supplanter, the half-Levantine.

The process was helped on by something which the French carry with them in all adventures overseas, to their good and to their evil. That unique Gallic power of assimilation which, after centuries, has reappeared in the relations between modern French and the Mohammedan world, had, by 1143, turned the Christian strip of Syria into something of a colony. It had produced a sort of social unity in so mixed a populace. It is a racial or cultural asset, against which must be set two heavy drawbacks: Gallic instability in policy, and the lower value of the mixed blood. The same qualities which make the French of today understand and largely be understood by the Mohammedan population, whom they with difficulty administer, were apparent in their ancestors of all those centuries ago: but then, so also were apparent the hesitations, sudden changes in policy, and personal feuds which are the eternal weakness of the Gaul. The same qualities which permit rapid welding of the conqueror and the conquered create also an increasing body of mixed blood [which] at last gives its tone to all society; and that new half-breed of Oriental and Westerner has not the political or military virtues of either.

Meanwhile, connected perhaps with this too-rapid mixture of blood, came a loss of fertility. Early in the occupation there began to appear a certain social phenomenon difficult or impossible to explain but plainly evident in date and fact: the great Crusading families were with difficulty maintained in being: they tended to die out.

It has been put down to climate, it has been put down to the impossibility of maintaining fortunes intact, but neither is a sufficient explanation. All we can say is that the fact was there. The first House of Tripoli ends with the third generation. The great-grandson of the original Count of Toulouse dies without issue and the land passes by adoption to the House of Antioch.

That House of Antioch is another striking example of the same thing. The Norman adventurers of south Italy, one band of them at least, came of a family of twelve, the most famous of that batch being the great Robert himself, the first, called Duke of Apulia. His son Bohemond, the man who founded the principality of Antioch, started a stock which ended without heirs almost at once; Bohemond's own granddaughter was the last of them. But the thing is most striking in the royal house itself. Godfrey of Bouillon leaves no heir. His brother, Baldwin of Edessa, succeeds him, marries three times, and leaves no heir. He is succeeded by a cousin, that other Baldwin (of the Borough). By *his* Armenian wife he had children enough, four, but all daughters, the eldest of whom, Melisande, passed on the kingship to her husband, Foulque of Anjou. But *her* first son has no issue. Her second son has in his turn one son only, who dies a leper just before the fall of the Holy City, and his sister by Foulque's daughter Sibyl (who marries Montferrat) has only one son, little Baldwin V, who dies a child. Sibyl's second marriage gave her second husband, Lusignan, his claim to the throne; he called himself King and had the honor to be ruling over the kingdom for a few months when Jerusalem was lost.

What a contrast to the Capetians in France going on from father to son, from Robert the Strong, to the Valois, four hundred years! What a contrast to the Plantagenets, already three generations old when Henry took over England, and ruling in England from father to son for more than three centuries—till the disaster of Bosworth![7]

But of these interior corrosions the gravest was the mixture of stock, aided by the effect of climate, and what it did we shall see in a moment. Hardly was Foulque of Anjou dead when a half-breed lost the first great bastion to fall to the Infidel.

---

7. For the Lancastrian usurpation, though of evil consequence, was no change of family or dynasty.

10

THE CRASH

The turn of the years 1143-1144 just at an active lifetime (fifty-four years) from the capture of Jerusalem, was not only "high tide and slack water" in the effort to hold the Levant by Western Christendom; it was not only the moment when the kingdom of Jerusalem with its vassal states had reached its widest extent; it was also the moment whence we date the disasters.

The realities of the situation were upon the point of piercing the façade of Crusading power. These realities were the climate undermining our Western men and gradually eliminating their superiority as heavily armored cavalry; the increasing admixture of Oriental blood of which so much has already been said and which will appear of greater and greater importance; and the very great superiority in numbers upon the Mohammedan side—all the near East—a countless reserve of power. That hopeless disproportion was rendered worse by the paucity of reinforcement from Europe and the long gaps between the arrivals of recruitment.

Things being so, all that was needed to crystallize the military situation and determine Moslem victory was unity of command on the Moslem side. So far such unity of command had menaced only, not yet appeared. Zengi had been held up for years by quarrels of rivals in Mesopotamia. These he had at last overcome. He ruled at Mosul as at Aleppo—but he had not acquired Damascus. He could not act towards the South. Damascus continued to withstand his ambition, and its independent ruler still feared absorption by Zengi even more than he did the attacks of the Christians on his borders. Damascus, having taken Baneas, the main castle on the southernmost slopes of Hermon right overlooking and threatening Tiberias and the Lake of Galilee, handed it back for the sake of Crusading support against the threat of fellow Mohammedans of the north, of Zengi's Aleppo.

More delaying to Moslem unity even than this division among Syrian Moslems was the sharp antagonism between Egypt with its Fatimite, that is, heretical, Caliphate at Cairo and the ortho- dox Caliphate of all that lay to the east of Jordan and Orontes, centered spiritually in Baghdad. Jerusalem could play off Damascus against Aleppo and Mosul, but as between all these three on one side and Cairo on the other, it must reckon with a permanent strong enmity. Zengi was advancing to stronger and stronger control. At any moment he might strike some blow under which the whole structure of the Crusading State would reel, and *then* it would be necessary to rely upon, and if possible master, Egypt. Hence the policy towards Ascalon.

For there was an exception to the hold of the Christians upon the seacoast belt—that exception was Ascalon, for Ascalon was an island of Egyptian power. That was the real, half-conscious reason for its being spared. Not until it became urgent to show Egypt the strength of Jerusalem in order to dominate a particular ally was Ascalon taken by the son of Foulque, but only after an interval of ten years, in 1153.

Yet another sign of ill ease, of the sense of possibly impending disaster, was the completion at this later date of the last great Crusading stronghold, thrust out with an excellent strategic judg- ment just at the point where such affirmation of a check to an invading power was needed. This new place was the second Kerak, Kerak of Moab, built by an officer of Foulque's court, Payen le Bouteiller, on the southeastern corner of the Dead Sea.

It has often been said that this marvel was put up to secure Transjordania and Moab; to expand the Christian State towards the southeast. That is a false judgment. No wide district was ever secured by the fortification, however heavy, of one point. All that belt of half-desert land south and east of the Dead Sea was not "held" by either Christendom or Islam, and was hardly worth holding. But what Kerak did do was to make difficult the passage of Moslem Syrian armies from north to south along the edge of the desert, and still more from east to west whenever they should attempt to master Egypt and unite it with themselves. Kerak of Moab was to prove for half a generation, after it was raised on its old Roman foundation, the irritant obstacle to easy passage for the armed Mohammedans of eastern Syria round the end of the Dead Sea towards the Nile Delta. Its splendid walls above the steep, walls six yards thick, high, impregnable, held till the very end of the Latin kingdom, a garrison which threatened all passing forces and levied tribute on commerce and intercourse between Syria and Nile. That the huge thing was built at such a moment and on such a scale is witness remaining to this day of the transition from the security and advance of 1100-1143 to the decline which ended, by 1187, in destruction.

We have seen upon another page to what that decline was due. We have seen that among other causes the mixture of Western with Oriental blood, especially in the case of the rulers, played a chief part. Now, it was precisely to this that the first of the great disasters was due. Allowing for other forces at work, the loss of Edessa at the beginning of the Mohammedan counter-offensive was mainly due to the character of its ruler, the second Jocelyn, the son of that first Jocelyn, the Courtenay, so typical a figure of the original triumphant advance. The mother of the second Jocelyn was an Armenian whom the great Jocelyn I, Lord of Edessa, by the grace of Baldwin, the King, took as wife. He did what Baldwin himself had done: to secure himself the better in that Armenian land he had married a native of high rank, but a native, and the mixture of blood did here what it so often does; it gave a certain brilliance to the character of the second generation, but that brilliance was accompanied by instability.

Jocelyn the Second was neither an Armenian, filled with the tradition of mountain resistance, nor a northern Frenchman of the West, alive with the energy of that blood; he had in him elements of both, but to the detriment of each. When we have made allowance for the difficult fitting in of the Latin with the

Oriental ritual and religious habits, and when we have allowed for the heavy handicap suffered ever since the last quarrel between Antioch and Byzantium, when we have allowed for the isolation of the county of Edessa through that quarrel, when we have allowed for the jealousy and competition between Edessa and Antioch, it is still the character of Jocelyn the Second half-breed, that determines the affair.

When any government suffers great misfortune the man with whom that government is identified will be reproached by history as a matter of course; weaknesses will be read into him unjustly and those with which he may be justly reproached will be exaggerated. There is also such ridiculous exaggeration today of the part played by race, or breed, in political affairs, that a writer hesitates to emphasize it in a particular case. Yet here it must be emphasized, for it underlay not only the tragedy of Edessa but all that followed, up to the loss of Jerusalem itself. We can still say that it was Jocelyn the Second, who with his contemporary, the half-breed Queen Melisande, so conspicuously typifies that new and too-sudden mixture of races which was largely responsible for the catastrophe.

In two things was he lacking, which things were determinant of the result. First, he had no continuity, sufficient will, or restraint in sensual action; second, he favored intrigue for the sake of intrigue instead of fixing a goal before himself and using intrigue only for the purpose of reaching that one goal. It was this non-Crusading appetite of his for physical self-indulgence, and this equally un-Crusading interest in, and mixing with, the shifts and countershifts of his Mohammedan neighbors—the chieftains upon his borders—this interest in Oriental haggling and bickering, which between them brought about the ruin of the northern province.

Moreover, Jocelyn II did not live in Edessa as he should have done, especially at the critical moment towards the end. It was a mountain town and thrust east towards the Tigris. There were more luxuries in the Euphrates valley to the west, and more security. Even when he was there his conversation was with the merchants, with commerce and news; he neglected, and lost

familiarity with, the fighting blood of the hill men and their tried
leaders, the natural defenders of all that frontier. The character
of the time was so personal that the physical absence of a leader
or his lack of interest in the garrisons of his province led at
once to a rapid fall in their military value. Jocelyn found life
easier further from the fighting frontier and in a better climate,
with pleasures around him, at Turbessel on the great River. At
last, in Edessa itself, there remained hardly any Western knights,
only mercenaries, and mercenaries who were ill paid. What is
more, their pay was falling into arrears.

It is true that apart from the defect of Jocelyn's character and
blood another prime cause of what was to come lay in the
minority of the kingship at Jerusalem. By kingship alone could
the unity of the whole Crusading State be preserved; strength
of kingship was vitally necessary and especially necessary to the
maintenance of that distant outpost, Edessa; to the regulating
of the quarrels between the great feudatories, between Antioch
and Edessa.

But kingship after the death of Foulque fell under eclipse. The
regency was in the hands of a woman, Foulque's widowed queen,
Melisande, half native; and the nominal King, her eldest son,
Baldwin III, was a child of thirteen. Jerusalem could give no
orders.

All this was an added weakness to the northern command;
but the root of the weakness at Edessa was Jocelyn himself. Had
some new adventurer come out of the West to inherit or seize
Edessa in that critical year after the death of Foulque; had some
fighter like Reginald of Chatillon[8] from the heart of northern
France appeared as a leader of arms in Edessa, the Moslem
would not have prevailed. But Reginald was as yet but a boy;
nearly ten years were to pass before, still in his very early

---

8. He was to found his fortunes on money, marrying the heiress of Antioch.
    It seems certain that the Chatillon from whom this great soldier takes
    his name was that same Chatillon in which Coligny, the Huguenot leader,
    was born 400 years later: Chatillon on the Loing. For Reginald was an
    ill-endowed younger son of the Lord of Gien.

manhood, he was to cross the sea, a poor cadet from the Loire country, to do so much for the Holy Land and be the occasion of its mortal wound.

As it was, the temporary failure of monarchy, so heavily apparent in Jerusalem (the principle, that is, of a united command), was beginning to pierce in Mesopotamia; and Zengi, the new manifestation of that principle, made Edessa his target.

He had fully understood the political weakness of the Christians at the time, not only in Edessa but at Jerusalem. He saw the opportunity afforded by such a salient as Edessa, presented, with his own town of Aleppo to the southwest of it, with his own recent conquests to the east of it, while to the south was the Moslem strip which united Aleppo to Mosul, where also he was ruler.

Zengi gathered a great force. He used, as had not yet been used, the vast numerical superiority of the Moslems; and just at the moment when Jocelyn II had left his capital and crossed the Euphrates to take his ease beyond the River, Zengi attacked.

It is probable that the fight he was conducting at the moment with Mohammedan rivals was emphasized in order to make the Christians believe him to be too much occupied to act, but in fact his name had become an inspiration to all Islam in those parts. There is a fine phrase of his spoken to his captains at the moment of his concentration: "None shall eat here with me save he be resolute to strike tomorrow with his lance on the gates of Edessa."

On November 28, 1144, that blow was struck; a month later, on December 23, by mine and sap rather than by ballistic, a breach was made. The wall fell over a wide gap of 100 yards and the Turks poured through. It was just over a year since Foulque had died and the kingdom of Jerusalem had seemed to have reached its highest.

The populace and priests of Edessa and their bishop fought desperately, crushed against the gates of the citadel. There was massacre and loot of course—when Zengi himself, though infamous for his cruelty even against his fellow Moslems—suddenly called a halt to it all. He desired to rally the Armenian Christians to his side in his coming efforts against the south, and he succeeded. He continued the murder of every Westerner he could find in the Province as he conquered it, but he spared the Syrian Christians. He gave over the local government of the captured city to its *Armenian* archbishop, whom he pitted against the Latin Christians and who fell in wholeheartedly with that scheme.

Zengi had, in that one day, laid the foundations of a new policy which was to sap the whole body of Crusading Syria. It was a policy of setting the native-born Christian against the chivalry from overseas, and that policy did its work.

The fall of Edessa aroused in western Europe, in all that part of Christendom which followed the Latin rite, a sudden and violent emotion.

It was the first sensational bad news to reach the West out of the East; the first dramatic evidence that what had been universally taken in Europe as the fixed triumph of the Cross was now imperilled. Edessa was an outlying northern mountain thing; it seemed to have little to do with the Holy Land, except, of course, that the name was familiar to all those who held by the traditions of Our Lord's life.[9] The population was mainly Christian. The establishment there of a Western feudal principality had been an accident of adventurous ambition. But it had

---

9. During Our Lord's predication [preaching] the local kinglet of Edessa, hearing of His miraculous cures and His fame, asked Him to come and preach at Edessa itself. Our Lord sent him an answer through St. Thomas, who wrote a letter conveying his Master's benediction and regretting that He could not make the journey. This letter was preserved as a holy object by the kings of Edessa for generations; and Eusebius testifies to its authenticity. There was no sort of reason why this should be denied, or why today doubt should be cast upon the fact of the letter's ever having been written or sent. The unreasoning skepticism of the eighteenth century ridiculed it, of course, but without grounds, not even the common (and insufficient) ground of its containing the miraculous. What could be more likely than that the preaching and healing which had made so great a stir in Palestine should have become famous in the near north; and why should the sending of a letter be regarded as improbable? Here, as in a hundred other instances, the denial of strong and continuous tradition is due to a vice of exaggeration, just as bad as the vice of credulity on the other side.

been the first conquest of the Crusaders. The Crusading house there first established had been the great house of Flanders, which had played so high a part in the Norman Conquest and which was so high a feudatory of the French Kingdom; the Courtenays who succeeded them were the Courtenays of Courtenay, born in the Orleans plain, of a lineage that went back to the roots of the French monarchy, to the earliest of the Capetians. But what moved men most was undoubtedly the contrast between the imagined security of the Latin East against Islam since the victory of the Crusade—the contrast between this security and the immediate obvious peril.

This kind of shock appears over and over again in history. It has been apparent with us today in the tardy, somewhat sudden awakening of sea power to the new influence of air power. Men linger for years, sometimes for more than a generation, under the influence of past conditions; and then are suddenly moved to belated action by a violent new experience.

Since the First Crusade had swarmed out from Gaul and from the Rhine, Western Christendom had gone through a change more thorough than any it had experienced since the Dark Ages; that is, since the period during which Europe had so nearly succumbed to anarchy and hostile invasion after the death of Charlemagne. That change had begun, of course, a whole lifetime before the First Crusade set out; but the Crusade itself had stirred Europe to a new life, and now, in the middle of the twelfth century, our society was rapidly forming upon the model it was to follow during the high life of the Middle Ages. The first gropings towards the architecture of the ogive, the high pointed arch characteristic of the new civilization, had begun; the life of the new universities was awakening. The Spaniards of the reconquest—Leon, Castile, Aragon—were taking on a color of their own. Northern France and in a lesser degree Aquitaine—all that held of the king in Paris—were rediscovering a certain Gallic unity. The now more civilized Germans beyond the Rhine, and in the upper Danube valley, though they had no nationality, had already a vague cultural sense binding them together.

The vernacular languages cannot be said to have yet appeared as literature, though they were beginning to take their first timid steps. Europe no longer had the simplicity of the large social body which had stirred on the appeal made at Clermont in 1095; it had not perhaps achieved a greater energy, but that energy had become more highly differentiated, more pointed. It was certain that if there should be a new movement for the succor of the distant Christian movement far away at the eastern end of the Mediterranean, that effort would be more highly organized perhaps, more rapid, than had been the original conquest of the Levant, but unfortunately it was also certain that the old single purpose of those who desired to rescue the Holy Sepulchre would now be confused with new issues.

The cry for a Crusade was not immediate. The news of the fall of Edessa reached western Europe in the spring of 1145; it was not till the end of winter that a first declaration was made suggesting reinforcement for the East. It was, of course, the King of France, Louis VII, who spoke first, for the Crusading work had been mainly done by those under feudal bond to his Crown.

His suggestion hung fire; western Europe was full of its own problems. Syria was far away. The Crusading State had got on very well so far with the increase of wealth through an expanding commerce, especially from the Italian merchants in its ports, with the constant stream of pilgrims, and with the arrival of many individual adventurers coming to try their fortunes with their swords in the Holy Land. The Pope, Eugenius III, was not eager for the move; and the man who counted most in Christendom at that moment, St. Bernard, doubted whether it should be made or no. After all, Edessa was not Jerusalem; it was not even part of the Holy Land.

But the instinct of our people did not fail them. There arose (as it was of the very nature of the Middle Ages that there should arise) a popular wave of feeling, and St. Bernard, as the animator of his time, fell in with the mood and consented to preach the Crusade.

He was the greatest orator of his time. He bore the most famous name in it. He was the leader of his generation. He roused an enthusiasm almost comparable to the spirit which had moved the crowds at Clermont half a century before. It was at the very end of March, 1146, that St. Bernard thus spoke at Vezelay, the great and famous monastery in the Aeduan Highlands, in his own Burgundy. Some months later, on the Rhine, it was he who persuaded the Emperor to raise a German army, and join with the King of France in going forward.

Should that going forward be by land or by sea? The decision was to prove of the highest importance. The Normans of South Italy and Sicily had ample shipping, and could transport great bodies of men. King Roger (Roger II) would himself have joined the Crusade. But what broke down an arrangement which might have made the whole thing successful was the same King of Sicily's claim to Antioch.

Antioch had been the fief of Bohemond, a prince of the Norman Sicilian house; hence Roger's claim, but the established families of the Christian Levant feared the newcomer. Raymond of Poitiers, now Prince of Antioch, especially stood in the way of accepting Roger's maritime aid. He was not only Prince of Antioch, he was the uncle also of the young French Queen, Eleanor, the heiress of Aquitaine, who would go with her husband to the Holy Land.

That was one set of obstacles to using the Sicilian fleet; another set was a corresponding quarrel between the Emperor and the Normans of Sicily. The original Knights Adventurers who had volunteered to help the Christian cause in Sicily and South Italy, who had there supplanted the ancient but broken-down Byzantine power, had further refused to fall under the Western Empire. He had supported by his arms the Pope against the Emperor; and though that standing conflict between the Papacy and the Empire was for the moment appeased, the head of the German feudatories would not lower himself to accept Sicilian aid.

The route taken, therefore, was not by sea where the Christians would have been secure, but the old way by land down the Danube valley, the same which had been followed by the First Crusade. Moreover, the start was made—too late—at the end of May, 1147.

They were regular armies that went out and they were very large: the French and the German in about equal numbers—each in the neighborhood of 70,000 men. They were not without discipline, though they included, of course, as the Crusades always did, considerable bodies of unarmed or half-armed pilgrims. Their government was regular and they were much more composed of true military units than ever had been the larger confused host which had gone out to victory a lifetime before. Yet they were to suffer even more severely, and their erosion was to be even more thorough than that of the earlier movement.

The King of France took up his banner at St. Denis at the end of the first week in June, made the concentration of his feudatories at Metz, and reached the Rhine at Worms before the end of the month. Conrad II, the Emperor, had gone before him by an arrangement clearly defined, to prevent confusion.

There was theoretically to be an interval of a week's march between the two columns; but in practice that was soon shortened and they bunched, the vanguard of one perpetually bickering with the rear guard of the other. It was inevitable that those who came after should quarrel with the denudation of the country, the buying up of provisions and the rest, by those who had gone first; and it is noteworthy that there had already appeared in Europe sufficient contrast in language and temperament to affect the relations between the two halves of that Crusade. The grumbling animosity between the two columns was a further weakness. Both parties, French and German, had their own quarrels with the Emperor of Byzantium.

For Byzantium, seeing these great hordes of the West appearing again under its walls, grew afraid. It tried to divert their march, especially that of the Germans who came first, by way of the Dardenelles. But Conrad would have none of it, it was for him a matter of prestige to go by way of the Imperial City.

There had already been all sorts of bad troubles between the Greeks and the Germans, the latter complaining that they were robbed: and it is certain that one of their lords, who had fallen ill, not only suffered robbery but (what was more serious for him) burning alive at the hands of the Greeks who had got his baggage. Wherefore Conrad asked young Frederick of Swabia (he who was later to be Barbarossa) to string up the aggressors—which he did. The tension was aggravated by all manner of dispute upon precedence between the one emperor and the other.

The upshot of the affair was that behind the back of the Germans the Greek Emperor made a peace of his own with the Turks against whom he had been recently fighting in Asia Minor. Whether the Turks were actually supported secretly by Byzantium or no, it was at any rate believed by the Crusaders that they were; and it was under these impossible conditions that Conrad crossed the Straits and engaged himself on the road to Antioch. Late in starting from Europe, he was inexcusably late in entering Asia; it was the middle of October before he was beyond Nicaea. It would take a good three weeks of marching to get him to Iconium, the Germans complained that they had been deceived as to the length of the journey—but that was nonsense, for the itinerary was by this time well known throughout Europe from the fame of Bohemond and Raymond, of Godfrey and Tancred half a century before. They marched slowly, and the Turks caught them near that same site of Dorylaeum where the great battle of the First Crusade had opened the way to the East.

Defeat followed. It was on October 26 that the Germans had broken down before the arrows of the light Turkish cavalry; a week later the poor remnants of Conrad's command were back, exhausted, in Nicaea. It was said, perhaps with some exaggeration, that not one tenth had escaped; it is certain that a huge booty was gathered and that the German army was ruined.

The King of France, following after, was still later than the Germans in passing over to the Asian side. He did not have his last interview with the Byzantine Emperor until the very day on which Conrad had been so disastrously beaten by the Turks. When Louis in his turn took the road, he naturally avoided the northern way, on which the Germans had been routed. He went down by the seacoast, by the main road through Ephesus. Conrad followed him at first with the poor, battered fragment of the

German forces, then lost his temper and went back to Constantinople, where the Emperor, Manuel Comnenus, looked after him and consented in the following March to take him by sea with such knights as remained to him and land him at the Crusading ports.

Louis VII and his French meanwhile fought his way through against efforts of the Turks to stop him at the Meander, but in the end fell upon much the same misfortune as had befallen the Germans. They struck him in the mountain gorges before he came to the Cilician Plain, not far from Adalia. He fell back upon that town, which was under Byzantine government, [and] accepted the Byzantine offer to transport such knights as remained to him. Those who remained behind suffered another defeat in their effort to go round by land.

In the upshot this Second Crusade, counting in fully armed and organized forces 140,000 men, appeared at last at the port of St. Simeon which served Antioch on March 19, 1148, with we know not how many survivors; but we can safely say not 15,000—the main part French.

It lay with the King of France, though he brought such meager reinforcement, to decide what should be put before the Crusade. The obvious, the crying thing, was to attempt a recovery of the land beyond the Orontes, where Zengi had pushed back the Christians. All the peril to Christendom lay from Zengi, and Zengi's land (or rather the land of his successor, for Zengi himself was dead) should have been the scene of the new victory—if that victory could be achieved. Nureddin, as we call him—Nur-al-din—Zengi's son, ruling in Aleppo, had for his mission the gathering together of Islam against Christ.

The issue was further complicated by the belated appearance of Conrad and his handful of Germans; the Byzantines landed them in St. John of Acre, just under four weeks after the King of France had appeared in Antioch. A larger division of Germans, who had not taken part in the first disastrous battle beyond Nicaea but had gone by the seacoast, had been brought overseas also by the Byzantines and had appeared in Jerusalem on Palm Sunday, a fortnight before—April 4, 1148.

Then began violent competition and discussion as to which route the new reinforcement and the lords of Palestine should take in their projected counter-attack against the Moslem to the east. The confusion of counsel was due to four causes, the first and most important of which was the eclipse of monarchy. From the death of Foulque until his young son, Baldwin (who at the moment when the Second Crusade arrived was only a lad), seized power, that is, during the eight years between 1144 and 1152, the normal monarchy, without which a Crusading realm could not be moved as a unit with one policy, lay with Foulque's widow, Melisande. This half Armenian was a woman direct, full of energy but violent, her judgment obscured by gusts of passion and an exaggerated appetite for rule. Nominal power in the hands of a woman was not real power in the twelfth century, because it was a century of soldiers perpetually in the field—and nowhere was this more true than in the Holy Land, where battle never ceased, where all life was a life lived upon a hostile frontier.

The second cause of confusion was the now established contrast between the Crusading State and the society of western Europe, whence the foundation of that State had come. It is true that there was perpetual recruitment from the West, but it was either impermanent, or on a scale insufficient to keep the three remaining Crusading territories (Antioch, Tripoli, and Jerusalem) identical in manners and blood with the Occident.

We must remember that it was now close on fifty years since the capture of Jerusalem; there were old men surviving who had ridden as young knights under Bohemond and Godfrey; but the mass of the fighting men who were native to Syria could remember nothing but Syria. A local leader forty years old in 1148, a lord representative of the twelfth-century Crusading world, would have been brought up among servants many of whom were local Moslems and in a household which had learned in great part the Oriental ways. He was familiar with a society in which the local Christians around him were mainly of another rite, and in which an understanding had arisen not only between the newcomers of the Latin Mass and the Oriental Christians of Greek

and Syriac rite, but in a great degree (especially along the central
part of the fluctuating frontier) between Mohammedan and
Christian. The men of 1148 thought of Damascus as a city with
plenty of Christians, though mainly Mohammedan; they thought
of Tiberias as a city not without Mohammedans, though mainly
Christian. They were concerned with the military power exercised in either place, in the one Mohammedan, in the other
Christian; but they saw no precise line of cultural cleavage.

Moreover, in that interval of nearly fifty years there had arisen
that large population of mixed blood to which we continually
return. Most of the half-breeds [were] born of Western fathers
and Eastern mothers; others, in somewhat smaller numbers,
sprung from the marriage of Eastern fathers and Western
women. Of these a due proportion were nobles: the social equals
of the ruling armed class throughout the feudal world. Some
of them (as we saw at Edessa) stood in the highest places. It
was inevitable that the pure-blooded Westerner should look down
somewhat on the men of mixed blood. He had to deal with them;
they were necessarily mixed up with his life, often claiming
equality and receiving all the outward marks of it. But behind
their backs they were now given a slang name—"the colts"—and
it was not meant to be flattering. Into all this already semi-
Oriental world came, upon the advent of the new Crusade,
nobles and their retainers direct from France and the Rhine,
fresh from that simple vision of the Holy Land which filled
men's minds in the Occident. They saw everything as a clear-cut
proposition—Christians against Paynims—the Lord's defenders,
and His foes. The greater shock did they receive when they discovered on arrival the social complexity of their new country.

The third cause of confusion was the divided nature and
divided ambitions of the German and French contingents. I
repeat, there was as yet no conscious national feeling, but there
were already the germs of such a national feeling. If you take
the list of the men who surrounded the Emperor Conrad you
find them nearly all German-speaking, in spite of their high
rank. There was young Frederick of Swabia, the Emperor's
nephew, later to be the great Barbarossa; there was the "Guelph"

of Swabia, Italian (an Este) in direct male descent but German-speaking now; there was Hermann of Bale, and D'Andeche, later to be Duke of Bavaria. From beyond the Alps there was William of Montferrato.

The common soldiers especially felt the contrast—unable to understand each other's dialects and irritated at the foreign jargon they heard. Between Conrad himself and Louis there was direct and striking contrast of interests, which showed itself as much in their relations with Constantinople as in any other way.

The fourth cause was more obscure, and yet it is one which we must especially bear in mind. There was always underlying whatever general movement was made, from the beginning of the Crusades to the end, the memory of Damascus.

It would be an exaggeration to say that the capital strategic importance of Damascus decided the objective of the Second Crusade; a dozen cross motives came in—including the quarrel of Louis VII with his wife and his reluctance to help the Lord of Antioch (his wife's relative and perhaps more) by attacking Aleppo. But it would be a worse exaggeration to say that the march on Damascus was a mere blunder. Had it succeeded and had Damascus been held—a thing perhaps impossible with the effectives available—not only this campaign would have been decided at a blow but the future of Palestine might have been decided in favor of Christendom. On the other hand, it was a heavy gamble. *If* Damascus were not taken, the attack would ruin the old alliance between it and Jerusalem. All Moslem Syria would unite.

At any rate the march on Damascus was decided, and for the warriors gathered at St. John of Acre, Damascus was the nearest and most obvious point against which a direct blow could be delivered.

The ban was proclaimed, the knights gathered from without the King's direct dominions—but it is ominous to remember that the county of Tripoli had no direct representative among those who planned the campaign, and still less the county of Antioch. Individual fighters came from the center and the north, but the direction was from the south.

The concentration was ordered to take place at Tiberias. Once more was an expedition to start in the very worst of the Syrian summer. The host marched by much the same direction as one may take today motoring from the lake to Damascus, except that they went round by the north to Baneas and the great castle there. Thence they went forward round the roots of Hermon, following the Roman road.

It was a four or five days' march at least, normally more like a week's journey for men on foot—and a week of hard going—before they pitched their tents in a wide sweep on the southwest of that city, which still is and has been throughout the ages the central military point of all that land. When they had thus arrived and looked over the gardens to the west of the city towards the domes and minarets of Damascus, it was the end of the third week of July. From the towers of their town and their high roofs the Damascenes looked across the plain to the southwest, newly covered with tents, and contemporaries bear witness to their fear.

Damascus has on this south and west side a large area of intensively cultivated land, the fullest use being made of that oasis character to which has been due for four thousand years the greatness of the city. The perennial torrents which rush down from the snows of Hermon and the Anti-Lebanon are canalized through a multitude of channels to water every kind of crop and in particular masses of fruit trees—the whole divided up by dried mud walls. Another much larger area of garden and orchards lay on the opposite side of the town, that is, the north and east; larger because there was a more ample supply of water. Flowing ditches which irrigated those gardens and orchards were all drawn from the Barada stream which pours, cold and rapid, throughout the summer heats, the natural reservoirs of the limestone continuing to supply its springs even after the snows on Anti-Lebanon have melted away.

The Crusading host thus planted on the south and west of the city had, then, the lesser area of orchards and gardens between them and the walls of Damascus. The mass of trees, the close division into tiny properties each with its mud wall, made a formidable obstacle; nonetheless it was decided to attack it and clean up whatever resistance might develop in its labyrinth. On the far side of the site, north and east, all the much larger body of cultivation and a forest (as it were) of fruit trees was left open; the Christian army was not sufficient for anything like encirclement.

That very difficult task of cleaning up the western oasis was accomplished; the task was given to the French, the Germans standing in reserve. Both together at the end of that first hard day found themselves standing on the banks of the Barada torrent, the creator and nourisher of Damascus, holding that stream two or three miles above the point where it enters the city: from one to one and a half miles above the point where it has been artificially divided into numerous small channels in order to water the large northern and eastern oasis.

During the first day's fighting it was remarked that Mohammedan reinforcement had come in from the north: the mounted Turks and footmen and a formidable body of archers from the internal valley between Lebanon and the Anti-Lebanon. It was this reinforcement which permitted the old and gallant Moslem lord of the city, he who had been the ally of King Foulque and whom so many among the native Crusaders still wished to have kept as an ally, to rally.

On the first day, the 24th, the Christian knights had been so successful that there had been the beginnings of panic within the walls; but they had not yet entered the city nor even attacked its gates. With the second day (the 25th) these Moslem reinforcements from the north arrived and joined the garrison and Damascus was able to launch a sortie.

The Moslems in their new strength counter-attacked during all Monday the 26th and Tuesday the 27th of July. The gates, which had been closed during the first violent effort of the Saturday, were now swarming again with the Damascenes themselves and the newly arrived Turkish cavalry.

In the night between the Monday and the Tuesday a decision was taken under the threat of this new pressure (which during the Tuesday was to increase), and the strategics of this new decision were so foolish that breakdown was unescapable and the inevitable rumors of treason grew loud. There was no proof of any treachery whether by bribery from the Mohammedans or on the part of the native Christians, and in spite of the divisions among the Crusading leaders it remains improbable. But contemporaries believed in it and have even set it down in their chronicles.

The disastrous new decision taken was this: Mohammedan reinforcement having come into Damascus through the open plain to the north and east, and through the much larger oasis there situated, the Council of War decided that the host should strike camp, leave the banks of the Barada, and come down to the north and east side of the city so as to prevent further Mohammedan succor from coming. They proposed to attack the walls from the far side.

There is no need to have recourse to the hypothesis of treason; it is enough to explain the fatal mistake by the motives which perpetually lead to strategic blunders—the mistaking of the immediate and obvious for the ultimate but indirect: the same mistake as made the troops of Savoy stand across the main road to Turin in 1796, instead of standing to one side and threatening Napoleon in flank.[10]

This change of front to the north and east, this decision to attack from the far side, did indeed prevent further reinforcement coming in; but it was too late. It was locking the door after the horse had been stolen. The reinforcement from the north, and especially the archers from the internal valley of Lebanon, had effected their junction with the Damascenes forty-eight hours before. Meanwhile by going round thus to the north and east and abandoning the upper banks of the Barada torrent, the Christians had lost the control of the water supply both of the

---

10. It will be remembered that after Napoleon had compelled the House of Savoy to make a separate peace, he very kindly explained to the general opposing him how much better it would have been not to stand astraddle of the road but to threaten him from one side; giving a neat little lesson in elementary strategy to his enemy.

orchards and of the town. From their former position upstream, above the point where the rivulets diverge to irrigate the great eastern and northern orchards, they could have held Damascus at their mercy. Now, short of water themselves, and quite unable to divert the main supply by which Damascus and its oasis lived, they were paralyzed.

Nureddin and the Zinghid army were approaching from Homs; there was nothing that the ruler of Damascus feared more than these—save indeed the loss of his city to the Crusaders. He had already told them a prophetic thing. He had said to the Christian leaders, "If you do not raise the siege, and I find I have not the strength to defend the town against you, I will give it over to my fellow Moslems. And then you will no longer be able to maintain yourselves in Syria at all."

That is what happened. The Christian host under the King of France and the Emperor struck tents at dawn on Wednesday the 28th of July; the blundering effort had lasted only four days, and in those four days Christendom in the Levant was ultimately lost.

It was the raising of the siege of Damascus, the breakdown of the Second Crusade, which had its final consequence at Hattin, forty years on.

11

SALADIN

THE ENCIRCLEMENT

The attack of Europe upon the Asiatic is over and has failed. The rest of the story is but one thing. It is the mortal sickness and death of the Crusading State.

The breakdown of the expedition against Damascus, "The Defeat of the Second Crusade," marks the outward, visible manifestation of that inward ruin of the Christian kingdom—the potential, impending ruin of it—which could be instinctively felt throughout the Holy Land ever since the fall of Edessa and even earlier: from the moment when the personality of Zengi had been thrown into the scales and when the unification of Moslem power against the now fated Christian effort had begun.

The retreat of the German emperor and the French king to the coast, their departure just before the middle of the century, was a symbol that our high Western civilization, pulsing higher year after year, was concentrated more and more upon its own life and would not nourish much longer the very difficult effort in the Orient.

From that day the whole character of the war was changed. The old episodes continued—the capture and the loss of strongholds, skirmishes and battles where victory falls to Islam or to Christendom, great men falling in disastrous fights, led away captive, ransomed again—all the refrain of all the Crusading time. But the *direction* has been reversed: and the initiative. The tide is now on the ebb and racing out.

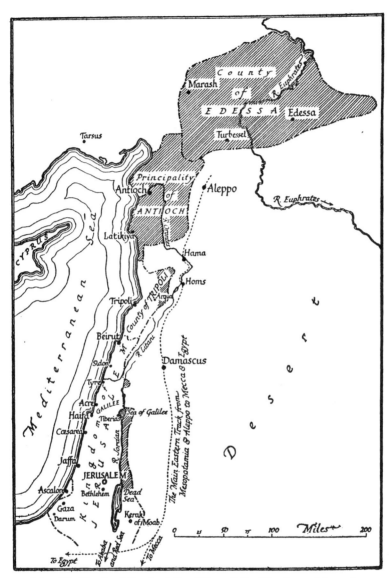

Map IV. Sketch of the Last Condition of the Kingdom of Jerusalem
when it was encircled: shaded portion shows lost territory.

Before the fall of Edessa the French action in Syria, based on the coast and fed from the sea, pointed inland and threatened further extension. After the fall of Edessa the minds of men were transformed. The confidence in further adventures disappeared, the fabric was shaken, and when, in that stifling Eastern night, the mixed host of half-breeds and of Western chivalry turned back from the orchards of Damascus, the whole spirit of the Holy War broke down. All now knew that Christendom in the Levant was on the defensive and all could feel that one issue dominated the future: whether, or rather when, the Mohammedan world of the Near East should achieve complete unity. By intrigue and policy, that unity might be postponed. It might be delayed; it could not be avoided. When it fully appeared, when there was one Mohammedan command all around, Jerusalem was doomed.

Now, whether Islam at the far end of the Mediterranean could achieve such unity or no depended on one thing: the linking up of Egypt with inland Syria, the linking up of Cairo and Baghdad, the putting of the wealthy and densely populated Nile delta and the tribute from the upper Nile valley under the same control as the revenues and government of Aleppo and of the Orontes and of Damascus and of Mesopotamia. The chance of life for the Frankish Christian Kingdom of Jerusalem depended on keeping apart the eastern from the western half of Islam, the country of the Euphrates and Orontes from the country of the Nile. The kingdom of Jerusalem lay geographically between the two; the holding of the ports along the Syrian shore by the Christian power and the long belt of Crusading territory with its fortresses from the Dead Sea to the Lebanon and from the Lebanon northwards physically separated the towns of the Orontes and the desert fringe, with great Damascus for its capital, and Mesopotamia, with its spiritual center in Baghdad, from Egypt.

But of more importance than the physical situation was the spiritual situation. The spiritual head of Islam upon the Nile, the Caliph at Cairo, was Fatimite, irreconcilable with the orthodox Caliph to the east.

The whole business of the lifetime to come, the period between the Christian failure in front of Damascus in 1148 and the wiping out of the Christian power in 1187, lay in the struggle of the Moslem rulers of Syria to unite with themselves the wealth and the population of Egypt: the Christian kingship at Jerusalem could live only by preventing that annexation. Whenever Egypt—schismatic Egypt—should fall into the power of orthodox Islam, whenever the Nile should be governed by the same authority as Syria, it was certain that the end of the Crusading power had come. Though the seacoast towns and the strip of Crusading territory physically intervened, it was possible for armies, and especially for native armies not too numerous, to turn the obstacle by the half desert marches to the south of the Red Sea, and cross the neck of the Sinai peninsula. Spiritual unity having been achieved, physical unity would follow, and when physical unity was founded, the Crusading State was encircled and could no longer permanently hold.

That encirclement ultimately took place. Moslem Syria and Moslem Egypt became one state under one control. The efforts of Christian Jerusalem and its feudatories to prevent such a coalescence failed, and when it had failed the end was clearly in sight. The Crusading State would be at the mercy of a surrounding Moslem world.

The stages of the disaster are clearly marked, and if we set them down here at the beginning of the story, that story will be the clearer.

The first stage is the unification of Syria.

Nureddin had not yet mastered Damascus. The city which withstood the Emperor and his Germans and Italians and the King of France and his army was still an independent state; but after so great a peril, barely escaped, it was bound to take refuge with the main neighboring Mohammedan power. That phase ended in 1154, when Nureddin rode in through the northern gate of the town, which acclaimed him and had not to be taken by force. It was just less than six years since Louis of France and Conrad of Germany had sailed away.

There followed ten years in which the opponents, now eager

Moslem, now anxious Christians, are watching each other with varied fortunes, ten years of balance, during which it is not certain whether Jerusalem will succeed in keeping Egypt free from Damascus or no. These ten years end in 1164, when the conquest of Egypt by Syria began. The Frankish influence was beaten back, Nureddin's officers commanded in Cairo; most important of all, the schismatic Caliphate was suppressed; and in the great mosques the prayers were said no longer for the spiritual head of the Fatimites but only for the orthodox spiritual head, common now to Syria and Egypt alike. The King of Jerusalem, struggling for life, had lost the game. One common enemy lay all around. So ended the second ten years when, in 1174, Nureddin died.

With Nureddin's death comes the next phase, the mastery acquired by him who had been till then Nureddin's vice-regent on the Nile, the man whose name will be associated forever with the destruction of the Crusading power, Saladin.

On Nureddin's death Saladin proposes to make himself leader of all the newly united Syria. He succeeds in that effort, he becomes the master of the whole Mohammedan world in the Near East. It is a matter of a dozen years.

Then, all being accomplished, Saladin is free to strike the final blow and to achieve his great purpose. The whole power is concentrated in his hands, and against such power the desperate kingdom of Jerusalem cannot stand. The decisive battle is fought at Hattin, right in the country wherein our religion arose, within sight of the Sea of Galilee, within a walk of Nazareth. At Hattin, in the summer of 1187, the Crusading State is killed in battle.

It is convenient to mark these steps by their place in the life of Saladin. He is a child of fifteen when his father Ayub (Job), Nureddin's right-hand man and Zengi's old captain, brings Nureddin into Damascus. He is a young man of twenty-five, still quite unknown, when the issue is joined on Egypt and Nureddin decides on the occupation of the Nile. He accompanies Nureddin's army, led by his uncle, and begins for the first time to show his strange quiet talent, and the good fortune to which he is predestined. He is a young man in his thirtieth year when he is given by Nureddin the command of Cairo itself. He is thirty-five years old when Nureddin dies. He is forty-seven when he has achieved complete rule, holding Mesopotamia with Syria and Egypt all in one hand. He is forty-eight when he wins his great victory over the last Christian army defending the Holy Places. Before he is fifty he has ridden in triumph through Jerusalem.

It behooves us, at the outset of that series, to understand what sort of man this was, he to whom such adventures happened.

Saladin was not of the type to which conform most great military leaders of history. Properly speaking, he did not achieve his results through the methods of a soldier so much as through the methods of a politician. He had in common with the great soldiers of history two things only: First, his ambition seems to have arisen late and accidentally, aroused by unexpected original success; second, he acted in any crisis immediately. He decided on what he had to do and, having decided, moved at once—*that* quality never fails in those who achieve such things.

We must remember that, of a hundred decisions so taken and rapidly acted on, only a few bear fruit. The greater part lead to disaster and many more to nothingness. There was therefore a preponderant element of good luck in Saladin's achievement: also he was very cautious. He ran no risks. Whether he should be accused of special cruelty it is difficult to say, so vilely cruel was the whole of his world. He was certainly quite indifferent to the sufferings of those whom he condemned to death and torture for the purposes of his policy.

He was, of course, fanatically anti-Christian: it is the character which has most recommended him to many of our modern historians. Islam always seems roused to a special anger against the organized religion of Christendom, but Saladin exceeded on this point. For him the Incarnation, priesthood, the Sacraments, "polluted the air."

Like all other fighting men in that mixed world, the mounted leaders on either side of that twelfth century, whether Western or Oriental, he took a certain pleasure in the ritual practice of chivalry. Too much has been made of his supposed respect for opponents of equal valor or of equal power. He would, like his predecessor, destroy them without mercy when they were within his grasp, and he would personally murder one against whom his personal passion was roused, as he murdered Reginald of Chatillon, his prisoner. But he was not a man whose common characteristic was either violence or the love of revenge. His common characteristics were, oddly enough, those of the scholar. His devotion to all the details of his religion was a scholarly devotion rather than anything else, and had not accident led him into such high places he would rather have spent his life among books and listening to disquisitions on theology than in the saddle; and as for the sword, he used it little himself—not from lack of courage, but from a preference for overseeing and managing. Mere fighting appealed little to him, but he enjoyed arranging the fighting of others.

His salient mark was a knowledge of man, and he loved to exercise this talent to the full. He was perpetually seeking out motives, and usually finding them accurately enough. He would deceive with skill and wait patiently, even for years, to reap the harvest of an intrigue. Yet he did not plan his own advancement: rather did he use it as it came, because all men, finding in themselves an aptitude, will naturally desire to express it and apply it.

One may sum him up by saying that he was a man upon whom most certainly a great part was thrust by fate, not a man who had sought it, but a man who, finding himself called upon to play that part, played it consistently and well. He owed much to birth and accident, the rest to calculation.

Without a doubt he was sincere in his religion, not only negatively in his hatred of Christian things, but positively in his simple and profound attachment to Islam. When he declared the Holy War it was a personal, unmixed emotion that drove him. He was in this a mixture of integrity and its opposite. No man was readier, in the chief moments of his life, to betray a bond of loyalty, to supplant one who had raised him, to oust the heirs of his benefactor or to lure men to destruction by pretended mercy. Yet he was genuine in praising adhesion to a pledged word, and he proved his honesty at times by foregoing advantage which he might have gained by betrayal.

To the major doctrines which the Mohammedan heresy had retained from Catholicism—the majesty of One, Omnipotent, and Beneficent God, the equal rights of His human creatures, the nature and destiny of man's immortal soul—he maintained a profound and unswerving attachment. He stood erect in the presence of Life and Death.

It was the question of Egypt—the all-importance to Jerusalem of keeping up the quarrel between Cairo and Damascus, the all-importance to Damascus of acquiring Cairo and welding all Levantine Islam into one body for the encirclement and destruction of the Crusaders—that was to bring Saladin on to the stage of the world. But this struggle for Egypt began long before he was heard of.

His father, Ayub, a Kurd of old family and distinction, Zengi's chief man, had ridden out to join that leader on the very night the boy was born—in 1138, the year before the capture of Baalbek whereof Ayub was made governor. It was not till fifteen years later, after the failure of the Second Crusade and the consequent recasting of all Syrian politics, that the Egyptian question grew urgent; and the first manifestation of its importance appears indirectly in the taking of Ascalon by the King of Jerusalem, Baldwin III.

When, in diplomacy or warfare, there is a force which you both desire to have upon your side and to prevent from joining your enemy, there are two ways of going to work. You may plan for an alliance binding that force to your own side by an agreement, which at the same time divorces it from your opponent; or you may intimidate, coerce, master to the best of your ability the element whose junction with your enemy you dread and whose support for yourself you need.

These two policies are not exclusive one of the other. They may be, and often are, worked side by side. So it was with the Egyptian Caliphate and the kingdom of Jerusalem after the crash of Edessa and the lamentable failure in front of Damascus. The kingdom of Jerusalem was now on the defensive and would be henceforward in permanent peril of destruction at the hands of the rapidly uniting Syrian and Mohammedan power which Zengi had formed, and his son Nureddin was continuing. It was vital to Jerusalem that Cairo should be if possible an ally; if not an ally, a sort of dependent; and at all costs that Cairo should not be absorbed by the power of Nureddin.

With that object Jerusalem might cajole, or coerce, or both. As a fact, after the first phase of intrigue, it turned to coercion. It ultimately failed in both. Cairo fell into the hands of Syria, and the encirclement of the Christian kingdom was accomplished. But it was a matter of sixteen or seventeen years before the failure of Jerusalem in this all-important point was complete.

The first sign, then, of the necessary new policy was Baldwin III's capture of Ascalon. It may seem far-fetched to ascribe that feat of arms to so deliberate a policy as that just described; but even if the motive were not yet fully conscious, it was certainly present.

The Crusading State had left Ascalon unconquered for a lifetime. Divisions among leaders, hesitation, occupation elsewhere, had all contributed to save the town. But it was not an accident that now that should be done which might have been done earlier. Earlier it was not vital. Now it was vital. Ascalon was one point on the Crusading seacoast still remaining as a landing place and stronghold in Mohammedan hands, and a Mohammedan-Egyptian garrison had held it uninterruptedly for all these years, after Gaza, and Jaffa, and Caesarea, and Haifa, and Acre, and Beyrouth, and Tripoli, and Tyre, and Sidon, and Tortosa, and Byblis, and Laodicea—all the string of ports and roadsteads along the shore—had long been in Christian hands.

Within four years of the great change Ascalon was seized at last. It was well fortified, the semicircle of its wall-crowned heights stretching from the sea to the sea again. The garrison was permanently reinforced from Egypt by water, and fresh contingents and relays arrived every three months. Its past immunity made its Egyptian owners think it impregnable. In this they were quite deceived, as people commonly are when they go by past form in military matters.

Ascalon, being thus mastered, was a warning on the part of

the Crusading King to the heretic Caliph at Cairo that he must regard Jerusalem as his superior. He might ally himself with Jerusalem if he would, or he might expect attack and compulsory subjection, which would serve the purpose as well or better than formal alliance. But by Ascalon he was both intimidated and warned.

The very next year, 1154, Damascus, which had so long cherished its independence and stood out against the growing rule of Zengi and his son—even during its great peril in 1148—gave way. The agent of this change was again Ayub. Partly by argument, partly by bribes he got the Damascenes to admit Nureddin, and thenceforward all the Moslem eastern half of the Syrian corridor was in one command with the wealth and central position of its chief city in the hands of Zengi's son. On April 25, 1154, Ayub's chief and lord, Nureddin of Aleppo, rode, acclaimed, into Damascus.

The second step in the "encirclement" had been taken.

It is typical of the military inferiority of the Crusading State after the great change of 1144-1148 that it dared not for some years provoke Nureddin on the main Egyptian question by a direct challenge: it was content to levy toll from the rival generals of the Caliph at Cairo and to make this a symbol of vague suzerainty.

Ascalon had indeed been seized, and there was of course throughout the ten years between the fall of that city and active operations in Egypt any amount of border warfare with varying fortunes between the two powers: Christian at Jerusalem, Moslem at Damascus. But during all those ten years neither Baldwin III nor his brother Amaury (Almeric) who succeeded him in 1162 attempted actual invasion. There was something like permanent or intermittent anarchy in the Egyptian government, the viziers succeeding each other by plot and counterplot, and murder. There was therefore recurrent opportunity for action by Jerusalem, yet none was taken until the year after Amaury's accession, that is, in 1163.

At the beginning of that year an Arab vizier who had worked his way up to the chief power under the Fatimite Caliphate after

having been governor of upper Egypt was attacked by a rival
general and driven out of Cairo. He had only held power for
just over six months.

The man thus driven out, the Arab vizier, was called Shawar.
He took refuge with Nureddin at Damascus and offered fantastic
terms for his support against his supplanter. He said that after
his success, should it come about, he would pay all the costs
of the Syrian King's campaign and pledged a third of the huge
Egyptian revenues as a regular tribute to be paid thenceforward:
for it must be remembered how in all this business the wealth
of Egypt, which was on a different scale from that of all the
rest of the Near East, played almost as great a part in the ambitions and rivalries of the two competing powers, Crusading-
Christian and Mohammedan-Syrian, as did its strategic value.

It must not be supposed that during all these years the various
competing, murderous, local commanders under the heretic
Caliphate of Cairo had not thought of appealing to Damascus;
but hitherto Damascus had not moved. It would be time enough
to move (thought Nureddin) when Jerusalem moved—if then.
Each was watching the other, as rival powers today in Europe
watch each other before venturing on actual hostilities. Moreover, Nureddin was growing older and dreaded the ambition of
his own generals.

An approach to Egypt could only be made by Damascus,
through the desert land beyond the Dead Sea, south of the
Crusading kingdom, which former lay right on the flank of such
an advance.

The new King of Jerusalem, Amaury, then, moved first.
Shawar's successful rival, Dirgham by name, was recalcitrant
over the payment of that tribute which the King of Jerusalem
regularly demanded as the symbol of his vague claims to protect
the Caliph at Cairo. With the failure of the tribute as a pretext,
the King of Jerusalem at once invaded. He was checked by the
flooding of the Delta. But the check came at that very moment
when Dirgham heard that Shawar, whom he had expelled, was
pressing Nureddin to strike. The King of Jerusalem had already
retired; he was followed by passionate, repentant pleadings from

Dirgham. Before these pleadings could be of effect, Nureddin had decided on war, six months after his rival, the Christian King, had first acted. He was persuaded to do so, rather against his will, by Ayub and by Ayub's brother Shirkuh. Nureddin sent an army round by the south of the kingdom of Jerusalem through the desert land and across the neck of the Sinai peninsula. That army he confided to one Shirkuh. Now Shirkuh being the brother of that same Job or Ayub who had been Governor of Baalbek for Nureddin and [who] had negotiated Nureddin's triumphal entry into Damascus ten years before, Shirkuh therefore was the uncle of the young Saladin, now just past his twenty-fifth year: a modest, bookish lad whom no one had yet noted in connection with arms or indeed in any other fashion.

Later in life Saladin told in striking words the story of that chance summons into Egypt; how he hated going, having no sufficient equipage or position. How he only at last reluctantly obeyed the command of Nureddin himself, who bade him join his uncle without delay.[11]

Shirkuh, then, took Saladin with him upon this expedition to Media which was to reinstate Shawar as vizier—and with that setting forth the story of Saladin begins.

Dirgham, hard pressed but not defeated, was turned upon by his own new subjects, thrown from his horse, and killed. Shawar, with the Damascene army at his back, was once more in power. It was the month of May, 1164.

Then came the habitual criss-cross of those purely personal intrigues among the rival Egyptian generals. Shawar, hoping to remain independent in spite of his ally Shirkuh, being at the head of a conquering army, kept the Damascenes out of Cairo; or, at least, out of the fortifications. He refused to pay the sums of money he had promised. Shirkuh replied by occupying the eastern side of the Delta.

It is at this moment that Saladin first appears in an important position. His uncle, Shirkuh, gave him the command of the local

---

11. Perhaps Saladin's second expedition. It matters not. The point is that Saladin did not seek his career but had it thrust upon him.

occupation in this eastern province. Shawar appealed to the King of Jerusalem, and Amaury marched against the Damascenes and their Egyptian entrenchments.

The thing ended in what was apparently a draw, but was really a preliminary defeat in this now open fighting for the possession of Egypt. Pressure having been put upon the far Damascene borders of Palestine by Nureddin, Amaury consented to a truce in Egypt. Shirkuh and his Syrian army, who were short of provision—they had been under a kind of siege at the hands of the Crusaders for three months—was ready enough for a temporary peace. The Syrian army went back to Damascus—but meanwhile Nureddin had taken the great castle at Baneas, the Christian outpost against Damascus, and carried off as prisoners the Prince of Antioch and the Count of Tripoli as well.

That was towards the end of 1164. Three years later Damascus, knowing its own power, once more took up the attack.

It is true that Nureddin again hesitated, but Shirkuh, feeling that his original expedition had been a success in spite of its inconclusive ending, pressed for a new campaign, and got his way. In the cold weather at the beginning of 1167, he made a desert march after a fashion in which the Mohammedans were ever superior to the Christians. It was only a small force of 2,000 mounted men, but carefully chosen. It turned at the Dead Sea, gave a wide berth to the Christian power on the north, appeared upon the Nile, crossed the river, well south of Cairo, and began moving against the capital. Amaury, hearing of the movement, had promptly followed.

Thenceforward, for two years and rather more, went on a dingdong struggle for Egypt. It was a struggle in which the two parties, Damascus and Jerusalem, might have seemed to some onlooker equal, and are treated as equal by more than one modern writer who fails to grasp the general sweep and outline of the time. They were not equal, and could never again be equal, because every factor of number, of time, of climate, of blood, was telling increasingly against the now beleaguered Western and half-Western Christian force in the Holy Land.

These campaigns led by Amaury, the King, the brother of Baldwin IV, lately dead, the younger son of Baldwin III, who had witnessed the great change, were really sorties. Nothing could have made them true campaigns with a chance of final victory but sufficient and sustained external aid—best of all, large and recurrent reinforcement from the vigorous chivalry of western Europe, particularly of France. The French nobles were the kinsmen of the men who governed in the now fatally imperilled garrisons of the Holy Land. The French language was still the language of all those commanders; but the French moved not. Those great recurrent but widely separated expeditions which are called each individually, "a Crusade," needed strong news to launch them. For a lifetime there had been no such movement after the First, until the catastrophe of Edessa had stirred not only the French but the Germans to a Second—and we have seen how that ended.

Nothing short of the fall of Jerusalem could launch another such effort, and then, of course, it was too late.

The two years opened by an indecisive action, after which the French forces and the Egyptians with whom they are in alliance besieged Alexandria, which Saladin was to defend. The siege came to nothing. And once again (August, 1167) Damascus and Jerusalem consented to abadon the battle for the moment and leave Egypt to itself until they should return. Late in the next year, November, 1168, helped by the cold weather, the King of Jerusalem came back—and this time the Caliph himself appealed to Nureddin at Damascus. Once more an army from Damascus set out. It was a small one, but it turned the King of Jerusalem's army, it entered Cairo, and the Christians went back to Palestine. For the second time they had retired before Shirkuh, but this time there was no truce—and no return. Shirkuh remained in Cairo as master. He died early the next year, and his death was the signal for the main opening of Saladin's career.

The Caliph, the Fatimite, the heretical Caliph, kept in fearful secluded pomp, a merely religious though still awful figure in his splendid palace, had taken Shirkuh, orthodox and emissary of Damascus, for his Vizier. Now that Shirkuh was dead, he, or rather his advisers, the clique within his palace (for the Cairene Caliph was quite young) chose Saladin to take his uncle's place, and to be Vizier in his turn. They chose him because Saladin "seemed to be unwarlike and easy to command."

Now, there was here an element which had appeared more than once in the brief life of this young man (he was only 30!), the element of chance—and what is more, of chance which, though favorable, the favored one neither desired nor sought for.

But it was part of the complex character of Saladin, a character so difficult to grasp and therefore of such interest to follow, that, an unexpected or even undesired opportunity being put into his hands, he could not but apply to it not only his industry, which was of the scholar's sort and therefore detailed and continuous, but also that most unscholarly quality, his cunning.

He made himself popular—it was a thing he did all his life, and a thing he was fitted to do. Having selected whom he should cow, he was ruthless; but with the undecided mass whose support he desired he was a smiling, generous, and even just figure. His first act on this elevation (he was appointed Vizier by the Cairene Caliph at the end of March, 1169) was to add to the prayers in the Mosque the name of his real master. Those prayers were still said for the heretical Caliph, his chief and nominator, but there was added to them the name of the orthodox Nureddin.

His next act was to destroy the armed guard of black Sudanese, who were the sole defense of the Caliph. He knew that they were secretly hostile. He discovered they were plotting against him, and he tortured, beheaded, and burnt them after defeat without mercy. There he showed again another side of his character, a calculated bloodthirstiness, which pierces time after time through his suave and sober bearing. Perhaps bloodthirstiness is not quite the word. There is no doubt he loved the suffering of enemies. But he loved to do nothing that was not calculated. He was determined that an act of terror should make future armed resistance impossible. And in this he was successful.

Amaury tried one more throw. The quite insufficient forces of Palestine were joined by the fleet of the Byzantine Christians. They besieged Damietta, which, with Alexandria, was the twin town commanding the mouths of the Nile. As with Alexandria the siege came to nothing. Most of the Byzantine fleet was wrecked. A counter-attack was the only fruit of this last serious effort on the part of the Crusading State to check the now almost perfect encirclement of which Saladin in Cairo was the symbol. Saladin raided against Gaza, and the whole year after, Damietta was filled with his activity for pressing in upon the threatened Crusaders.

That was 1170. The following year a last decisive step was taken. In September, 1171, prayer was called in the Mosques of Cairo for the Caliph of Baghdad—it was as though prayers in the name of the pope had been ordered by the Government of Belfast.

But the thing had been long prepared; the wrestling out of sight between the newcoming Damascene power and the old unwarlike Egyptian state—very wealthy but unfitted for arms— had wearied out the less virile party, and they accepted their fate. Within a week the poor young Fatimite Caliph was dead.

The religious revolution, which was the decisive battle in all this affair, which put one spiritual force in command of all local Islam, to the south and to the west as well as to the east of the Holy Land, which later was to put all the revenues and all the recruitment from the wealthy Delta and valley of the Nile to wealthy Damascus and Aleppo and wealthy Mesopotamia in one hand, was accomplished.

Some thought that Saladin, with his old father, Ayub, still by him, might, in his triumph, attempt to supplant Nureddin—who was still their lord. But cunning was still the strongest force, and time was a sufficient ally.

Saladin, moreover, had been unsuccessful in following out Nureddin's own orders to attack that master castle, Kerak in Moab, south of the Dead Sea, which still interfered with the roundabout half-desert way between Cairo and Damascus, and next Ayub was thrown from his horse and killed outside the gate of Cairo. All this made for delay.

There was one last insurrection by the relics of the black troops and of native Egyptians; it was put down with the usual complement of barbarity—everyone was crucified. It had been subsidized from Jerusalem, and on its failure Jerusalem was too weak to move. There was an abortive assault on Alexandria by the King of Sicily, who learned the news of the plot's failure too late, and meanwhile that thing had happened which had been so patiently awaited—on May 15, 1174, Nureddin, after a short illness, was dead.

KINGSHIP

The doomed kingdom of Jerusalem being now encircled, the next progress towards its destruction would be the gathering of that encirclement into one military command.

For those who admire craft in public affairs, a perfect spectacle is presented by Saladin immediately upon his hearing of Nureddin's death. Nureddin had left a little son, eleven years of age, to continue the dynasty of his grandfather, the great Zengi. Saladin at once had coins struck in the image of that royal boy and had prayers said in his name, public prayers in the Mosque at Cairo, which ceremonial act was the recognition of royalty.

He did more. He sent a letter to confirm and to make permanent the record of his loyalty to the great house which had made his father, Ayub, and his uncle, Shirkuh, and himself. This letter he dispatched straight to Damascus. In it he blamed other magnates for having taken over the guardianship of the young king and affirmed his own special devotion, saying that he saw with pain how they had arbitrarily taken over guardianship of "his Master, my Master's son." He went on to say that he, Saladin, was coming at once to do homage and to show his gratitude for the good things the boy's father had showered upon him.

Whereupon dissension having arisen (as a matter of course) between Damascus and Aleppo, to which the young heir of Nurredin had been taken, he chose the best seven hundred out of his mounted men and made off across the desert fringe round by the south of Palestine, slipped through the widely separated posts and small thin garrisons of the Christians south of the Dead Sea, and rode into Damascus on November 27, 1174.

He had come to break his word with that thoroughness and foresight which both belonged to his inmost self.

To us of the West such hypocrisy is revolting; but then, we have difficulty in apprehending the Oriental mind.

Here let us note in connection with that small column of seven hundred light-armed men on their light swift Arab horses, what was one chief factor in all the success that lay before Saladin. *He now possessed the permanent nucleus of an army.* The troops whom he had maintained and drilled after regular fashion in Egypt had become, as it were, professional, and in that fluctuating fluid world of Islam such a solid kernel was of incalculable value.

It is something that appears fairly often throughout history in places and times where social habits and political institutions do not lend themselves to standing armies and trained bodies of soldiers. By having to maintain a prolonged, uninterrupted effort a leader finds himself, without having perhaps at first intended it, possessed, at the end of some years, of a true army, a body of men steeped in the habits of military life and obedience: separate, increasingly superior in quality to the unorganized bodies whether of civilians or of men temporarily armed whom they have to meet. Of such a sort were Cromwell's cavalry regiments at the end of the Civil War when the great powers of Europe competed for his alliance. Of such a sort were the formations of the French Revolution within some few years of its outbreak, and especially after the campaign of Lombardy. Of such a sort now, in this late autumn of 1174, was the immediate command of Saladin.

He went forth at once to besiege Aleppo, and that young "My Master, my Master's son," to whom he had been so devoted on paper a few weeks before. He did not immediately succeed, but he beat off the young heir's cousin, another grandson of Zengi, who commanded in Mosul to the east, and was lord of Mesopotamia. The combined troops of Mesopotamia and

Aleppo attacked Saladin near Hama. His veterans cut the attackers to pieces.

After that victory Saladin went the whole hog, a thing he never did in all his life until he felt certain. After such a period of intrigue he declared himself king, had his name put into the prayers as sovereign and struck coins whereon the name of Nurredin's son no longer appeared, but only his own, "Yussuf (Joseph), Ayub's son."

Though he felt himself so far secure, he was still on the defensive, with enemies all around. They had already made an attempt upon his life by that strange sect of dissenting fanatics, the "hashash eaters," of whom we have made the word "assassin." These men were a small group, Ismailite in tradition, who hated both orthodoxy and a strong government in any hand. They were half brigands, half a secret society. They had come from the north to fix themselves in the difficult mountain tangle lying between Antioch and Laodicea: a country difficult to penetrate, even today. Their castles were built on the peaks of those hills, inaccessible, reputed impregnable. They sent out men to murder Saladin, and in an attempted campaign against them in their own wild country he failed altogether. His failure had one good result, it produced fine daemonic legends. In order to account for the ill success, those about him spread supernatural stories which have about them the flavor of the Arabian Nights.

He was opposed also by sundry in Damascus itself, but his trained troops were invincible and were so dreaded that he counted confidently on his future. That future seemed specially prepared for him and for that scheme of a final Holy War against the Christians and their Faith, which had begun vaguely to take shape in his mind.

What made him thus confident was the disaster that had fallen on Jerusalem and the Crusading State. Less than two months after Nureddin's death his rival, the Christian champion, King Amaury, had died—on July 11, 1174. Like Nureddin, Amaury had left no heir but a child: a boy of 13 who was called King under the title of Baldwin IV. During those two years, therefore, which were filled by Saladin's seizure of Damascus and successive attempts upon Aleppo, the hazarded Christian realm between him and the sea was stricken in its vital element, the element of monarchy.

For not only was the new king a boy under regency and [the Crusading State] in peril of political chaos thereby, but the East had done its work upon him, and he was known to be already a leper.

As against the enormous numbers of Islam, the masters of the Crusading State, the French nobility, and the merchants of the seaports—themselves hampered by Mohammedan subjects and functionaries—had one force which Islam has never had: the Roman conception of a *State,* and with it the Roman inheritance of a continuous single central command; the great legacy of the Empire to us Europeans. It did not suffice.

Islam did indeed know monarchy in fits and starts; Zengi had been an example of that, and now Saladin was already another. When Islam thus produced an ephemeral local dynasty it enjoyed single command, but it never conceived the political idea of political continuity. Just as its religion was all-pervading, so its lay controls were personal and passing. Leaders in Islam, warriors whom others would follow, rose like a wave of the sea and they or their descendants sank again as do waves. So it had been with Zengi, so it was to be with Saladin.

As against such instability the Western tradition had rooted a dynasty at Jerusalem. The poor sick lad now on the throne was the fifth in succession from the first Baldwin who had made the monarchy more than seventy years before. It was but a spiritual force to set against the overwhelming masses that could be gathered against it from all around. It was not sufficient to save the Crusading State, but such as it was it was a strength sufficient to bolster up the few last years of the Cross in Jerusalem.

At the end of the following year, 1177, there fell an incident which shows at once what the dying Christian monarchy could still do with its still superior type of fighting man, the mounted knight, at its orders—*and* how pressing the power of Saladin had become.

On November 25, 1177, Saladin with something like 12,000

behind him led a raid right up to the seacoast, pointing at Ascalon. Outside the walls of Ascalon, to the east, the young leper King, vastly outnumbered, won a victory against the raiders from which Saladin barely escaped on a fast camel.

But the significance of that fight, of that local Christian success which bore no fruit, was not the irresistible charge of a few Christian knights affirming itself once more over the Orientals; it was rather the fact that Saladin should take it for granted that he might at will ride at the head of troops right up to the coast of the Mediterranean. In the next year he won a victory in his turn against the Christians outside Hama, notable for the massacre in cold blood (by Saladin's orders) of the prisoners. The year after, 1179, he again rode right up to the seacoast at the head of an army, passing through northern Galilee unchecked and menacing Sidon itself. In the fighting he took prisoner the chiefs, the masters of the military orders, the young leper King himself, and netted enormous ransoms—Baldwin alone paying over 150,000 Tyrian pieces of gold.

Not only could the Mohammedan now almost at will pass through the whole breadth of the Christian kingdom and come up to the shore, but the rapidly uniting kingdom of Saladin could bring up the fleet from Egypt, and, a couple of years later, he nearly captured Beyrouth, after bombardment from the sea by machines mounted on the decks of his ships.

The whole story, then, is of continual, increasing, and soon to be intolerable, pressure; and the end might have come even then, five years before it did, had not Saladin been diverted for the time by threats of attack from the east. The ever-swirling Mohammedan world of armed horsemen, changeful in allegiance, prepared to attack him from Mesopotamia. He turned his back to Palestine and rode for the great rivers.

He did not take Mosul, but he cowed it, and he exchanged with it as against such places as he had seized during his Mesopotamian invasion the, to him, all-important fortress of Aleppo. He rode into that town on June 12, 1183. It was the crown of his long effort, and yet he had to wait somewhat before he could deliver the final blow. For though Mesopotamia had bowed before him he did not feel that he could yet use it as a recruiting field, nor even that he was fully safe for the future against attack therefrom. Once more he marched against Mosul, fell ill, and was on the point of death. Once more he avoided direct attack upon the walls, but this time he had no fears for what was to come. All Mesopotamia accepted him for suzerain, and the ruler of Mosul was ready to follow him in war. Therefore, by the spring of 1186 things were ready for the last phase.

During this eastern diversion there had been a truce patched up with the kingdom of Jerusalem. That truce is yet another proof of the relation between all that was left of Christian power and the now consolidated Mohammedan organization around it.

There was indeed among the vassals of the poor, dying young leper King only one man left whom Saladin feared as a fighter and who for the vigor of his temperament, the determination to keep up the resistance, was feared upon the other side. That man was the savage, but most capable, soldier, Reginald of Chatillon. Other barons the Moslem knew and respected as great fighters still; Hugh of Toron, the Constable, who had fallen where the Damascus road crosses the upper Jordan, where now the frontier bridge is at Jacob's Ford; or that unfortunate but valiant lover and knight, the lord of Ramleh. Saladin took him prisoner, too, and thereupon showed his chivalry by pulling out the Christian noble's teeth until he was ready to promise a fantastic ransom. There was the Master of the Templars, whom perhaps Saladin hated most of all for wearing the Cross and for his monastic vows, but the man whom he feared most was still Reginald of Chatillon.

He was that Reginald who had come as quite a young man from the Loire valley, sailing out East on quest, and had enjoyed and suffered such astonishing adventures, committed so many atrocious crimes, and fought like a lion in the marches of the north. He was that Reginald who in youth had mastered and married the heiress of Antioch and had ruled there. He had fallen prisoner to the Moslem twenty-five years ago, and of those twenty-five had spent sixteen as a prisoner in Aleppo castle. After his release, and now elderly as the lives of fighting men

in Syria then went, he had married the heiress of the Transjorda-
nian barony and had become lord of the strongest castle, and
the one most boldly fronting Saladin's power, the great Kerak
of Moab, the stumbling block on the roundabout way from
Damascus to Egypt.

Saladin would have given his left hand for Kerak. He besieged
it on its precipice, once and once again, bringing all his power
against it and the strongest siege train men had yet seen. But
the twenty-foot walls of stone stood on their height in that
wilderness and still defied him, and Reginald carried on there,
the chief menace, or at least challenger: a man who had actually
dared to attempt a raid on Mecca, and who refused to despair
even now of the Christian power. But he should have despaired,
had he used his reason, a thing so wild a man would never use
save immediately and tactically in the field. For, indeed, there
was already no hope, and once the Mesopotamian affair was
settled, once Saladin's hands were fully free and all Syria, all
Egypt, mobilizable at his command, the final blow would fall.

In the midst of all this the poor young leper King died. He
had been holy as well as gallant, and, in the midst of his fearful
trial, constant in gallantry as a soldier and in cares as a king.
He was not twenty-five when they buried him on Golgotha, by
the side of the kings, his forerunners, and now was Jerusalem
abandoned and lacking all guidance.

Baldwin IV, dying, had pointed out as his successor the little
child, his nephew, the son of his sister, Sybilla, a boy five years
old. The little fellow died after a few months, and what authority
was to be found? What command over the predestined victims
of the Holy Land? Who could rally them now?

In feudal law, by all the customs of France and of the West,
the tall, fine young knight, Guy of Lusignan, was heir; for he
was the new husband of Sybilla, the daughter of Baldwin III
and the sister of the dead leper King: the mother of the child
who had just died in his turn.

But the strict law of heredity, if such an idea may be said
to have already crystallized as early as 1184, did not hold in
the Holy Land as it did in western Europe, for the Holy Land

was under siege, and needed the best soldier it could find. All the Lusignans were of good blood and proper soldiers, but a better leader was Raymond of Tripoli, the third of that name to rule the vassal state of the mid-coast, the Phoenician shore.

Moreover (what was of the highest moment in such a crisis), Lusignan was a newcomer. That would not have mattered a generation earlier, but the Syrian-born nobility was beginning to have a national feeling of its own. The great bulk of the lords of castles and of land were for Raymond.

What turned the scale was the intense will power and thrust of two men, the Master of the Templars and Reginald of Chatillon: the first as an enemy of Tripoli, a violent personal enemy; the second, because he desired to be master, supported Guy. Guy was crowned, but crowned under the protection of Reginald, that is, of Kerak of Moab.

Raymond, persuading himself perhaps that it was policy of a sort and a postponement of doom for the Christian kingdom, entered into a peace with Saladin upon his own initiative: a peace that might be called an alliance. Whereupon men called out treason upon him.

Against Guy thus apparently isolated, Saladin still held his hand; but he was sending out his messengers to his vassals, his preparations were made, he only waited the occasion. Nor was occasion necessary to him. Yet occasion was afforded him: fortune gave him his excuse with both hands.

Sometime early in the year after Guy's coronation (or possibly a few days before the turn of the year), Reginald of Chatillon had issued from his stronghold and swooped, not for the first time, upon the caravan for Mecca, the largest and the richest of all. He held it to ransom prodigiously, and now the enemy could energize all his forces with moral indignation for the Holy War upon which he was determined, and the time for which was ripe.

The lord of Kerak refused any compensation for his deed, though the King whom he had made begged him to yield. If he must go down, he would go down fighting. He said he was lord in his own house. The Count of Tripoli had made a truce with Saladin; he was free to do so if he willed; but Reginald thought nothing of such arrangements, and trusted them and Saladin not at all. Towards Easter, which fell in that year, 1187, on March 29, Saladin, pleading virtue and honor and resenting in particular the detention of his sister by Reginald during that or some previous raid, mobilized all Islam from the Tigris to the Nile.

The spring days were full of the gathering. By the last week of June the Sultan could review a force of perhaps 100,000 men, such a force as none had seen since the First Crusade; and 12,000 of them were fully armed, mail-clad chiefs and leaders, corresponding to the knights of Christendom. In a crisis so mortal Raymond of Tripoli, who had a few weeks before allowed the entry and passage of Saladin's men through his lands, rallied to the common cause, whether from shame or from policy.

He, Reginald of Chatillon, the Master of the Templars, and the King, perhaps 1,000 knights, or at the most 1,200, some 15,000 to 20,000 all told with the footmen and mercenaries, began their concentration. By cutting to the bone all the garrisons and leaving walls almost defenseless, by spending all the money in the treasury of the Templars for the hire of Moslem troops as well as Christians, there may have been got together a fifth or a quarter in mere numbers of what Saladin was bringing against them; but in the decisive arm, the fully equipped, mailed Knights, they were only one to ten.

12

HATTIN

As a man goes up the fine new road from Tiberias and the shores of the Sea of Galilee towards Nazareth, he mounts ever upward into the Galilean hills, and shortly, on the shoulder thereof, but when he has already lost sight of the lake below, he will note upon his right to the north a rising slope of strange formation. It is a bit of sward, not steep, but rather in the shape of a wave mounting to its crest, and on that crest against the sky two low hummocks of rock stand out through the turf, marking a sort of double summit above the field. The green sward sweeps on beyond the road, which here cuts through it, so that the traveller upon it has a complete view of the wide-flung open grass.

That field now so empty, on which he gazes, should be as famous as any field in the world. For it is the field in which Christ and His Cross went down before Islam: it is the battlefield of Hattin.

* * *

One cannot say, "Hattin! Hattin! Hattin!" as the poet could say, "Salamis! Salamis! Salamis!" The rhythm is not right. It is a pity; for if ever a battlefield deserved to be regarded as Salamis was regarded it is the battlefield of Hattin. Indeed, it was the reverse of Salamis. It was the revenge of Salamis. At Salamis the East was defeated; and the thrusting back into Asia of the Oriental, which Alexander was to complete and crown and fix for a thousand years, was begun.

With the Arab conquest of Syria and the West, the Orient

235

came back as in a tidal wave. With the First or Great Crusade a second thrust back begins, and it seemed at one moment as though we had restored our race to its ancient dominion over all the shores of the inland sea. But the high adventure died and Hattin was the grave thereof.

On Thursday, July 27, 1187, under the burning Syrian sky, more fierce even than its wont (for all men record the furnace breath of those days coming in from the desert to the east and shifting to Galilee), the countless army of Saladin lay in its tents all around the sacred water of Galilee where that lake lies in its mountain hollow far below the sea.

The innumerable infidel host covered all the rising slopes whereon the ruins stand of those places whose names have transformed the world—Capharnaum and Magdala and the rest. The Moslem had seized and burnt the town of Tiberias itself, closely besieged the castle wherein the Countess of Tripoli lay defending her husband's fortress. But for the threatening of those walls only a detachment was needed. The great mass of the Moslem army covering the parched lands which swell up towards the Galilean heights from the lake shore faced westward, awaiting the movement of that Christian victim State which they were marching to destroy. One who looked down upon the swarm of men and sea of canvas said that it was like the Assembly for the Day of Judgment, so great were the numbers. Up over the lift of the hilly land which gradually rises more than 2,000 feet over the waters, down on the further slight decline of its westward drop towards the sea plain are the pasturage and springs of Saffuriya, 15 miles and more in direct line from the lake's edge; by the stony track which made its way through the Galilean uplands it was nearer 20 miles: *and between those wells of Saffuriya and the lake there was no water.*

On that same Thursday council was held over there at Saffuriya a forced march away, a long day's going, and the chiefs of the Christian army consulted on their plan.

There were two policies. One policy was to march with the next dawn right east over the parched upland and make straight for Tiberias, in spite of the magnitude of Saladin's forces which

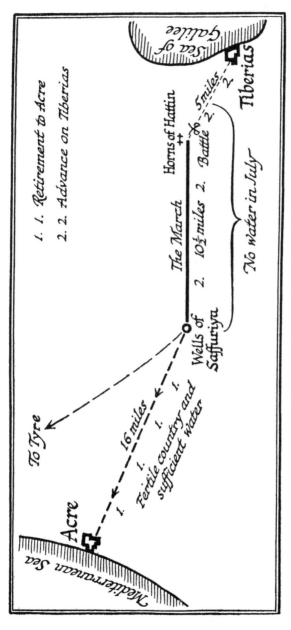

Map V. Sketch showing the alternatives of retirement to Acre and march to Hattin.

barred the way. So spoke the Grand Master of the Templars; so spoke Reginald of Chatillon; and Guy, the King, was molded by their insistence.

It was a hazard, but all was a hazard, since they were at odds of 5 to 1 even in foot, and in mounted fully accoutred cavalry—altogether the decisive arm of the moment—at odds of 10 to 1. Over and over again Western chivalry had been able to break through and ride down the Eastern men, even where, as at Ascalon, the odds had been on this scale. It would not be victory, still less would it be a decision, but they could stand behind walls in Tiberias and the shock might raise the siege.

The other policy was earnestly pleaded in that fatal night by Raymond, the Count of Tripoli, suspect for his quarrel with the King and with the Templars, but still more suspect for his recent alliance with Saladin and his half-desertion of the Christian cause.

Now, what Raymond proposed was this: to march with the dawn, not east but west, not on Tiberias nor towards the Mohammedan myriads, but away from them downhill to the seacoast, a shorter march and an easier one, and to stand behind the defenses of Acre.

The fortress of St. John of Acre was not only the chief emporium of the Christian coast, full of provisionment for the maintenance of an army on the defensive, but the nearest place of refuge. Raymond spoke earnestly; but he did not convince. His record was against him.

"Though my wife is within those walls of Tiberias," he said, "and my children there and my goods, and though it is my own castle in my own land, yet I would rather all those were lost, my wealth there and those of my blood, rather than that the Kingdom itself should be thrown away; and surely if you march on Tiberias you will destroy the realm forever. I know the Turkish armies, I have seen them for a lifetime—and never was there gathered such an army as this."

After a disaster the policy which led to it is met with execration and condemned for folly. Any other alternative policy then looks better, and men marvel that the right line was not taken.

But if historians would consider the problem calmly, they would see that the arguments for marching on Tiberias and against the retreat on St. John of Acre were stronger than men in the agony of subsequent defeat allowed for.

In order to gather even this Christian force now present at Saffuriya, in its crying inferiority to Saladin's, Palestine had been swept bare. There was nothing that could certainly hold, not Jerusalem itself, not even Kerak of Moab. All the defenders of the State were gathered there, at the wells of Saffuriya. If the army refused battle and fell back behind the defenses of St. John of Acre, they left the whole land at the mercy of the invader. And was it so sure that the army could fall back in safety? Saladin's riders would press them hard. The Moslem foot would follow on their heels. The chances were for an action outside Acre's walls in which the Christians would be swamped, or, if they had the luck to get behind those walls before the pressure was overwhelming, how long could they there hold out, with all the strong places and castles of the land falling around them? Time pressed, as did money for the mercenaries. It might be best to hazard all upon one blow and break through to Tiberias, if the thing could be done.

Raymond of Tripoli, knowing what that burning land would be in the next torrid morning, after the furnace night under the desert breath, foreseeing what their most terrible foe and Saladin's chief ally, mortal thirst, would do, despaired. He cried out through the night, "The Kingdom is lost!"

With the dawn of the next day, Friday, July 3, 1187, they set out. King Guy in the center of the column, Raymond of Tripoli in the van, the Templars, the Christian foot and mercenaries following last: Nazareth to their right and Cana of Galilee. All that Friday the torture of thirst increased upon them. Man and beast were maddened for water.

They should by the rules have pushed on and made a forced march of it in the darkness, but no military rule held. The strain was too great. They could no more. It was Raymond of Tripoli who advised the halt or gave way to the demand for it. So they bivouacked, save such few as were in tents upon the slope which rises to the horns of Hattin. Already while the daylight lasted skirmishers from the Arab host had harassed them and in their exhaustion after that pitiless day, stumbling over the limestone and the dried shrivelled grass of summer, their hearts were already failing.

So the night passed, with the oven air from the desert filling it. With Saturday's dawn they formed, to see whether it might be possible, in spite of exhaustion, to battle through to the water, to the lake which lay so many hundred feet below.

But already the outflanking had begun. And as the gradual light broadened they saw that the immensely greater numbers of the infidel were about to surround them. Up under the rocky point of the horns on the top of the gentle slope sweeping north-ward King Guy had pitched his red tent, and round it rallied the chivalry of the Holy Land. At his orders were the much greater body of footmen, but though greater how much less than the Moslem all around! And from that Moslem circle there poured successive flights of arrows. Saladin, careful in all his organization, had his munitionment of missiles calculated and ample and borne by scores of camels, and not only the loads on the beasts but great reserves of further shafts—hundreds of loads of them.

As the sun climbed higher, the damnable heat still grew. The old tactic repeated once again, as it had been so often since the first march of the Crusaders and since Antioch—the setting on fire of the dead grass—filled the air with smoke under that slight hot easterly air. In such a pass the King and the great barons about him tried a last throw. They charged. Their unfortunate mounts had still the energy to gallop in line down the slope and, exhausted as they were, the Western blood still told. The encir-cling line reeled. Saladin, tugging at his beard, called on God to confound the demon. The mounted knights summoned the Christian infantry in vain. These, huddled together like beasts for the slaughter, drooped and did nothing. They could not even drag themselves forward; and soon all was a confusion of the Saracen thousands breaking into the formations, separating knots of staggering Christian men, pressing inward on all sides, slaughtering and gathering prisoners by scores. Then the red tent of the King on the furthest of the slope, under the rocks, was seen to waver and to go down. And he himself and all those about him were caught as in a net, and the struggle was over.

Raymond of Tripoli, charging once more, broke through westward towards the coast and rose with those about him till he had thrown himself into Tyre, nearly 50 miles away. It was a mere flight, but it was to prove of service, for Tyre remained in consequence the only port in Crusading hands and through it there came later that attempted relief and that partial reconquest of the coast which we call the Third Crusade, but which indeed was but the confirmation of failure.

* * *

Up on the battlefield, under the horns of Hattin, King Saladin had ordered his tent to be pitched and summoned his chief prisoners to be brought before him. King Guy, the legendary Chatillon, the Master of the Templars, and the rest. And when Saladin saw this Reginald the victim, for whose blood he had thirsted so long, he burst into a fury, taunting him and challenging him. That soldier, the lord of Kerak, was offered his life if he would renounce his faith. He refused, and Saladin, shouting "swine," drew his sword and cut the man down at the shoulder. The guards dispatched him. To the King, Saladin said, "Kings do not kill kings," but murder was in his heart, and that intense hatred of Christian things which made him especially the murderer of the military orders, for they were dedicated to God, celibate, and armed: their whole mission was religious, and, therefore, he must destroy them. He had every Templar and Hospitaller murdered.

So ended the day of Hattin, and with it the glory of the Crusade. The True Cross was gone. Later, men saw that fragmentary beam of wood dragged at a horse's tail through the streets of Damascus.

* * *

The task remained to rid the Holy Land of Christ, of Christ as God, and our worship of all that for which we had gone out into Asia and to the rescue of the Sepulchre. All the ports went, one after the other, for their garrisons had been reduced to next to nothingness in the effort to gather every available man for the last struggle with Saladin: all save Tyre. King Saladin rode into Acre to desecrate the church there which had replaced the former mosque. He sent his horsemen to hold Nazareth, others swept down the seacoast through Haifa onwards, and Saladin's subjects from Egypt came up to join them, taking Jaffa by storm. Beyrouth went, and Sidon, Ramleh and Darum, and then with the Egyptians helping, Ascalon was entered two months after the victory. There remained Jerusalem. Jerusalem without the means for defense, yet attempted defense. It held out for a week, with the Sacrament borne in procession through the streets and desperate men, newly levied, trying to hold a great breach which had been made in the walls. It was not till the twelfth day after the first appearance of Saladin's army before the Holy City that the surrender was admitted. All ransom and toll that could be taken was taken, save that the very poor were not all enslaved. The liquidating of the victims and the gathering of that spoil took up the whole month and more, and by the early days of October the thing was over.

Nor has Jerusalem since returned to Christian men, though today after a fashion their descendants hold it precariously in fee—but not for themselves.

EPILOGUE

Hattin was the end. After Hattin there were expeditions of every size, generation after generation, for centuries, and the name "Crusade" still attached to them so long as they were connected, directly or indirectly, with attacks on the Mohammedan hold upon the Mediterranean coasts. But they were not what the expeditions of the twelfth century had been, between 1095 and 1187, for Jerusalem was lost.

Without Jerusalem, without the Holy Sepulchre, the meaning of the fight had changed.

The most famous of these expeditions was that which set out for an attempted reconquest of the Holy Places when all Europe had been appalled by the news of the fall of Jerusalem. It bears the general name of the Third Crusade. It has been written about more fully, and described in greater detail, than either of its predecessors. On this account it takes a large place in literature. For most readers of fiction, and even for many readers of history, it seems the most important of all the expeditions. But it is not part of the true story, for it failed to regain Jerusalem.

A dozen years later, another host set out from the West on Venetian transports. Venice, desiring to recover a debt from Byzantium, deflected this Fourth Crusade against her fellow Christians on the Bosphorus. Constantinople was sacked, a Latin dynasty was put upon the throne of the Greek emperors, the Latin Mass was said in St. Sophia. That experiment ultimately failed. It lasted one long lifetime, and no more. But as a Crusade the Fourth Crusade was less of a Crusade than any. It never even reached the Holy Land.

Frederick II attempted a compromise. It was disingenuous and bound to fail, if for no other reason than because he was fighting the Church and because his success in any field meant the breakup of Christendom. Later in the same century Louis IX of France, the Saint, struck against the Mohammedan power in Egypt and failed. At the end of his life he returned to strike against it again, in Tunis, and there died, having effected nothing. Not long after that, the last of the seaports on the Syrian shore was surrendered to the Mohammedans. Antioch lingered on. That went, in its turn, and after it had fallen to the Moslem no Western ruler had power in the Syrian land.

The struggle against the Mohammedan did not cease, though he pushed on to Constantinople and to the islands of the sea, swept over the Balkans, seized the Hungarian plain, and at last threatened Vienna. But the name "Crusade" died out, and the spirit died with it.

There was, indeed, but one Crusade, that of which I have sketched the main outline in this book: it was the great breaking out of all western Europe into the Orient for the rescue of the Holy Sepulchre, and within one very long lifetime it had failed; for with Jerusalem in the hands of the Infidel the purpose of the original great campaign was gone, its fruits were lost.

It had all been one continuous battle, wherein lesser reinforcement was continual and one main reinforcement in the middle of its century failed before Damascus. That battle, which has been the subject of this book, began with the triumph of the Crusading State, the setting up of the kingdom of Jerusalem and its vassal Christian principalities. It seemed at first secure. It maintained the offensive for over forty years, crashed at Edessa, and then fought a continuously losing fight until the decision at Hattin. That historic episode, 1095-1187, was the true Crusade, from its inception to its final failure. All that followed was of another kind.

I have said that the expedition immediately following the loss of Jerusalem, known as the Third Crusade, was of all the Oriental wars that one which modern men best know. There is good reason for its fame. It gathered larger armies than had been seen since the first great march of a hundred years before; the Plantagenet King of England, and the Emperor with his Germans and Italians, each took part therein. It was full of pageantry. It had hoped to recover what had been lost. But it was, under the surface, no more than a forlorn hope. The seacoast towns were for the most part recaptured. Richard of the Lion Heart, the Plantagenet, founded his legend. The Emperor died upon that pilgrimage. It was like a great drama, played out upon the stage of Syria before the eyes of an attentive Europe, and the memory of it has survived most vividly; but it could not, and did not, effect anything permanent.

King Richard did, indeed, come almost in sight of the Holy City, and many have asked why, after his victories along the coast, he did not proceed to occupy Jerusalem and to restore what he and the French King and the Emperor and all Europe, you might say, had set out to restore. A dozen reasons have been given for the hesitation and the retreat of the Lion Heart and for his abandonment of that by which the whole matter was to be tested—the place of the Crucifixion, of the Sepulchre, and the Resurrection.

Many have even said that the problem is insoluble and the retreat inexplicable; but if you will read what the barons of the land said to King Richard in that wild winter night when his army and his pilgrims crouched under the ruins of Ramleh, you will find the answer there, plain enough. These men, who knew the land and had the military situation before their very eyes, answered: "Even if we enter the City, we could not hold it." The Third Crusade, the forlorn hope, failed as all the rest of the great battle had failed, from lack of men. Commonly, the kingdom of Jerusalem was starved for men. Even when the rare larger expeditions came out, they melted on the road, and their remnants melted faster still in Syria itself. Christendom could not, or would not, supply with sufficient regularity and in sufficient amount the recruitment necessary to holding its bastion in the East; and that is why the Crusades failed.

When they had thus failed, and when our people were reconciled to what seemed an irrecoverable loss, there came belatedly a turn of the wheel which no one of the men who had lived and died under that Syrian sun, battling for the thrusting back of Islam, could have imagined possible. Christendom, now no longer Christendom: Christendom, wherein the Faith by which it had lived was dying, became, suddenly as it were, the master of the Mohammedan world. What all the intense valor of the twelfth century had failed to achieve, arrived of itself, as it were, through the physical science of the West and the use of the new machines of transport and of war. The descendants of those who had found it possible to hold their garrisons in one corner of the Moslem world now administered the whole of it, or nearly the whole of it. By another avenue and in another spirit Europe, if not Christendom, had come in the nineteenth century to master Islam; we are well on in the twentieth century, and of twelve Moslems ten are still under English government, one under French, and only the remaining twelfth under fully independent Mohammedan rule.

But will that state of things endure?

The men from what used to be Western Christendom, the men from the Channel, the Atlantic, the Balearic, and Tyrrhenian seas, have returned to Syria. The French idioms which were universal to the Crusading garrisons and dominated the varied hosts of reinforcement are heard again in the streets of Damascus, of Homs, of Aleppo, as in Tripoli, Antioch, and the hamlets of Lebanon. The local dialects of England, coalesced with the French of the English noble class which ruled all English villages in the Crusading days, have long formed the English language; and that language is heard throughout the Levant as the language of an occupying power. It is the tongue of those who govern Palestine. Men coming from Paris and Rheims, from Toulouse and Flanders and Normandy, speak with authority in the administration of those hills and plains where the monster castles of Crusaders and Moslem, hardly ruined, still face each other; and in Palestine men of the same authority, speaking not indeed the tongue of Richard and his knights but sprung from the soil of which he was King, establish their rule.

So Europe has returned to this vital meeting place, this bridge, or crossroads, where East and West debate. Our first and noblest effort to re-establish European order and tradition therein ended after the triumph of the Moslem in disaster, decline, and complete failure at the last. When the successive, sporadic, uncombined thrusts at Islam which bear the false name of the Crusades in Egypt, Tunis, and where you will, when even these had ceased, it seemed evident, part of the nature of things, that that whole Orient world had been mastered by the spirit of Mohammed.

That spirit had slowly and stubbornly yielded in Spain alone; elsewhere it was politically the master. With the failure of the Crusading charge, and the extinction of the Crusading soul, all Barbary, all hither Asia, Egypt, Greece itself, and the half-barbaric but Christian world of the Balkans sank under the still flowing Mohammedan tide. The Turk who had conquered at Hattin conquered again at Constantinople itself, conquered all up the Danube valley, conquered the Hungarian plain, besieged Vienna. It lay within a narrow margin of defeat or victory whether he should appear upon the Rhine not much more than two hundred years ago.

Jonathan Swift as a young man, Louis XIV as an old one, might have wondered whether the peril to Christendom were not still destined in their day to return. The Mohammedan had, upon the whole, the greater unity, he had the more living faith, and he still had superior armament.

The Crusades had indeed failed, and our blood was thrust back out of the Orient forever.

But not forever, not even for much more than a lifetime. So little do men know of the future, so little can they conceive it, that almost unperceived by them a profound revolution transformed the relations between East and West. A child who could have heard in France, when just old enough to note the news, how the Polish King had saved Vienna and Christendom and checked the high tide of the Turkish advance, might have lived to speak to some other child who in his turn could in late middle age have heard of that great action in which men suddenly awoke to the now complete superiority of Western over Mohammedan armament—that battle of Aboukir in which Napoleon's expeditionary force completely destroyed, wiped out as a matter of course, the Turkish army.

Thenceforward the thing was decided. There were rallies, the defense put up by Turkey against Russia sixty years ago was an example; but the material power of Islam was receding at a catastrophic pace and today the whole band of territory from the Atlantic round by Egypt to the Armenian hills, even to Baghdad itself, is under the administration or overlordship of western European men. "Islam has no guns." One might add, what is more important than guns, no machinery, moral or material, for the making of them or the throwing of them into action.

The West has returned, and one might say that the work of Saladin was plainly undone.

Now the future is as hidden from us as it was from those fathers of ours who, barely three lifetimes ago, still feared the further advance of the East. But when we consider the major forces at work before our eyes, though we cannot conclude upon their results we can at least estimate their immediate proportion and value. The comparatively recent domination of western Europeans, English and French, over Mohammedan lands, is due to causes mainly material and therefore ephemeral. One must always look to moral (or, more accurately, to spiritual) causes for the understanding of human movements and political change. Of these causes, by far the most important is the philosophy adopted by the community, whether that philosophy can be fully expressed as a religion, or [be] taken for granted without overt definition.

Now, it is true that on the spiritual side Islam had declined in one factor wherein we of the West had not declined, and that was the factor of energy allied to and productive of, tenacity and continuity of conduct. But on the other hand, in the major thing of all, Religion, we have fallen back and Islam has in the main preserved its soul. Modern Europe and particularly western Europe has progressively lost its religion, and especially that united religious doctrine permeating the whole community, which unity gives spiritual strength to that community.

There is with us a complete chaos in religious doctrine, where religious doctrine is still held, and even in that part of the European population where the united doctrine and definition of Catholicism survives, it survives as something to which the individual is attached rather than the community. As nations we worship ourselves, we worship the nation; or we worship (some few of us) a particular economic arrangement believed to be the satisfaction of social justice. Those who direct us, and from whom the tone of our policy is taken, have no major spiritual interest. Their major personal interest is private gain, and this mood is reflected in the outer forms of government by the establishment of plutocracy.

Islam has not suffered this spiritual decline; and in the contrast between [our religious chaos and] the religious certitudes still strong throughout the Mohammedan world—as lively in India as in Morocco, active throughout North Africa and Egypt, even inflamed through contrast and the feeling of repression in Syria (more particularly in Palestine)—lies our peril.

We have returned to the Levant, we have returned apparently more as masters than ever we were during the struggle of the Crusades—but we have returned bankrupt in that spiritual wealth which was the glory of the Crusades. The Holy Sepulchre has become a petty adjunct, its very site doubtful in the eyes of the uninstructed mass of Christians. Bethlehem and Nazareth are held, but they are not held because they were each the cradle of Divinity. Damascus is held, but it is not held as the key of a Christian dominion, nor is the Levant held as one whole, but divided between separate nations to whom the unity of Europe has ceased to be sacred. We are divided in the face of a Mohammedan world, divided in every way—divided by separate independent national rivalries, by the warring interests of possessors and dispossessed—and that division cannot be remedied because the cement which once held our civilization together, the Christian cement, has crumbled.

These lines are written in the month of January, 1937; perhaps before they appear in print the rapidly developing situation in the Near East will have marked some notable change. Perhaps that change will be deferred, but change there will be, continuous and great. Nor does it seem probable that at the end of such a change, especially if the process be prolonged, Islam will be the loser.

If you have enjoyed this book, consider making your next selection from among the following . . .

At your Bookdealer or direct from the Publisher.
Call Toll-Free 1-800-437-5876.

Prices subject to change.

ABOUT THE AUTHOR

Hilaire Belloc
1870-1953

The great Hilaire Belloc was likely the most famous and influential Catholic historian of the past two centuries. His rare understanding of the central role of the Catholic Faith in forming Western Civilization—from the time of Christ up to our own—still opens the eyes of many today.

Hilaire Belloc was born in 1870 at La Celle, St. Cloud, France. His father was a distinguished French lawyer; his mother was English. After his father's death, the family moved to England. Hilaire did his military service in France, then returned to Balliol College, Oxford, taking first-class honors in history when he graduated in 1895. It has been said that his ambition was to rewrite the Catholic history of his two fatherlands, France and England. In 1896 he married Elodie Hogan of Napa, California; the marriage was blessed with two sons and two daughters.

During a period of 50 years—until he suffered a stroke in 1946—Hilaire Belloc wrote over a hundred books on history, economics, military science and travel, plus novels and poetry. He also wrote hundreds of magazine and newspaper articles. He served for a time as a member of the English House of Commons and edited a paper called the *Eye-Witness.*

As an historian, Belloc is largely responsible for correcting the once nearly universal *Whig* interpretation of British history, which attributed Britain's greatness to her Anglo-Saxon and Protestant background.

Hilaire Belloc visited the United States several times, giving guest lectures at both Notre Dame and Fordham Universities. Among his most famous books are *The Great Heresies, Survivals and New Arrivals* (something of a sequel to the above), *The Path to Rome, Characters of the Reformation,* and *How the Reformation Happened.* Hilaire Belloc died in 1953, leaving behind a great legacy of insight regarding the true, though largely unrecognized, inspirer of Western Civilization—the Catholic Church.